THE ELUSIVE BRAIN

JASON TOUGAW

The Elusive Brain

LITERARY EXPERIMENTS
IN THE AGE OF
NEUROSCIENCE

FOREWORD BY JOSEPH E. LEDOUX

Yale
UNIVERSITY PRESS
NEW HAVEN & LONDON

Yale University Press books may be purchased in quantity for educational, business, or promotional use. For information, please e-mail sales.press@yale.edu (U.S. office) or sales@yaleup.co.uk (U.K. office).

Printed in the United States of America.

Library of Congress Control Number: 2017946588
ISBN 978-0-300-22117-6 (hardcover : alk. paper)
A catalogue record for this book is available from the British Library.

This paper meets the requirements of ANSI/NISO Z39.48-1992 (Permanence of Paper).

10 9 8 7 6 5 4 3 2 1

For Nancy,
whose brain has etched so many tracks in mine.

CONTENTS

FOREWORD

Joseph E. LeDoux

THE HUMANITIES AND SCIENCES HAVE OFTEN been at odds, sometimes at war, in modern times. Philosophers and poets have seen scientists as hopeless reductionists, and scientists sometimes assume that in the humanities "anything goes," since there is no requirement for grounding in reality, since "reality" is, for the humanist, a relative proposition. While I can't speak for all scientists, my personal view is that both approaches have more to gain than to lose by interacting in an open-minded way.

As a scientist, I have tried to cross the great divide between the sciences and humanities in my books, especially in *Synaptic Self* and most recently in *Anxious*. Traveling in the other direction, Jason Tougaw's *The Elusive Brain* is exemplary in treating science and the humanities as complementary endeavors. Both enable us to extract meaning about our inner selves and the physical and social contexts in which we exist.

Our ability to explore how the brain works is only as good as our understanding of what we are trying to learn about the brain. We can pinpoint exactly what it is we are measuring when we study how an external stimulus, say an apple, is processed by the brain. The apple has certain features (shape, color), the processing of which can be understood in fairly precise terms. We can also explore how features like shape and color come together to give rise to a visual representation of the object. These processes are now well understood.

Less is known about how first-person subjective experience comes about in the brain. As the philosopher David Chalmers has noted, this is a "hard problem" for science. To paraphrase Descartes, you can't see inside of me; only I know the content of my conscious experiences. Yet, neuroscience and philosophy are joining forces to seek answers to the problem that follows from Descartes's soul-searching analysis.

For example, the rise of functional imaging has allowed scientists to make some progress on solving the hard problem. An impressive amount of data now suggests what goes on in the brain when people can give introspective reports of stimuli (usually visual stimuli) and when they cannot, due to subliminal stimulus presentations or brain damage. This work shows that when people can report on seeing a stimulus, both the visual cortex (necessary for representing the visual stimulus) and prefrontal and parietal cortices (involved in such processes as attention and working memory) are active. However, when they are not aware, then only the visual cortex is active.

The conclusion from these data is that prefrontal/parietal circuits make possible introspective access. While some theories argue that these circuits are necessary for subjective experiences, others claim that the subjective experience only requires the visual cortex, and the other areas merely allow introspective access. While I side with the former view, the key point here is less about which theory is correct than about the fact that the theories can be proposed and tested in laboratory studies.

But clearly, we have not solved the hard problem. Perhaps the humanities can help in ways that science may be limited. For example, in *The Elusive Brain*, Tougaw's analysis of subjective experience in literature, especially in brain memoirs and neuronovels, provides useful insights into our experiences that may provide principles that can bridge humanist and scientific views and may help refine our questions about what to look for in the brain when we study subjective experiences.

Another way of looking at the humanist-science divide is to recognize that the old fault lines of academic debate are tumbling down. The turf wars that protect the sanctity of academic disciplines are giving way to cross-discipline interactions. Indeed, philosophers are not the only ones embracing neuroscience. Today neuro-fields are sprouting everywhere: neuroaesthetics, neuro-literary criticism, neuro-economics, neuro-politics, neuro-marketing, and on and on. This neuro-mania has been criticized, and some of the criticism is well deserved. But we have to avoid throwing the baby out with the bathwater, as there are genuine benefits to intellectual sharing and collaboration across diverse disciplines. As

Tougaw notes in his introduction, "[I]f we dismiss neuromania's circulation of ideas too quickly, we miss opportunities to glean its productive, instructive, and pleasurable energies. We miss what it enables us to think and feel."

To illustrate my own efforts to come to terms with how the mind works via the brain, I'll describe how, as a young scientist, I turned a vague interest in the topic of emotion into a research problem. During my PhD studies in the 1970s, I noticed that one of the most important aspects of mental life was being ignored during the heyday of the so-called cognitive revolution in psychology—emotions. I therefore turned my research toward questions about the brain mechanism of emotion. Based on the assumption that emotions are often elicited by trigger stimuli, I employed a behavioral paradigm through which a neural stimulus could be converted into a threat. This was simple Pavlovian conditioning in which a tone was paired with an electric shock, making the tone a harbinger of harm. I studied how the brain processed the tone and elicited behavioral responses and physiological changes in the body (like increases in blood pressure and heart rate). A key finding was the role of the amygdala as the centerpiece of the brain system involved. This led to the idea of the amygdala as a "fear" center.

Though my work had helped shape that idea that the amygdala was the brain's fear center, I had always felt uncomfortable with the idea. Fear, I believed, was a conscious experience that emerges through complex cognitive processes. But I nevertheless said the amygdala was at least part of a fear system.

Recently, however, I've come to terms with my discomfort. I now argue that the amygdala is not part of a fear system but is instead part of a *defense* system that nonconsciously detects and responds to threat. Fear is what happens when the conscious brain becomes aware that the defense system is activated. But it is important to note that the amygdala is not necessary for the brain to make fear. We can be afraid of not being a good person or of not leading a meaningful life, qualities that do not depend on the amygdala but do depend on our being aware that we are facing some kind of threat, existential threats in these examples.

To think about emotions this way takes us out of the realm of reductionist biology and into the realm of subjective experience. My personal approach to emotion these days builds on Claude Lévi-Strauss's notion of *bricolage*. In French this means to put something together from things that happen to be available. The individual, in this context, is the *bricoleur*, the one who assembles. In this view, our emotions are not predetermined states of brain areas but experiences that are built from the objects and social contexts we encounter and from the memories we have of what emotions are like. To some extent, brain memoirs and neuronovels use literary techniques to portray the self as a kind of bricolage.

As I noted above, our ability to explore how the brain works is only as good as our understanding of what we are trying to learn about the brain. We have to narrow the problem down when we start a scientific project, but at some point it is important to look back up and see how the data helps us with the big questions. Scientists are not necessarily in the best position to figure out what those big questions are. Fortunately, this is just what the humanities are all about. Tougaw discusses wonderful examples of literary explorations into brain and mind: Siri Hustvedt's *The Shaking Woman* examines how to live with neurological symptoms that defy diagnosis; David B.'s *Epileptic* assesses the ways that epilepsy comes to define identity; Alix Kates Shulman's *To Love What Is* focuses on aspects of her husband's identity that survive the amnesia caused by his memory loss; Ian McEwan's *Saturday* is the story of a day in the life of a neurosurgeon. A number of other relevant literary works contain scenes in which characters fantasize about finding selfhood in physical brains, such as Hustvedt's *The Sorrows of an American,* John Wray's *Lowboy,* and Maud Casey's *The Man Who Walked Away.* If we scientists are open to what the humanities have to offer, we will surely benefit in our conceptions of how the human mind works. We may not always be able to turn these conceptions into ideas for experiments, but at least we will think more broadly about the larger problem at hand.

ACKNOWLEDGMENTS

THANKS FIRST TO NANCY K. MILLER FOR insisting this book was in me and it was time to get it out. I'm grateful that it's no exaggeration to say that I work with beloved people at Queens College. Thank you to those of you who read parts of the manuscript in progress: Annmarie Drury, Gloria Fisk, Carrie Hintz, Steven Kruger, Amy Wan, and Karen Weingarten. Thanks to Kevin Ferguson for finding and sharing so many images of brains with me (and for taking me down a peg and making me laugh). Thanks to Seo-Young Chu for changing the way I read Richard Powers and for lessons in lyricism. Thanks to the many colleagues at Queens whose integrity, intelligence, and compassion motivate me every day—and for helping me with a particularly messy draft in our faculty seminar, including Ryan Black, Jeffrey Cassvan, Caroline Hong, Richard McCoy, and Siân Silyn Roberts. Thanks to my editor, Heather Gold, for "getting" the project before it was a book and for her insight in its development. Thank you to Kate Davis and Dan Heaton, whose eagle eyes make all the difference.

Special thanks to Sebastian Groes and Stephan Besser for inspiring my thinking, offering camaraderie, and inviting me into your Amsterdam world. Thanks to Patricia Pisters and everybody involved with the Neuroaesthetics and Neurocultures Research Group at the University of Amsterdam. Thanks to Victoria Pitts-Taylor for the Neurocultures Seminar at the CUNY Graduate Center and for writing a book that helped me write this one. Thanks to the anonymous reviewers whose invaluable insights sharpened my thinking and gave me new ideas. The support from a Mellon Foundation Fellowship in Science Studies at the CUNY Graduate Center made this book possible in so many ways. Thanks to students in seminars at Queens College and the Graduate Center who dug into these books with me: Hillel Broder, Yulia Greyman, Erin Spampinato, Joey Cannizzarro, Amelia Daly, Jenn Forese, Assely Etienne, Jay Kim, Colin No, Natasha Rankine, Sahla Zawril, Michael Coccia, Chris Vitale, Sara Bowne, Shane Hanlon, Danabelle Ignes, and Shannon Ritchey. Special thanks to my research assistant, Jacob Aplaca, whose care for the work has been a special kind of consolation.

Thanks especially to David Driver, for everything, every day.

And thanks to all the living writers whose voices appear in these pages.

THE ELUSIVE BRAIN

Introduction: You Are Your Brain,
You Are Not Your Brain

IN DAVID B.'S GRAPHIC MEMOIR *EPILEPTIC,* HE portrays an impossible fantasy: that he might find a doctor who could "transfer" his brother Jean-Christophe's epilepsy into him. He fantasizes that an exchange of brain matter might enable him to feel what it's like to be his brother. It's a fantasy of overcoming the *explanatory gap,* a term coined by philosopher Joseph Levine to describe a persistent obstacle to understanding consciousness from a neurobiological point of view: Nobody can explain how immaterial experience—self, consciousness, cognition, memory, imagination, affect—emerges from brain physiology, from synaptic networks and brain regions, groups of neurons oscillating in and out of synch, stimulating each other with varying amplitudes of electricity, circulating chemicals that change each other's behavior.[1]

"I fantasize," David B. writes, "that I could take on my brother's disease if a resourceful scientist were to transfer it into my skull"[2] (fig. 1). Throughout *Epileptic,* he struggles to empathize with Jean-Christophe. In his fantasy, brain science will rewrite his failure and undo the mutual alienation of two siblings. But no scientist is that resourceful. Readers don't need to see David B.'s imaginary scientist to know he's a quack (though versions of him *do* appear in other panels). The trappings of his steampunk lab undercut the fantasy with irony and despair. David B. draws Jean-Christophe's epilepsy as a serpent that slinks from panel to panel and page to page. In this particular panel, the serpent fuses with the characters' brain matter and the wires of retro machinery of a mad scientist's laboratory. In others, it slips out of the brain through scenes of family domesticity, medical clinics, and characters' dreams and memories, to become

Maintenant que je suis fort, j'imagine que je pourrais prendre sur moi la maladie de mon frère si un savant habile pouvait la transvaser dans mon crâne.

Fig. 1. English translation: "Armed with my newfound strength, I fantasize that I could take on my brother's disease if a resourceful scientist were to transfer it into my skull." From *L'Ascension du Haut Mal* by David B., © 1999, David B. and L'Association.

a recurring image of epilepsy's reach beyond the brain. Epilepsy is a brain disorder, but it affects the whole of Jean-Christophe's body and life. He suffers physically and emotionally; his family is defined by the helplessness it makes them feel; his community ostracizes him. Neurology can't eliminate Jean-Christophe's seizures, and the constellation of their effects is surely beyond the power of biomedicine. *Epileptic* reminds readers of a fact that's easy to overlook: The brain reaches through the whole body, through selfhood, touching identity, family, social life, and the physical environment.

As an impetus for narrative, epilepsy entangles brain, body, self, and world. As a literary response to the age of neuroscience, *Epileptic* tells a characteristic story about *what it feels like to live in and with the explanatory gap.* If *Epileptic*'s story of the explanatory gap is characteristic, it's because it is so particular. A family story becomes a quest to restore equilibrium to their collective life—with little success—through neurology, macrobiotics, alchemy, and art. The physicians, philosophers, healers, and occult leaders they turn to for help consistently offer the reassurance of certainty. *We can heal Jean-Christophe,* they say, *because we have knowledge others lack.* When one technique after another fails, David B. makes a vocation of graphic storytelling, a medium that enables him to explore his brother's devastating story with no claim to putting it right, or even understanding it.

Like many works of contemporary literature, *Epileptic* asks, in philosopher Catherine Malabou's words, "What should we do with our brain?"[3] How might we understand its relation to identity? How should we live with it, study it, or write about it? These are pervasive questions in twenty-first-century literature. *Brain narratives* have emerged in large numbers, in both nonfiction and fiction. *Brain memoirs* and so-called *neuronovels* conceive the physical brain as central to the stories they tell, the conflicts they plot, and the characters they portray; both genres engage brain research, translating neurobiological theories into literary experiments. These writers experiment with narrative forms that may frame new views around the relationship between brain matter and the immaterial experiences that compose a self—the stuff philosophers call "phenomenology."

The age of neuroscience compels people to think about this extraordinary organ inside our skulls, its intimate yet remote location, its role in animating us, in making us human—and what happens to us when its ordinary functions are disrupted by disease, injury, or biological difference. By implication, neuroscience reminds human beings that we are organisms, shaped by dense relationships among biology, self, and culture. Theoretical neuroscientists are increasingly likely to assert, as Antonio Damasio does, that "biology and culture are thoroughly interactive."[4] Despite aspirational claims like this, no neuroscientist would suggest that empirical methods or existing theoretical models can account for the bewildering complexity of relations among body, mind, self, and world. To do so would require an integration of physiological, psychological, social, and ecological variables whose complexity—and, in many cases, elusiveness—cannot be accounted for with the empirical tools of the laboratory. But narrative, whose emphasis on *particular experience* and *speculative knowledge,* makes for a different kind of investigation—what literary critic Heather Houser has called a "a laboratory for perceptual and affective changes that can catalyze ethical and political projects."[5]

Levine coined the term "explanatory gap" in a 1983 essay entitled "Materialism and Qualia: The Explanatory Gap." The concept of *qualia*—the subjective, first-person, and ineffable qualities of perception—has been a cornerstone of debates about consciousness ever since. Philosophers Daniel Dennett and Patricia Churchland argue that there simply is no gap, that qualia, or feelings, are explained fully by the neural activity associated with them—a view echoed by "you are your brain" neuroscientists like Francis Crick and Dick Swaab. Philosopher David Chalmers coined the term the "hard problem" to counter purely physicalist arguments like these. Building on Thomas Nagel's famous essay, "What Is It Like to Be a Bat?," Chalmers insists that neural correlates do not explain what "it is like to be a conscious organism"—a view echoed by theoretical neuroscientists who describe consciousness as emerging from but not fully explained by brain physiology alone, including Antonio Damasio, Stanislas Dehaene, Michael Gazzaniga, Joseph LeDoux, Jaak Panksepp, and Sebastian Seung.[6] While some philosophers argue that qualia represent an intractable epistemological problem, that we probably will never understand the precise relation between matter and mind, most theoretical neuroscientists take the position that we don't know enough yet, but we will one day. Literary writers tend not to engage the debate so much as use it as a source for material. The unresolved debate makes space for the literary representation of the relation between matter and mind. Brain narratives offer simulations of qualia, streams of them, represented in the contexts of their characters' lives. Readers find themselves tossed into the explanatory gap, their minds hijacked by the qualia provoked by the black marks on the page.

Literary responses to twenty-first-century neuroscience are part of a broader cultural trend, looking to the neurosciences for explanations about the brain's role in aspects of life you might expect, like the cause of a seizure, and some you might not, like the emotional distance between siblings. In that sense, they participate in what critics have called "neuromania," a term generally used as pejorative shorthand for a host of institutions—including neuro-education, neuro-marketing, neuro-economics, and neuro-self-help movements—that bypass the explanatory gap, exaggerating and oversimplifying recent developments in neuroscience. The term suggests a culture in thrall to "the seductive appeal of mindless neuroscience," to quote the subtitle of Sally Satel and Scott O. Lilienfeld's book *Brainwashed* (2013). Mania can be dangerous, especially when it becomes the basis for education, law, or propaganda. But the danger is only part of the story.[7] I aim to reclaim *mania*'s positive meanings, following the lead of brain memoirist Kay Redfield Jamison: "My manias, at least in their early and mild forms, were absolutely intoxicating states that gave rise to great personal pleasure, an incomparable flow of thoughts, and ceaseless energy that allowed the translation of new ideas into papers and projects."[8] Of course, Jamison is describing psychological mania. Cultural neuromania is a metaphor, describing the rapid and enthusiastic circulation of ideas about the brain. The dangers of personal mania are direct and severe, its benefits unpredictable but genuine. The dangers of cultural mania involve widespread exaggerations and distortions of brain research. Still, if we dismiss neuromania's circulation of ideas too quickly, we miss opportunities to glean its productive, instructive, and pleasurable energies. We miss what it enables us to think and feel. While many works of literature can be described as direct responses to neuroscience, just as many represent the brain without engaging science directly. In that sense, it may be more accurate to describe them as responses to neuromania than to neuroscience.

Literary Laboratories

In *The Elusive Brain,* I examine literary experiments in neuromania to suggest how they might restore difficult philosophical and social questions overlooked in the rush to valorize the brain—as well as the vicissitudes of feelings provoked when we think about the organ that enables thinking and feeling. Houser's laboratory metaphor, from her book *Ecosickness in Contemporary U.S. Fiction: Environment and Affect* (2014), focuses on ecological fictions that portray relationships between human bodies and their physical environments.[9] Nonetheless, her scientific metaphor—the lab—is easily adapted to describe the work literature does in the world, particularly when that literature gives narrative form to questions central to science. A laboratory is a place for investigation, obviously, but also for daily work, collaboration, and conceiving methods that might yield answers to elusive questions as well as applications for treating illnesses, forestalling environmental disasters, or enhancing the quality of lives. Of course, those applications might just as easily lead to ecological destruction, the proliferation of disease, or ever-increasing disparities between wealth and poverty. If brain memoirs and neuronovels are laboratories, they work by telling stories about brain-related experiences that invite readers to consider a full range of philosophical and social implications of the relations between their brains, minds, bodies, and worlds.

My aim is to account for a broad range of literary responses to neuroscience and neuromania—and to contextualize them in relation to philosophical, social, and scientific debates about the brain's role in the making of life and self. Brain memoirs can be understood as belonging to a number of overlapping categories:

- **Chronicles of lived experience of neurological difference:** Ellen Forney's *Marbles* (2012), Naoki Higashida's *The Reason I Jump* (2013),

Siri Hustvedt's *The Shaking Woman* (2010), Stephen Elliott's *The Adderall Diaries* (2009), Tim Page's *Parallel Play* (2009), Daniel Tammet's *Born on a Blue Day* (2007), Tito Rajarshi Mukhopadhyay's *How Can I Talk If My Lips Don't Move?* (2008) and with Lorna Wing, *Beyond the Silence* (2000), Lauren Slater's *Prozac Diary* (1999) and *Lying* (2001), Kay Redfield Jamison's *An Unquiet Mind* (1996), and Temple Grandin's *Thinking in Pictures* (1995) and with Margaret Scariano *Emergence: Labeled Autistic* (1986/1996).

- **Reflections on the aftermath or recovery from brain illness or injury:** Karl Ove Knausgaard's "The Terrible Beauty of Brain Surgery" (2015), Jill Bolte Taylor's *My Stroke of Insight* (2009), and Jean-Dominique Bauby's *The Diving Bell and the Butterfly* (1998).

- **Accounts by caregivers, family members, or witnesses:** Derf Backderf's *My Friend Dahmer* (2012), Patrick and Henry Cockburn's *Henry's Demons* (2011), Darryl Cunningham's *Psychiatric Tales* (2011), Alix Kates Shulman's *To Love What Is* (2009), David B.'s *Epileptic* (2006), Jonathan Franzen's essay "My Father's Brain" (2001), and John Bayley's *Elegy for Iris* (1999).

- **Chronicles of neurological practice by physicians or researchers:** Paul Kalanithi's *When Breath Becomes Air* (2016), Henry Marsh's *Do No Harm* (2015), Oliver Sacks's *On the Move* (2015), and James Fallon's *The Psychopath Inside* (2013).

- **Philosophical reflections on the distinctive contours of neurotypical experience:** Douglas Hofstadter's *I Am a Strange Loop* (2008), and Steven Johnson's *Mind Wide Open* (2005).

Similarly, neuronovels come in a variety of forms:

- **Fictions that appropriate neurological symptoms as mimetic experiments in narration:** David Mitchell's *Slade House* (2015), Kazuo Ishiguro's *The Buried Giant* (2015) and *The Unconsoled* (1996), Maud Casey's *The Man Who Walked Away* (2014), John Wray's *Lowboy* (2010), Rivka Galchen's *Atmospheric Disturbances* (2008), Tom McCarthy's *Remainder* (2005/2007), Mark Haddon's *The Curious Incident of the Dog in the Night-Time* (2004), Jonathan Lethem's *Motherless Brooklyn* (2000), and Lauren Slater's *Lying* (2001).

- **Fictions whose protagonists witness intimates suffering from severe neurological disease or injury:** Eimear McBride's *A Girl Is a Half-Formed Thing* (2014), Lisa Genova's *Still Alice* (2009), Richard Powers's *The Echo Maker* (2007), and Nicole Krauss's *Man Walks into a Room* (2002).
- **Narratives featuring protagonists whose medical professions, scientific research, or abiding interest in neuroscience put them in contact with the minds and brains of others:** E. L. Doctorow's *Andrew's Brain* (2014), Teju Cole's *Open City* (2011), Siri Hustvedt's *The Blazing World* (2014) and *The Sorrows of An American* (2009), Ian McEwan's *Saturday* (2005), and David Lodge's *Thinks . . .* (2001).
- **Sensational or speculative fictions that use the brain as a theatrical plot device:** Haruki Murakami's *1Q84* (2011), Paul Beatty's *The Sellout* (2015), Robin Becker's *Brains: A Zombie Memoir* (2010), Octavia Butler's *Fledgling* (2005), M. T. Anderson's *Feed* (2012), Thomas Harris's *Hannibal* (1999), Ian McEwan's *Enduring Love* (1998), and Richard Powers's *Galatea 2.2* (1995).

Despite their diversity, neuronovels and brain memoirs tend to share common aims, which underscore the questions this book explores. They

- revisit the representation of consciousness in response to developments in brain research;
- provoke debates about determinism and reductionism, asking readers to reconsider simple cause-and-effect relationships between biology and experience;
- reflect and challenge cultural assumptions about neurological difference—underscoring commonalities in disability activism and philosophy of mind;
- experiment with literary conventions to foreground the bewildering complexity of relations between brain, body, and world;
- challenge the equation of consciousness and "interiority," suggesting that conscious experience is dynamic and relational, emerging through interactions between an organism (or protagonist) and its environment, including other organisms, cultural products, and social relationships—a move whose implications seem primarily literary but are profoundly social because they challenge widespread cultural assumptions about the

brain, assumptions that influence the direction of scientific research, medical practice, social policy, and general prejudice.

Even texts easily critiqued for social or aesthetic shortcomings (for example, the reinforcing of stereotypes about autism in Haddon's *The Curious Incident* or the patent sensationalism of Harris's *Hannibal*) stimulate debate about topics ranging from neurological difference to the embodied aesthetics of horror. In that sense, they are productive contributions to the cultural dialogue catalyzed by the collective work of neuronovels and brain memoirs.

Brain memoirs and neuronovels offer an antidote to polarizing debates, in the form of stories that emphasize the stakes of understanding the brain's relation to self in particular bodies living in particular worlds. In *The Brain's Body: Neuroscience and Corporeal Politics* (2016), feminist sociologist Victoria Pitts-Taylor examines the social implications of "the centrality of the brain in contemporary thought and public life." Taking a wide view, she argues that "The social brain, in sum, is equated with mind and self, is understood as the product of embodied experience, is seen to provide the foundation for (and is reflected in) social structures, and is subject to intervention and transformation. In these ways the social brain collapses the distinction between nature and culture." Pitts-Taylor urges brain researchers to eschew the "dual specters of biological determinism and neuroreductionism." Like Damasio, when he describes the imbrication of brain and culture, Pitts-Taylor describes the scope of the brain's meanings beyond the empirical neurosciences, but she tasks the *theoretical* neurosciences to grapple with the brain's meaning in actual bodies living in social worlds and physical environments: "the multiplicity of the neurobiological body and the specificity of embodied lives." Building on the work of disability studies scholar Rosemarie Garland-Thomson, Pitts-Taylor is particularly interested in brain research that reveals "cognitive and affective 'misfittings' of body-minds and worlds"—misfittings "that can occur when variant bodies meet constraints in the built world."[10]

Literature is one cultural arena in which the enormous variety of brain-body-world relationships are already being explored, their personal and social stakes emphasized, their multiplicity represented, and their myriad misfittings examined. Like *Epileptic,* many brain memoirs and neuronovels find impetus in the pragmatic stakes of understanding the brain—to improve lives, alleviate suffering, or enable new ways of thinking. Neuroscience and clinical neurology improve the lives of people suffering with brain injuries or illnesses. Of course, some illnesses—Alzheimer's, to name one—remain mostly untreatable, and some forms of neurological difference, such as autism or Tourette's, are too often mistaken for diseases, their personal and social dimensions medicalized into invisibility. While these complexities are very real, they don't obviate the material benefits of brain research. Brain memoirists take the material stakes of their brains seriously. They tend to begin with personal motives and proceed toward social and philosophical questions raised by quests to understand partic-ular brains in relation to general knowledge about the brain. Neuronovels tend to explore these philosophical and social questions through fictional stories that demand specificity in terms of character and speculation in terms of plot. Both genres dramatize the literal touching or probing of physical brains with the intent of learning about immaterial qualities of self or experience—including affect, memory, imagination, identity, and aesthetic pleasure; others touch brains more indirectly or metaphorically by making the relationship between brain and mind central.

When writers dramatize fantasies of finding selves in brain physiology, they respond (indirectly) to arguments made by theoretical neuroscientists like Antonio Damasio, Gerald Edelman, Jaak Panksepp, and Mark Solms—all of whom take the liberty of stepping outside the laboratory to speculate—or fantasize?—about relationships between biology, self, and culture. These neuroscientists are interested in sealing the explanatory gap. The confidence of their language might fool a reader into believing they've sealed it already, but this is not the case. Damasio's theory of consciousness hinges on the dynamic relationship between "organisms" and "objects," a relationship that produces the mental "images" that comprise subjective experience. One of Edelman's several books on his theory of neuronal group selection, or "neural Darwinism," is entitled *A Universe of Consciousness: How Matter Becomes Imagination.* The first chapter of Panksepp's book *Affective Neuroscience: The Foundations of Human and Animal Emotions,* begins with the sentence, "Our emotional feelings reflect our ability to subjectively experience certain states of the nervous system." In *The Brain and the Inner World: An Introduction to the Neuroscience of Subjective Experience,* his collaboration with Oliver Turnbull, Mark Solms seeks to build on "new insights into the natural laws that govern our inner life" in order to resolve long-standing conflicts between neuroscience and psychoanalysis.[11]

While they often use language and rhetoric that suggest a physicalist stance, implying that brains determine fate, end of story, the details of these writers' theories reveal much more interesting attempts to grapple with questions about how matter and mind, or physiology and consciousness, shape each other. For example, LeDoux ends his book *Synaptic Self* with two pithy declarative sentences: "You are your synapses. They are who you are."[12] However, he begins the book by acknowledging critics of this view: "Many will surely counter that the self is psychological, social, moral, aesthetic, or spiritual, rather than neural, in nature. My synaptic theory is not proposed as an alternative to these views. It is, rather, an attempt to portray the way the psychological, social, moral, aesthetic, or spiritual self is realized."[13] Similarly, Sebastian Seung makes what sounds like a "you are your brain" claim in his book *Connectome: How the Brain's Wiring Makes Us Who We Are* (2012): "This book proposes a simple theory: Minds differ because connectomes differ. . . . Personality and IQ might also be explained by connectomes. Perhaps even your memories, the most idiosyncratic aspect of your personal identity, could be encoded in your connectome." Your connectome is the "totality of connections between the neurons in a nervous system," and that totality belies the simplicity of Seung's rhetoric. Turn the page, and you'll find this: "your connectome changes throughout life." That would suggest that the "wiring" metaphor—a familiar one to most readers, no doubt—is misleading because it doesn't account for the fluidity and flux of neural interaction. Read on for a couple of paragraphs and you'll find this: "Both genes and experiences have shaped your connectome. We must consider both historical influences if we want to explain how your brain got the way it is."[14] Genes imply that the whole of the organism is involved in making the connectome; experiences become meaningful in the context of the whole of social life and culture. We already know our connectomes change throughout life, so "how your brain got the way it is" is not quite right either, since it was not quite that way a minute ago, or yesterday, or last year, and will be different tomorrow or next year.

If brain memoirs and neuronovels work like cultural laboratories, they make plenty of room for contradiction. When neuroscience writers contradict themselves, they make room for more complicated and interesting stories. I don't see their contradictions as fatal, or even as mistakes. Instead, I want to suggest that these contradictions arise through writing that involves collisions of epistemological hope, rhetorical stance, professional affiliation, and public personae. It's easy enough to locate the contradictions—or, more commonly, to critique half a contradiction and ignore the other. I believe we will learn more by reading the contradictions as the product of language and rhetoric grappling with the uncertainties of rapidly advancing and evolving disciplines. If writers of brain memoirs and neuronovels can tell us anything, it's that mystery defines the epistemology of relations between brain and self; and where you find mystery, you'll find contradiction too.

Your Brain and You

I believe debates about whether or not persons equal brains have outlived their usefulness, but they rage nonetheless. Famously, in his book *The Astonishing Hypothesis: The Scientific Search for the Soul* (1995), Crick dismissed the explanatory gap: "You, your joys and sorrows, your memories and ambitions, your sense of personal identity and free will, are in fact no more than a vast assembly of nerve cells and their associated molecules."[15] Crick's assertion initiated vehement discussions in disciplines as disparate as philosophy, anthropology, sociology, and literature. The debates are variations on similarly circular discussions of nature and nurture. Literary narratives about the brain offer an alternative to this circular rhetoric, which has become a chimera that even those who wield it don't believe in. The inflammatory titles of two controversial books illustrate a major—and I would argue, false—divide raised by all this neuromania: Neurobiologist Dick Swaab's *We Are Our Brains: A Neurobiography of the Brain, from the Womb to Alzheimer's* (2010/2014), and American philosopher Alva Noë's *Out of Our Heads: Why You Are Not Your Brain, and Other Lessons from the Biology of Consciousness* (2009). The "you are your brain" / "you are not your brain" divide is possible because of the paradox created by rapid advances in the neurosciences that raise more questions than answers. But neuronovels and brain memoirs offer a way out of the binary installed by the rhetoric of philosophers and neuroscientists. Of course, their writers have varying motives and methods for making brains central to their literary experiments, but nearly all of them use narrative to ask a set of questions the laboratory sciences are not equipped to answer: *What roles might the brain play in the making of identity, the experience of embodiment, and the shaping of social relations?* Put more simply, they emphasize the "you" in the "you are or aren't your brain" discussion. They invite readers to consider vicissitudes of identity more

capaciously represented through story, rather than argument, by linking the experience of living with a brain to particular characters, voices, and plots.

The subtitle of Swaab's international phenomenon of a book anthropomor-
phizes the brain. Swaab is going to tell us the life story of our brains: "Everything
we think, do, and refrain from doing is determined by the brain. The construction of the fantastic machine determines our potential, our limitations, and our
characters; *we are our brains.* Brain research is no longer confined to looking
for the cause of brain disorders; it also seeks to establish why we are as we are.
It is a quest to find ourselves."[16] Swaab's invocation of a literary genre—the
biography—seems consistent with his argument. But there's a side effect to his
rhetorical frame. The theatricality of the literary device reminds readers that
brains don't in fact have biographies. When neuroscience "seeks to establish
why we are as we are," it wanders into questions literary writers have been
exploring for centuries. When Swaab invokes metaphor to describe the brain as
a "fantastic machine," he lands on one of the most pervasive modes for representing the brain in literature: mystery. Despite his confident italics, in his
preface Swaab indicates a more contingent story about the brain. "The question
I am most frequently asked," he writes, "is whether I can explain how the brain
works. That's a conundrum that has yet to be fully solved, and this book can of
course only provide a partial answer."[17] Here again, Swaab is on a par with
authors of neuronovels and brain memoirs who represent the relationship
between brain and self as a fascinatingly complex conundrum.

Noë responds to assertions like Swaab's—though his direct target is Francis
Crick—with rhetorical confidence on a par with the neuroscientists he critiques:
"In this book I advance this truly astonishing hypothesis: to understand
consciousness in humans and animals, we must look not inward, into the
recesses of our insides; rather, we need to look to the ways in which each of us,
as a whole animal, carries on the processes of living in and with and in response
to the world around us."[18] Noë's hypothesis may be too commonly accepted to
be as astonishing as he suggests. Similar arguments—that the brain is only
meaningful when it's embodied and only works in relation to other organisms
and objects in the environmental contexts in which embrained creatures live—
have been made in particular by many social scientists.[19] You wouldn't know it
from Noë's book, but similar ideas are also emerging from the neurosciences.
As Nikolas Rose and Joelle M. Abi-Rached argue in their book *Neuro: The New*

Brain Sciences and the Management of the Mind (2013), the neurosciences "at their most sophisticated . . . are struggling toward a way of thinking in which our corporeality is in constant transaction with its milieu."[20]

In conceptual terms, the epistemological struggle Rose and Abi-Rached describe—with its vast social, philosophical, and aesthetic implications—has outpaced the chimera of the "you are / you are not your brain" debate. Even the staunchest reductionists don't believe that anybody is simply a brain. But the rhetoric persists. Neuroscientists and some philosophers make claims like Swaab's routinely, even if reading the details of their work makes it clear that, like him, they acknowledge both the epistemological limits of their own theories and the many dimensions of self that can't simply be reduced to brain—for example, the rest of the physical body, the vicissitudes of perception or memory, or the influence of family and culture. Without setting out to do so, philosopher Patricia Churchland, well known for her staunch "you are your brain" reductionism, offers some indications about how and why the debate rages in her book *Touching a Nerve: Our Brains, Our Selves* (2014).[21]

1. When reductionists confront the explanatory gap, their rhetoric tends to breed contradictory statements.
2. Debates about the origins and meaning of selfhood become heated, often intensely emotional, because they are so closely tied to existential questions about life and mortality.
3. Emotional intensity motivates disciplinary rancor between the sciences and the humanities and the social sciences.
4. Relations between scientific research and science journalism often lead to oversimplification and distortion when promising lab results are translated for popular audiences.

Fortunately, the theoretical neurosciences frequently approach the question with new ideas and new rhetorical frameworks. For example, early in *Who's in Charge?: Free Will and the Science of the Brain* (2011), Michael Gazzaniga encapsulates the epistemological conundrum: "The physiochemical brain does enable the mind in some way we don't understand and in so doing, it follows the physical laws of the universe just like other matter."[22] Gazzaniga's concern is a social one. A strictly determinist interpretation of his claim that the "brain does enable the mind" might suggest humans are not responsible for our actions. To counter this idea, Gazzaniga argues that "the mind . . . constrains the brain." In order to explain mind, he argues, we need to think in terms of layers, including "the micro world of subatomic particles" and "the macro world of you and your buddy high-fiving over the Super Bowl." If mind is composed of tiny particles and social relations that do not obey the laws of physics, then it is a "dynamic system" requiring some mechanism to give it coherence.[23] For Gazzaniga, that mechanism is the self, the responsible agent. The self inhabits social and environmental worlds whose input enables it to think and feel—in other words, have a mind—that "constrains" the brain's physiology, which at the level of the subatomic, must already be disobeying laws of matter anyway. For Gazzaniga, you are not simply your brain.

Like Gazzaniga, Antonio Damasio and Joseph LeDoux both identify as materialist neuroscientists, but also like him, their theories do not simply reduce selfhood to brainhood. Damasio argues that consciousness arises when an "organism" interacts with "objects"—and in the process creates images of that object that alter the organism's "map" of its own physiology and its relation to the world around it.[24] The map, of course, is a representation, composed of neural networks but also what Damasio calls the "chemical bath" or "internal milieu" of bodies.[25] Bodies regulate life through making patterns of meaning, but those patterns mostly elude consciousness. LeDoux, the original author of the sentence, "You are your synapses," has recently turned to anthropology to refine his explanation of the brain-self relationship. In his most recent book, *Anxious: Using the Brain to Understand and Treat Fear and Anxiety* (2015), LeDoux invokes Claude Lévi-Strauss's concept of *bricolage* to explain how fear and anxiety may be "assembled from nonemotional ingredients." LeDoux includes among the items of social life "persons, objects, contexts, the sequence and fabric of everyday life." He argues that "In the brain, working memory can be thought of as the 'bricoleur,' and the content of emotional consciousness resulting from the construction process as the bricolage."[26] While LeDoux's focus is on the physiology of feeling, he does more than create an illustrative analogy when he casts working memory as the bricoleur. He suggests that neuroscience benefits from sociological and anthropological theories of the self. Like Damasio, LeDoux is building a theory to account for the interplay of biology and culture in the making of self—an interplay fundamental to contemporary brain narratives.[27]

5

Rhetorical Brains

The title of Patricia Churchland's book—*Touching a Nerve*—initiates a rhetorical situation that can't be contained through empirical methods. Its simplest meaning is double: Touching a nerve means making people uncomfortable by speaking the truth, but it also implies touching nerves directly, via dissection, or indirectly, via brain-scanning technology. The title implies disciplinary precedence for neuroscience, the domain of the disconcerting truths touching the rest of our nerves, but Churchland muddies this precedence in her opening paragraph: "My brain and I are inseparable. I am who I am because my brain is what it is. Even so, I often think about my brain in terms different from those I use when thinking about myself. I think about my brain as *that* and about myself as *me*. I think about my brain as having neurons, but I think of me as a having a memory. Still, I know that my memory is all about the neurons in my brain. Lately, I think about my brain in more intimate terms—as me."[28] Few would argue that Churchland's brain is separable from her self, though many would take issue with the idea that she is who she is solely because her "brain is what it is." Take Churchland's example of memory. By now, it's doctrine in memory research that the present informs our recollections of the past; experience primes memory retrieval. In that sense, memory is not "all about the neurons" in anybody's brain, a fact Churchland surely understands. Memory is a process that entwines experience and physiology, in ways that are not reducible to neuronal activity. Churchland and her brain are surely inseparable. That much is uncontroversial. But she proceeds to exaggerate the claim, albeit in subjective terms. She imagines her brain as her self; she hasn't quite stated that she is her brain. Nonetheless, she comes close to offering what she calls "hypotheses about the brain ... marketed by self-promotional writers who exaggerate what we actually know, thus causing a sensation"—as in "the self is an illusion" or "love is just a chemical process."[29] Later in the book, Churchland argues that scientists have an ethical obligation to help journalists report accurately, but that sometimes "baser impulses" like a desire to see one's name in print or to appease a campus public-relations department may lead to a scientist "cranking up the story to get the journalist's attention." In other words, social impulses may shape the communication of scientific ideas.[30]

The social motives Churchland describes—desire for acclaim, pressure from institutions—are fairly base, but also very real. She doesn't consider the emotional charge of subjects like self or love or the possibility that brain research itself may be shaped by both base and subtle social motives, as likely to be unconscious as conscious. These are the kinds of insights that "you are not your brain" proponents would be likely to raise. Churchland frames her book with caricatures of such proponents, in the form of unnamed but assumedly real colleagues—a philosopher and an anthropologist. Churchland describes the philosopher in order to demonstrate how difficult the truths of neuroscience can be: "a renowned if rather melodramatic philosopher hoisted himself up in a conference I attended and, hands gripping the chair in front of him, hollered to the hushed crowd, 'I hate the brain; I hate the brain!'[31] Toward the end of the book, she describes an awkward elevator ride with an anthropologist: "My very presence brought her to fury, and she hissed, 'You reductionist! How can you think there is nothing but atoms?' Who, me? I was flabbergasted. It was as though the word *reductionist* was in the same league as *Gestapo* or *arsonist* or *hired assassin*." Churchland makes an explicit connection between the melo-dramatic philosopher and the furious anthropologist, informing readers that they both "motivated some inquiry." In the case of the anthropologist, the inquiry reveals some possible misconceptions about reductionism. In defense of reductionism, she explains that it can be helpful to "understand a macrolevel thing in terms of microlevel parts." The stakes of doing so can be high, as her example demonstrates: "If we understand that epilepsy is owed to the sudden synchronous firing of a group of neurons, which in turn triggers similar synchro-nous firing in other areas of the cortex, this is an *explanation* of a phenomenon; it is not a denial of the *existence* of the phenomenon."[32]

The language and rhetoric here indicate an unfortunate failure of communi-cation between Churchland and her unnamed colleagues. In laboratory research, empirical reductionism is a necessary and useful tool that can help explain the role of the brain in seizures—and, hopefully, lead to therapies that may alle-viate the suffering of the people who experience them. But while the synchro-nous firing of neurons may be a central factor in the cause of many seizures, it cannot explain or alleviate the full spectrum of experience described in a literary text like *Epileptic*. To describe epilepsy as "owed" to them is to obscure the fact that a seizure is a whole body phenomenon as well as a social one. Churchland's anti-reductionist colleagues would likely argue that in physiological terms, epilepsy owes as much to genes as neurons, or that understanding the stigma of seizures should be fundamental to medical therapies designed to treat them.

When Churchland caricatures other thinkers, or characterizes them as intellectual opponents, she forestalls multidisciplinary inquiry that might yield productive collaboration and models for using language and rhetoric supple and
capacious enough to avoid oversimplifying the complex, overdetermined, and
little-understood relations between brain and self.

Contrary to Churchland, Noë is adamant that you are not your brain: "If there
is one thing we now know, it's that the character of experience is not fixed by
individual neurons. The neuron is just the wrong unit of analysis. . . . You can
no more explain mind in terms of the cell than you can explain dance in terms
of the muscle. If the character of our mental lives depends on what's going on
in the brain—and it does—then we need to turn our attention away from individual neurons. It is now accepted that if we are to have any chance of understanding the brain basis of consciousness, we need to widen our gaze to
encompass large-scale populations of neurons and their dynamic activity over
time."[33] Noë is persuasive when he argues that a dynamic approach must
conceive "neural systems as elements of a larger system that includes the rest
of the animal's body and also its situation in and interaction with the environment."[34] The brain doesn't do its work in a vacuum. This is the consensus in the
field of the philosophy of mind these days, and it's an assumption in most work
in the neurohumanities. Critiques like Noë's may provoke new methodologies
in the sciences. Nonetheless, it's important to remember that *reductivity,* a casti-
gating term in the humanities and theoretical social sciences, describes fundamental practices in the sciences—practices without which it would be
impossible for research programs to proceed. Empirical studies are reductive
because they work under the guiding assumption that it is only possible to
investigate parts of any given problem—but that other scientists in other labs
will contribute by investigating related parts of the same or similar problems.
The scientific method works through reduction, but that does not mean that the
motives of scientists or conclusions drawn from their research must be reductive. Empirical research requires a community of readers who will interpret
results and follow through with related inquiries. This scenario is complicated
by the fact that future research will almost certainly demonstrate that previous
research got quite a bit wrong.

With this in mind, it seems unlikely that many brain researchers will be
hospitable to the conclusion Noë draws from his astute analysis of contemporary neuroscience's tendency to overlook the environmental contexts in which

the brain works: "But if I am right, whole research programs have to be set aside. It is misguided to search for neural correlates of consciousness—at least if these are understood, as they sometimes are, to be neural structures or processes that are alone sufficient for consciousness. There are no such neural structures. . . ."[35] This rhetorical flourish reads like a twenty-first-century articulation of the hostility to science C. P. Snow ascribes to the old humanities. Whole research programs set aside? What about the emergence of new research programs, or the revision or evolution of existing programs?

Noë isn't claiming that neural structures are not involved in consciousness. Surely these neural structures must be studied if we are to understand "the whole of mental experience." Noë uses Crick as his example of the reductive "you are your brain" neuroscientist, but he ignores the fact that plenty of theoretical neuroscientists acknowledge and examine the crucial interaction of brains, bodies, and worlds. The work of Jaak Panksepp, Mark Solms, Gerald Edelman, and Antonio Damasio come to mind. Damasio is the most public of these figures, and he has been focusing for years on the relationship between the "organism and the object," which he argues is essential to understanding consciousness.[36] In fact, he suggests, like Noë, that there can be no consciousness without an object—in other words, we must understand the interaction of brain and environment and, ultimately, culture and biology. With somewhat different rhetoric, Noë would be much more likely to garner and persuade a scientific audience.

While critiques like Noë's are valuable, they risk reinforcing the "you are your brain" / "you are not your brain" binary and masking the epistemological impasse of the explanatory gap. Brain imaging and other technologies can correlate physiology and experience, crudely, but they cannot identify cause-and-effect relationships between the neural networks that seem to be active when we read or get angry and what it feels like to read or be angry. This is not merely an abstract philosophical debate, because it's linked to high-stakes questions about embodiment, medical practice, and social policy. The etiologies of most mental illnesses and neurological disorders are not well understood. Nobody knows what causes autism, synesthesia, schizophrenia, or migraine.

Philosopher Catherine Malabou offers a model for toning down the rhetoric and clearing intellectual impasses. Malabou asserts that she isn't interested in "playing the game of anti-reductionism."[37] Instead, she seeks to delineate the claims of contemporary neuroscience and their social implications. She admires advances of reductionist neuroscience, which "has enabled us to approach phenomena such as memory, perception, learning—even psychical and behavioral problems—more and more precisely and objectively. In the most general way, it constitutes a new approach to the subject by affirming the existence of a 'neuronal self.'" However, she argues, "the continuity between the neuronal and the mental can never be a strictly scientific postulate." When she elaborates, she may as well be describing Churchland's rhetorical convolutions: "It necessarily constitutes a philosophical and epistemological position and such positions are not always clearly articulated." If neuroscience is struggling toward convincing accounts of our bodies' relationships with culture, it will need to contend with some of the conceptual and social obstacles Malabou describes. She argues that when the "theoretical fissure" of the explanatory gap "is not recognized as such . . . it runs the risk of being overwhelmed by brute, naïve ideology." This is where the perspective of the philosopher and the anthropologist—not to mention the literary critic or the novelist—help to refine collective understanding of the brain *and* the self. As Malabou writes, quoting LeDoux, "'You are your synapses': I have nothing against this sentence. I simply want to understand the meaning of 'being' here." The irony of the word "simply" here is palpable—and might be read as a jab at staunch reductionists—but what Malabou is proposing is a materialist stance that values reductionism for what it can accomplish and that recognizes its theoretical limitations, its social and philosophical implications, and the rhetoric that enables the translation and dissemination of its findings. Malabou opens her book with a two-part claim: "The brain is a work, and we do not know it. We are its subject—authors and products at once—and we do not know it."[38] Building on the work of Damasio and others, Malabou emphasizes the fact that the brain works through representation, registering and representing stimuli in the world through neural reconnections. The brain's plasticity, its capacity to change, imbricates its *representation* of the world with that world. It raises cultural and political questions in addition to scientific ones.

In fact, neuroscience writers tend to be frank about the gap between their dramatic hypotheses and the available evidence. Even Swaab acknowledges that "how the brain works" is "a conundrum that has yet to be fully solved, and this book can of course provide only a partial answer."[39] In *The Tell-Tale Brain: A Neuroscientist's Quest for What Makes Us Human* (2011), V. S. Ramachandran articulates neuroscience's epistemological limits and aims as an exciting motive for research, rather than a deficit. Following upon the allusion to Edgar Allan Poe in his title, he does so by way of an explicit analogy to mystery as a literary genre: "As heady as our progress has been, we need to stay completely honest with ourselves and acknowledge that we have only discovered a tiny fraction of what there is to know about the human brain. But the modest amount we have discovered makes for a story more exciting than any Sherlock Holmes novel."[40] Scholars—or lovers—of literature might wince at the implicit competition between the affective pull of brain science and detective fiction, but the competition is a phantom, a product of rhetoric. While there is very real competition for resources among these disciplines within universities and the various institutions that fund them, this should not be mistaken for or projected into a competition when it comes to the pursuit of heady questions about the meaning of physiology, the affective experiences that motivate behavior, or the dense relationship between biology, identity, and culture. Like literary writers, neuroscientists are taking the liberty of speculating based on what we do know, in part to spark cultural dialogue and in part to suggest avenues for research that may provide some of the elusive answers. Literary writers exploit the explanatory gap with somewhat different intentions—to propel plots that emphasize phenomenological experience and cultural anxieties that ensue from the bold propositions emerging from the neurosciences. These multiple, intersecting modes of inquiry represent the promise of contemporary neuromania.

The Literary Labs of Siri Hustvedt and Richard Powers

Among novelists interested in and influenced by neuroscience, Siri Hustvedt and Richard Powers share at least two distinctions: They are widely respected by critics, and they are more involved with and committed to contemporary brain research than most. In Hustvedt's novel *The Blazing World* (2014) and in Powers's novel *The Echo Maker* (2006), these two authors engage contemporary neuroscience in explorations of the mutability of identity. While their novels explore some common ground—embodiment, preconscious affect, or relationality—they diverge in ways that make it clear that the neuronovel, as a genre, is far from uniform in its themes, aims, and forms. Hustvedt's novel focuses on questions about embodied aesthetics, and Powers's focuses on neurological collisions (involving humans, other species, and physical environments). Reading these two novels together demonstrates a central quality of literature's contribution to conversations about what the brain means: the variety of questions they engender through the creation of *particular* narrative worlds and characters.

In *The Blazing World,* Hustvedt tells the story of Harriet Burden (Harry for short), an artist who takes elaborate revenge on the sexist art world by borrowing the bodies and identities of three different male artists—and disseminating her work under their names. As one of the novel's narrators describes Burden, "The woman was chin-deep in the neuroscience of perception, and for some reason those unreadable papers with their abstracts and discussions justified her second life as a scam artist."[41] Harriet is interested in making art that elicits discomforting eccentric neurological experience. She uses aesthetic means to put audiences in the position of defamiliarizing their own neurologies.

Burden exhibits a series of sculptures she calls "metamorphs" as the work of queer performance artist Phineas Q. Eldridge, who describes his response to the "homemade critters" she's been sculpting: "When I arrived at the lodge, Harry was tending to her own characters, a group of stuffed figures—cold, coolish, warm, and hot. I became fond of her 'metamorphs' (as Harry called them), even though a good number of them were injured or deformed. I take that back. I liked the hurt metamorphs most, the ones with missing legs and arms, with braces and slings, humps, or rashes painted on them. They did not look real, but they felt more human than a lot of humans I know, and Harry was gentle with her homemade critters." The exhibition is an installation entitled *The Suffocation Rooms,* a series of rooms, each a little warmer than the last, amplifying the metamorph's peculiar range of body temperatures. Burden has placed critters made from beeswax in boxes, "trying to get out," and populated the rooms with other metamorphs, who grow larger as visitors walk from one room to the next. In Eldridge's words, "The metamorphs were big, goofy-looking, lumpy things, who sat at their tables in all seven rooms." The seventh room is the warmest and most startling: "Because she did want the person to look like an alien in some 1950s sci-fi film, the model became more and more realistic: skinny, eerily transparent (liver, heart, stomach, and intestines just barely visible), hermaphroditic (small breast buds and not-yet-grown penis), frizzy red human hair. The creature is strangely beautiful, and when you see him/her in the seventh room out of the box, standing on a stool to look out the window, or rather into the mirror, you can't help feeling touched somehow. The really large (by now) metamorphs have finally noticed that the personage is out and have turned their heads to look at it."[42]

The Suffocation Rooms elaborates and complicates a foundational experiment in the history of cognitive science—Fritz Heider and Marianne Simmel's opaquely titled "An Experimental Study of Apparent Behavior" (1944).[43] In their lab at Smith College, Heider and Simmel showed an animated film to experimental subjects. In the film, triangles and squares move around the screen. All but one of thirty-four viewers described the film as a narrative and endowed the shapes with subjectivities, motivations, and emotions. Triangles became bullies or heroes, squares became houses or traps. Viewers established affective connections with the shapes. Burden's metamorphs play on a human penchant to endow inanimate objects with mental lives, but they also respond to and revise twentieth-century cognitive science's tendency to examine minds as though their basic functions can be disconnected from the bodies that enable them to function and the worlds that give them meaning. *The Blazing World* dramatizes a fantasy of overcoming the explanatory gap, a fantasy figured as impossible but irresistible. The metamorphs will never be alive, but they will provoke audiences to consider themselves as organisms. Hustvedt emphasizes Burden's didactic mission. She conceives her exhibitions quite literally as laboratories: She wants her audiences to feel, in a visceral sense, the fundamental relationality involved in being an organism—a relationality that entwines biology, identity, social life, and culture.

The Echo Maker tells a different story about the explanatory gap—one about a man with a rare neurological syndrome called "Capgras Syndrome," embedded in another about a breed of crane whose nesting habitat is threatened by real estate development. As a result of brain injury sustained in a car accident, Mark Schluter awakens with the delusional belief that his intimates—especially his sister Karin, are imposters. Where Hustvedt uses multiple first-person narrators to emphasize the relational identities of her characters, Powers uses a third-person narrator who roves in and out of his characters' partial minds, emphasizing the unconscious motives, affiliations, and conflicts. Where Hustvedt emphasizes fantasy and ekphrasis, Powers imbues apparently realist narrative with an insistent lyricism that throws the realities it represents into ever-receding relief.

Powers's lyricism is key to understanding his novelistic response to neuroscience. Powers begins the novel not with the accident, the coma, or the awakening, but with a lyrical description of cranes returning to the small midwestern town where the Schluters were raised, a passage that begins with a "sky, ice

blue," that "flares up, a brief rose" as the "nervous birds, tall as children, crowd
together" on a river "they've learned to fly by memory":

> They converge on the river at winter's end as they have for eons, carpeting the
> wetlands. In this light something saurian still clings to them: the oldest flying
> things on earth, one stutter-step away from pterodactyls. As darkness falls for real,
> it's a beginner's world again, the same evening as that day sixty million years ago
> when this migration began.
>
> Half a million birds—four-fifths of all the sandhill cranes on earth—home in on
> this river. They trace the Central Flyway, an hourglass laid over the continent.
> They push up from New Mexico, Texas, and Mexico, hundreds of miles each day,
> with thousands more ahead before they reach their remembered nests. For a few
> weeks, this stretch of river shelters the miles-long flock. Then, by the start of
> spring, they'll rise and head away, feeling their way up to Saskatchewan, Alaska,
> or beyond.[44]

Lyricism condenses meaning, as dreams do. In this passage about nesting
cranes, the sky morphs into a rose, frozen plant life is stubble, the birds become
human children. The world to which Mark awakens is defamiliarized through
lyricism. Questions about memory link his story with the cranes'. For him, as
for them, "it's a beginner's world again."

Lyricism becomes literal as Mark emerges from his coma. When he begins to
awake, Powers describes him with subjectless sentences: "Rises up in flooded
fields. There is a wave, a rocking in the reeds. Pain again, then nothing."
Gradually, pronouns signal the reemergence of his feeling of selfhood:

> Where his mouth was, just smooth skin. Solid swallows up that hole. House
> remodeled; windows papered over. Door no more a door. Muscles pull lips but no
> space to open. Wires only, where words were. Face bent wrong and folded up into
> his own eyes. Slipped in a metal bed, the hell he must be in. His smallest move a
> pain worse than dying. Maybe death is done already. Done all ways, in one tip of
> his life and lifting. Who'd want to live after such a fall?
>
> A room of machines, the space he can't reach. Something splits out from him.
> People move in and smooth away too fast. Faces push up against his mouthless
> face, pushing words into him. He chews them and puffs sound back. Someone
> says be patient, but not to him. *Be patient, be a patient* is what he must be.[45]

Powers shepherds readers through a swift trajectory of phenomenological experience. An awakening that would take hours, days, or weeks in life becomes a

few paragraphs in fiction. The subjectless verb "rises up" indicates Mark's initial experience of awakening with a sort of premonitory subjectivity. He doesn't experience a difference between himself and his environment. His "beginner's world" is portrayed like that of an infant, thrust into a world of stimuli on the fringes of meaning. He becomes a toddler, drowning in the river where the cranes nest, before exploding into a hospital room, a badly injured adult, in terrible pain, kept alive by machines and air, people "pushing words into him." His first expression of language is portrayed as internal dialogue, folding into free, indirect speech: "*Be patient, be a patient* is what he must be." The narrator borrows Mark's echolalia, the apparently meaningless repetition of language that attends many brain injuries and neurological disorders. But in this case, nonsense becomes sense. Mark hears somebody say the words "be patient," and he elaborates and transforms the language into a realization of who and where he is: a patient—a person whose brain injury reminds him how fundamental it is to the making of identity, without any suggestion that physiology works in isolation.

When Mark finally speaks, his sister asks his neurosurgeon a crucial question about the combination of his echolalia and disorderly speech:

> "If he can say a word, it must mean *something*, right?"
> "Ah! You're pushing up against questions neurology can't answer yet."[46]

And that's where literature comes in. Powers opens his book with a lyricism that depends on the interplay of words to create novel meanings, to transform skies into roses and cranes into human children. Literary language, he seems to be suggesting, shares with Mark's echolalia a capacity to blur the boundaries between sense and nonsense—or to create speculative knowledge that works as much through feeling as it does through thought. Literature pushes up against questions neurology can't answer. As the narrative develops, the cranes continue to frame the story about the mysteries that entail the relations between Mark's physiology and his identity—as well as the more literal mystery plot focused on finding out what caused his accident.

If neurological stories take many forms, they also represent a variety of affects and philosophical convictions. Where Hustvedt asks readers to attend to the relational qualities of our biology, Powers's entwined narratives of two species experiencing "a beginner's world again" invite readers to consider interspecies relations—and, more than that, to reconsider the commonly held assumptions about human exceptionalism. When cranes and humans collide in *The Echo Maker,* their modes of perceiving their worlds defamiliarize one another. Just as cranes can't experience what it feels like to be human, humans cannot experience what it feels like to be a crane. What's common to these very different neurological stories is a refusal of simplistic cause-effect relations implied by "you are your brain" arguments. Like so many writers engaging neuroscience, Hustvedt and Powers substitute particularity for reductionism and the partial views of subjective narration for objective empiricism. They write fiction that foregrounds the overdetermined relations among brain, mind, identity, social relations, and physical environment—and they do it by imagining characters and scenarios that represent what it means and feels like to live in slices of those relations, slices whose particularity makes them knowable without suggesting they represent all there is to know.

A Brief History of "Neuro Lit Crit"

In 2010, neuromania emerged—or came out—into the world of literary studies. The most public sign of the coming-out party was *The New York Times*'s publication of a series of articles debating the question "Can 'Neuro Lit Crit' Save the Humanities?"—yoking a variety of critical methods under the umbrella of "neuro lit crit," including those informed by evolutionary psychology, cognitive science, and the neurosciences. Two of the six contributors—William Pannapacker and Marco Roth—answered with an emphatic (and even mocking) "no." Pannapacker compares neurohumanists to previous generations of literary scholars he casts as "amateur historians, sociologists, or philosophers," suggesting the approaches are faddish vehicles to advance careers rather than genuine intellectual inquiry. Roth argues that they're "depressingly determinist": "Learning about which part of your brain lights up when you come across a passage of free indirect discourse seems less interesting to me than learning what free indirect discourse is, how and when it emerged, and why a novelist might choose to use it, as a free and conscious choice."[47]

Critiques of "neuro" and cognitive approaches to studying the arts and culture share a number of valid concerns—though, in their rhetoric, they still tend to reinforce the gulf between science and the humanities that C. P. Snow lamented (famously) in the 1950s in his essay "The Two Cultures" (first published in *The New Statesman* in 1956 and subsequently expanded as a lecture and book in 1959 and as second book in 1963). Today, as in the fifties, literary intellectuals and scientists often display "a curious distorted image of each other."[48] Critics of neuroscience worry that reductive and determinist approaches to understanding the brain oversimplify subjective experience, underestimate individual difference, diminish agency, and obscure the role of social, cultural, and political forces in the shaping of individual experience. Critics of the neurohumanities worry that these same tendencies will reduce art to a biological or evolutionary imperative—and that scholars and artists who employ brain research in their work are capitulating to the empirical bottom lines and cultural capital of neuroscience.

Two contributors to the *Times* debate—Blakey Vermeule and Michael Holquist—write as neuro-enthusiasts, about the possibilities of overcoming divides between the sciences and humanities, without rising to the headline's bait about whether the humanities need saving or whether they, as cognitive critics, would be its saviors. Vermeule applauds "a new openness to scientific ideas and methods," describing their influence as "practical, positive, coopera-tive, and empirical" research projects that can help us understand why people are "passionately moved" by art. Holquist emphasizes literary study as a way of understanding complex forms of literacy and argues that "trying better to grasp what it is that we do when we read works having advanced levels of intricacy is the kind of study that reaches out to a wider community." Neurocognitive approaches to literature can and do lead to new insights like these, but within the context of a debate about "saving" the humanities, the neuro-enthusiasts become accidental voices for an unproductive division between the *neuro*hu-manities and its many other forms. The remaining two contributions read like a corrective to the enthusiasts. William Chace and Elif Batuman articulate meas-ured, equivocal responses. Chace expresses a "hope that the relationship with brain research will prove a productive meeting of equals." Batuman cautions that what literature does "better than anything else" is to provide "a detailed representation of the inner experience of being alive in a given time and place"—and therefore "a good cognitive theory of the novel has to involve the historical conditioning of mental processes."[49]

As Rose and Abi-Rached argue, "a number of key mutations—conceptual, technological, economic, and biopolitical—have enabled the neurosciences to leave the enclosed space of the laboratory and gain traction in the world outside."[50] Neuroscience's migration into literary criticism and the pages of *The New York Times* would seem to indicate some evolution beyond the intractable divide between Snow's "two cultures," but it's an evolution that requires careful rhetorical and conceptual attention to the very real tensions that keep the divide alive. The implications of neuroscientific understandings of the self or art raise a host of ethical and philosophical problems. In *Neuromania: On the Limits of Brain Science* (2011), Paolo Legrenzi and Carlo Umiltà trace the history of this migration and the ethical questions it raises, about personal agency, life and death, social responsibility, and biopolitics. In *Brainwashed: The Seductive Appeal of Mindless Neuroscience* (2013), Sally Satel and Scott O. Lilienfeld observe that "The key problem with neurocentrism is that it devalues the importance of psychological explanations and environmental factors." Feminist anthropologist Emily Martin has argued that the "dominance" of neuro-reductionism threatens to overshadow qualitative or "non-reductionist" academic discipline.[51]

Literary critics such as Marco Roth, Francisco Ortega, and Fernando Vidal have expressed skepticism about the neurocentrism of recent developments in contemporary literature, arguing that they may capitulate to or reinforce the bold speculations and reductionism of so much recent neuromania. Roth makes the extreme claim that "the new genre of the neuronovel" may be a sign of the novel's "diminishing purview" because it replaces what he sees as the complexity of psychological realism with neurological reductionism. Ortega and Vidal are more careful to delineate a range of literary responses to neuroscience: "neuronovelists differ—at least in their writings—in their commitment to treating humans as 'cerebral subjects' characterized by the fact of *being* brains."[52] Ortega and Vidal are critical of a tendency among literary writers and scholars to defer to neuroscience's empirical aura, and they object to representations that reduce human beings or literary characters to "cerebral subjects," but they don't see these problems as a defining feature of literary responses to neuroscience.

As Ortega and Vidal observe in their influential article "Brains in Literature / Literature in the Brain," "neuro lit crit" has appeared at a time when some distinguished writers have depicted their protagonists using neuroscientific vocabulary."[53] Like brain memoirs and neuronovels, literary criticism informed by "neuroscientific vocabulary" is arguably a contribution to neuromania as a larger cultural phenomenon, but at its strongest it offers a synthesis of multidisciplinary inquiry about how the brain and mind make meaning through representation, as literature does. As Alan Richardson observes in his epilogue to a recent issue of *Modern Fiction Studies* on "Neuroscience and Modern Fiction," cognitive approaches to literature do not enjoy "key signs that usually accompany widespread institutional acceptance"—for example, a journal or designated faculty positions. Despite *The New York Times*'s description of "neuro lit crit" as "The Next Big Thing in English," the neurohumanities remain controversial and somewhat marginal. Richardson argues that "theory-driven venues . . . have not welcomed cognitive studies the way they have, say ecocriticism, disability studies, or animal studies" at least partly because of a "lack of a common program, shared methodology, or unifying theoretical framework."[54]

While it's true that the methods of the neurohumanities diverge at least as much as they cohere, it's also true that they are haunted by the legacy of Snow's two cultures and by a suspicion among humanities scholars that the neurosciences are wedded to reductive, deterministic views of the mind (and the world in general). Broadly conceived, the neurohumanities—neuroaesthetics, cognitive literary and cultural studies, neurocognitive theories of reading and narrative—ignite ideological and political flashpoints that fields like ecocriticism or disability studies do not. Key texts in this history—published by scholars like Ellen Spolsky, Mark Turner, Paul John Eakin, Lisa Zunshine, Blakey Vermeule, and Paul Armstrong—seem to push against the grain of literary studies, by engaging with science rather than critiquing it and by suggesting that it may still be valuable to consider universal qualities of literary experience. However, these scholars were among the first to recognize convergences between the post-structuralist theory dominating the humanities and new ideas about the physiology of self that were emerging from cognitive science and neurobiology during the 1980s and 1990s.

In the opening essay to her edited collection *Introduction to Cognitive Cultural Studies* (2010), Lisa Zunshine names Marxist literary critic Raymond Williams as a central influence. As Zunshine observes, Williams argues in *The Long Revolution* (1961/1965) that human experience is a "creation" built from "two main sources: the human brain as it has evolved, and the interpretation carried by our cultures."[55] It's a savvy rhetorical move. Zunshine defines this emerging field as a response to a call heralded by one of the most respected cultural materialist critics in the history of literary theory. Zunshine is aware that a significant thread in neurocognitive approaches to literature emphasizes universalism, an idea largely eschewed by literary studies in the decades after post-structuralism displaced traditional humanism's ethos and methods for understanding literature. While many neurocognitively minded critics have emphasized universal qualities of literary experience, they have also developed increasingly nuanced arguments about the complexities of brain physiology, arguments that resist determinism and account for the dramatic variations in the actual brains of living people. Productive tensions between general universals and attention to particular differences have been central to the relatively brief history of the neurohumanities.

Mark Turner and Ellen Spolsky became voices of the first wave of cognitive literary studies during the 1990s—famously declared "The Decade of the Brain" by George H. W. Bush. Both critics worked on the margins of literary studies but situated themselves in relation to the centrality of cognitive science in the development of intellectual and academic thought more broadly. In the process, they published work whose ethos was at odds with norms in literary studies. A decade before it became fashionable in literary criticism to question "the hermeneutics of suspicion" that had become a side effect of post-structuralist theory, Turner and Spolsky emphasized literature's power to help people think—and feel—and cognitive science's capacity to help us understand that power.[56] In 1989, Turner collaborated with cognitive linguist George Lakoff on *More than Cool Reason: A Field Guide to Poetic Metaphor,* arguing that metaphor is a cognitive phenomenon—rather than a purely linguistic or literary phenomenon. In his subsequent two books, *Reading Minds: The Study of English in the Age of Cognitive Science* (1993) and *The Literary Mind* (1996), Turner built on the idea that what we call "literary experience"—particularly narrative—is in fact a "fundamental instrument of thought."[57] In other words, literature is central to culture, rather than a rarefied or elite by-product of it. In 1993, Ellen Spolsky published *Gaps in Nature: Literary Interpretation and the Modular Mind,* making two bold claims: "the gaps in human cognitive structure—the vacancies between fragments of understanding—not only permit but actually encourage transformation and innovation and, furthermore, this state of affairs is the logical outcome of evolutionary development."[58] Spolsky acknowledges the fact that her hypothesis is rooted "fragilely" in tentative and evolving research in cognitive theory and neurobiology—and, in fact, the idea of modularity has been largely displaced by models of mind and brain that emphasize widespread connectivity among systems. Ironically, that paradigm shift in the cognitive neurosciences bolsters Spolsky's most valuable contribution to literary studies—the way she transforms the gaps and fissures central to deconstructive reading into tools for thinking about reading as a constructive enterprise. Even while Turner and Spolsky espoused ideas unpopular in literary studies—that there might be something like a universal experience of literature or that the humanities have some things to learn from the sciences—they were bumping up against conceptual resonances between the post-structuralist humanities and the cognitive sciences that were difficult to see because of pervasive differences in vocabulary, methods, and rhetoric.

At the end of the 1990s, autobiography theorist Paul John Eakin described a convergence between theories of the self emerging from the neurosciences and the humanities. Eakin drew on the work of Ulric Neisser, Antonio Damasio, Oliver Sacks, and Gerald Edelman to offer a new angle on post-structuralism's central tenet, that the self is socially constructed:

> Post-structuralist thought in the last twenty years . . . has delineated the manifold ways in which cultures shape the individual subject. Inevitably, resisting the more deterministic forms of social constructionism, others have sought to reaffirm the possibility of an individual's agency. The issues in this debate look quite different when we shift from cultural theory to neurobiology. Whereas post-structuralism postulates a subjectivity that is "split" or "decentered," the point of departure for neurobiological accounts of subjectivity is "the binding problem." Which "poses the question of how different stimulus inputs to different parts of the brain are bound together so as to produce a single unified experience, for example, seeing a cat." The link between the neurobiologist's concern with seeing a cat and a cultural theorist's account of the individual's relation to the world is precisely the interface between organism and environment.[59]

In Edelman's theory of neuronal group selection, sometimes called "neural Darwinism," and in Damasio's theory of consciousness, perception is the key "interface between organism and environment." If selves are socially constructed or consciousness culturally inflected, the brains of the organisms feeling selfhood are surely fundamental to the construction. The implication is that empirical and theoretical research on the brain and cognition may yield greater understanding of the lived realities of people described by the abstractions of post-structuralist accounts of selfhood—and of literary experience.

During the first decade of the twenty-first century, a number of critics inspired by these unexpected disciplinary consonances undertook the challenging work of devising methods and vocabularies for articulating their implications—Patrick Colm Hogan, Alan Richardson, and Zunshine. In 2003, Hogan published two books, *The Mind and Its Stories: Narrative Universals and Human Emotion* and *Cognitive Science, Literature, and the Arts: A Guide for Humanists.* In the latter, Hogan wrestles with the disciplinary divides that tended to obscure the interdisciplinary consonance Eakin observed. Hogan calls for the institutionalization of these consonances: "It is crucial for humanists and scientists to recognize that the arts should not be some marginal area to which cognitive discoveries are imported after they are made elsewhere. Arts are central to our lives."[60] Why is it crucial? Because, as Hogan observes in *The Mind and Its Stories,* literary genres like narrative and lyric are vehicles for what he calls "emotion prototypes"; literature gives concrete form to phenomenological experiences. For example, "the prototype for sorrow is roughly 'what you feel when someone you love dies and express through weeping.'"[61] If, as Eakin observed, the cognitive neurosciences cannot solve the "binding problem," or if they haven't overcome the explanatory gap, reading is a kind of laboratory for exploring what's involved when feelings acquire names, become concepts, and then shape new feelings. The sum of all these feelings is, plausibly, something very similar to what post-structuralist critics call the "socially constructed self."

The first decade of the twenty-first century saw the publication of several books that represent a second wave of the neurohumanities, characterized by a diffuse set of methods that would later come to be yoked by the category cognitive literary studies. Three books in particular became influential exemplars of this second wave in the neurohumanities: Zunshine's *Why We Read Fiction: Theory of Mind and the Novel* (2006), Suzanne Keen's *Empathy and the Novel* (2007), and Blakey Vermeule's *Why Do We Care about Literary Characters?* (2009). Like many of their contemporaries, Zunshine, Keen, and Vermeule synthesize cultural studies methods with increasingly sophisticated and multidisciplinary research emerging from the cognitive neurosciences and the philosophy of mind. Their titles represent the clarity of their purposes, their shared interests, and their emphasis on cognitive and literary universals like empathy, theory of mind, and identification. Zunshine draws on theory-of-mind research in cognitive science to argue that literary texts satisfy, create, and test "cognitive cravings," focusing mostly on cognitive capacities to imagine other people's mental experiences—and the centrality of doing so to navigating social relations. Keen emphasizes neurocognitive research—especially the fMRI studies of Tania Singer—that link empathy to so-called mirror neurons.[62] Responding to influential research on empathy and mirror systems by Tania Singer, Keen observes that "Singer and her colleagues conclude that empathy is mediated by the part of the pain network associated with pain's affective qualities, but not its sensory qualities."[63] In other words, we can imagine other people's pain, but we can't feel it. As a result, Keen's conclusions are multifarious—and not entirely rosy: It may be easier to empathize with fictional characters than real people; novelists (and writers and artists in general) may be more empathetic than the general population; empathetic responses occur more readily in response to negative emotions; empathy does not necessarily lead to altruism or action; and empathy can lead to an aversive response as well as a sympathetic one. Vermeule focuses on literary characters, as "tools to think with": "Literary narratives probe us and make us worry about what it is to interact with fictional people. And we should worry, because interacting with fictional people turns out to be a central cognitive preoccupation, one that exposes many of the aspects of how our minds work."[64] Vermeule's "fictional people" include characters, like Clarissa Dalloway or Humbert Humbert, but also representations of actual people we don't know, like Barack Obama or Caitlyn Jenner, and people we do know, even those we're intimate with. When we imagine the mental lives of others, we create a kind of productive fiction. Vermeule emphasizes the productive necessities of such fictions. Literature, she argues, makes us attentive to forms of representation that shape the ways we live. If we don't recognize the role of representation in the shaping of social relations, we will mistake our mental reproductions of others for "the real properties" of those people, rather than recognizing the cognitive filters that enable us to relate to them.

In *How Literature Plays with the Brain: The Neuroscience of Reading and Art* (2013), Paul Armstrong observes that "the divide between the so-called two cultures . . . can be crossed by conversations between both parties on both sides who share common interests and find mutual benefit from discussing them."[65] Armstrong's key words are "common" and "mutual." Cross-disciplinary encounters like the ones he describes are increasingly common in public forums like conferences and symposiums, but still rare in day-to-day research or scholarly publications. Until recently, most neurohumanities research has drawn on the cognitive neurosciences to frame arguments about the arts. Genuinely multidisciplinary inquiry is still rare. Two recent (and very different) publications offer promising examples of multidisciplinary research paradigms: Gabrielle Starr's *Feeling Beauty: The Neuroscience of Aesthetic Experience* (2013) and Sebastian Groes's edited collection *Memory in the Twenty-First Century: New Critical Perspectives from the Arts, Humanities, and Sciences* (2016).

Starr collaborated with Ed Vessel and Nava Rubin in the Center for Neural Science at New York University to design a series of empirical studies to investigate questions about aesthetic experience, both ancient and contemporary. As Starr conceives it, "In turning to the tools and methods of cognitive neuroscience I am continuing, in new form, the fundamentally multidisciplinary inquiry that has obtained since the early years of modern aesthetics. As Alexander Baumgarten put it in his Meditations of 1735 (the text that introduced the term aesthetics into the modern lexicon), aesthetic experience is a blend of sensation and knowledge such that we almost feel thought itself."[66] In pragmatic terms, Starr's collaboration confronts the explanatory gap directly: "The key problem . . . is how we bridge the gaps between knowledge of matter (neurons, networks), experiences of works of art, and the works themselves." Her answer is a hybrid of traditional literary criticism, philosophy, and empirical research focusing on brain activation during intense aesthetic experience and relations between the experience of imagery and perception.

Based on her blend of empirical research and literary analysis, Starr argues that aesthetic experience activates new relations among networks of brain activity (for example the default mode network, commonly theorized to be fundamental to identity *and* reward systems). Because she is a deft critic of art and literature, Starr is careful to acknowledge "that not all aesthetic experience is the same, and being moved by a work of art means different things to different people." Nonetheless, she argues that her multidisciplinary approach enables a new hypothesis about art's power to reorganize identity. "[T]he arts," she argues, "mediate our knowledge of the world around us by directing our attention, shaping perceptions, and creating dissonance or harmony where none had been before." Through her collaborations with Vessel and Rubin, Starr comes to a conclusion that bridges traditional, universalizing views on the humanities and more recent, theoretically driven critiques of those views: "what aesthetics thus gives us is a restructuring of value."[67] The experience of art changes us, by enabling new experiences and judgments. The contents of those experiences and judgments vary with time, context, and mood.

Rather than systematizing multidisciplinary inquiry, Groes's *Memory in the Twenty-First Century* creates a dissonant montage of new research from disparate fields. The anthology juxtaposes "a series of experimental, creative, and critical interventions as dynamic and protean as memory itself"—and puts them into dialogue through Groes's synthetic introductions to the book's sections. As he writes, "It is in this . . . interdisciplinary spirit that this book seeks to do a number of things differently, so that various reductive dialectics that inhibit current debate and scientific research on memory can be transcended."[68] While the dialogue is mostly hypothetical, it occasionally becomes literal: "In discussion with a neuroscientist [novelist Will] Self made an extraordinary claim about plotting and writing a novel—a process that demands him to keep control over 100,000 words: 'I can feel my hippocampus throbbing.' Spiers [the neuroscientist] wanted to find out whether Self's psychogeographizing would make him stand out from the control group of 24 average participants" involved in his hippocampal research.[69] The result became an ongoing collaboration between Self and Spiers—a largely hypothetical, if not fantastical, one. Spiers and Self know very well that fMRI scans generate statistical knowledge about groups of people. It's dubious to draw conclusions about the significance of one writer's brain from them. In that sense, their experiments resemble the cultural laboratory of literature, exploring its personal meanings for Self rather than advancing hippocampal research.

When Self describes his throbbing brain, it's *his brain* touching *him*. As Starr's research suggests, aesthetic engagement—for example, reading one of Self's novels—touches readers, changing those readers via little-understood relations between immaterial experience and material physiology. The brain, in the twenty-first century, is compelling just about every discipline to attend to it—and to touch each other's methods and debates. Literature's contribution is a diverse set of aestheticized narratives that invite readers to explore the vicissitudes of the explanatory gap. Starr argues that aesthetic experiments invite us to attend dissonance in harmony and harmony in dissonance. If she's right— and I think she is—they are ideal laboratories for making sense of the paradox of neuroscience: We have learned so much and still know so little about relations between brain and self.

"All Manner of Neurologies"

The number 2 is a very dangerous number: that is why the dialectic is a
dangerous process. Attempts to divide anything into two ought to be
regarded with much suspicion.
—C. P. Snow, "The Two Cultures"[70]

As "neuro lit crit" has been establishing itself, a small but growing number of critics have begun taking it in a slightly different direction: studying the representation of brains in literature. Their work is related to—but also distinct from—the field that has come to be called "cognitive literary studies." As Ortega and Vidal explain, "A neural turn has also been taken in some quarters within the literary field. The neurosciences have provided writers of literature with resources for depicting characters and psychological processes and states; at the same time, they have inspired new interpretive approaches within literary studies. A twofold motif structures what might be called the 'neuroliterary field': brains in literature / literature in the brain. There has been a certain convergence between the rise of 'neuronovels,' on the one hand, and the neurologization of literary analysis, on the other."[71]

In an article on the role of neuroscience in *The Echo Maker*, Charles B. Harris declares it "the first fully realized novel of *neurological realism.*"[72] Even though he wants to avoid the assertion of a binary relationship between psychological novels and neurological ones, Harris—like Roth—contrasts neurological realism with the psychological realism of predecessors like Henry James. In fact, the attributes of the genre, as he articulates them, describe the commitments of most neuronovels (and many brain memoirs). As he argues, neurological realism

- "foregrounds the effects of largely unconscious neurological activities";
- challenges "the concept of a solid and continuous 'inner' self" and replaces it with portraits of fluid, multifarious, and fragile identity, described by Powers as "a committee of millions" or "like coral reefs, . . . complex but fragile ecosystems";
- "dismantles . . . dualisms on neuroscientific grounds," including "inner and outer, mind and body, reason and emotion, self and other";
- represents fuzzy "boundaries between self and world" as positive (rather than "threatening").[73]

In literary theory, *realism* is a rhetorical black hole, because what's *real* depends on a reader's frame of reference. A novel like *Middlemarch* might be described as realist on social grounds, *The Portrait of a Lady* on psychological ones, or *The Sound and the Fury* on phenomenological ones. I have little interest in adjudicating the realism of neuronovels as different from each other as Lethem's *Motherless Brooklyn* or Casey's *The Man Who Walked Away,* nor do I have much interest in debating what makes a "fully realized" work of fiction in any genre or subgenre. Nonetheless, Harris's description of Powers's neurological realism describes many of the core qualities that make neuronovels and brain memoirs cultural laboratories for exploring questions about what to do with or about the fleshy matter in our skulls. Andrew Gaedtke addresses the neuronovel—especially Lodge's *Thinks* . . . and McEwan's *Saturday*—in terms of formal experimentation and its relation to epistemology: "the explanatory gap between first-person and third-person accounts of cognitive phenomena is both a philosophical and a narratological problem that defines this emergent genre. While addressing the problem of qualia, these novels also turn toward renewed concerns about the status of narrative as a procedure of knowledge, identity, and self-delusion—concerns that have also been raised by contemporary neuroscience."[74] In general, brain narratives tend to represent conscious, unconscious, *and* embodied cognition; offer portraits of fluid, fragile, and multiple identities; resist dualisms or binaries that fuel debates about the explanatory gap; emphasize the dynamic interplay of self and environment; and create explicit connections between the epistemological complications of narrative and the brain research they respond to. In addition to all this, they emphasize neurological difference, rather than norms, and they wrestle with ironies and paradoxes that arise from giving linguistic and narrative form to unconscious or preconscious experience that precedes or eludes language. As laboratories, they pick up the brain where brain research tends to put it down—at its epistemological limits. For a neuroscientist like Damasio, the idea that "biology and culture are thoroughly interactive" is an implication of his research, both a guiding assumption and epilogue to his theories. For literary writers, it's a starting point that initiates the complications of story.

The urgency of the questions at stake here is most vivid in memoirs written by people whose experience has confounded clinical neurology. When David B. writes about his brother's epilepsy, autobiography becomes a form of reflection on the uncertainties and pain of living with an incurable brain disorder; when Temple Grandin writes about her autistic experience, she becomes a public advocate for neurological difference; when Jean-Dominique Bauby uses blinking eyes to dictate his story about the daily experience of "locked-in syndrome," his writing is a means of personal expression, communication with friends and family, and a contribution to medical science. In a published conversation with Lisa Zunshine about the need to create dialogue between cognitive studies and disability studies, Ralph James Savarese describes the work of autistic memoirist Tito Mukhopadhyay, who learned through writing to "translate the experience of alternative embodiment into evocative language."[75] Mukhopadhyay's writing compels neurotypical readers to reconceive their assumptions about cognitive norms—and the social practices that follow from them. In this dialogue, Zunshine acknowledges a mistake in her earlier work: equating autism with so-called mindblindness, or an inability to imagine the mental states of others. A host of memoirs by autistic people published in the last ten years have—along with the voices of activists in the neurodiversity movement—made it stunningly clear that autistic people think routinely about the mental states of others. The attribution of mindblindness is a neurotypical misreading of autistic experience. Most writers of brain memoirs and neuronovelists link questions about cognitive norms to the explanatory gap—and ask readers to question or examine their own cognitive eccentricities. They model a combination of intellectual humility and curiosity that acknowledges all we don't know about physiology's role in the making of self and values the neurological differences that define the experience of particular selves.

Brain memoirs and neuronovels, understood as comprising a loosely structured literary movement, assume a cultural force with a message similar to Savarese's: "If cosmopolitanism is the idea of a trans-national community, the feeling of being respectfully at home everywhere in the world, then neurocosmopolitanism is the idea of a trans-neurocommunity, the feeling of being respectfully at home with all manner of neurologies. By 'neurocosmopolitan' I mean not just an openness to neurological difference but, rather, a denaturalization, even a dethronement, of privileged neurotypicality."[76]

In *The Elusive Brain,* I show how writers grapple with representing both the explanatory gap and neurological difference, foregrounding the strangeness of every brain and the elusiveness of the brain, body, world relations through which identity seems to emerge—in ways that dethrone simplistic myths about "cerebral subjectivity" and neurotypicality. These writers transform neuromania into productive cultural dialogue about what it means to be an organism, helping readers imagine a near future in which many more of us are "respectfully at home . . . with all manner of neurologies."

1

Before Neuromania

Even someone who has modeled the function of the inferior frontal gyrus
might still be plagued by monsters that gyrus modeled.
—Richard Powers, *Galatea 2.2*

THE CHARACTER PLAGUED BY THOSE MONSTERS OF the inferior frontal gyrus is
Phillip Lentz, the voice of science in Powers's *Galatea 2.2,* a novel that dramatizes Snow's argument about the two cultures of the sciences and humanities
through a story about teaching a computer to pass graduate exams in literature.
Lentz's collaborator in this experiment in artificial intelligence is Richard P.,
fictional novelist and voice for the humanities. As narrator, Richard P. has the
power. In his telling, Lentz's scoliosis, which sometimes takes the form of a
neuromuscular condition, becomes a monster; like Helen, the computer, he's
got something in common with Mary Shelley's creature in *Frankenstein.* Lentz,
a neuro-linguist who models neural networks with computational ones, suffers
from a condition related but not reducible to his brain—one whose mysterious
effects reach throughout his body. His condition signals the problem that
prevents Helen from becoming human: She has no body. With Lentz, with his
"kinked walk," Powers crystallizes a theme in neurological narratives of the
1990s: No matter how much Lentz knows about brains—and he knows enough
to believe he can build one from computer chips—he still has to live with his
body, including the three pounds of flesh in his skull. And that means living
with its fundamental but elusive relation to every detail of his existence: his gait
and gestures, his moods, his intellectual work, and his tendency to be what

39

he calls a "social maladroit."[1] We must learn about the brain, these narratives suggest, but we must also learn to live with our brains—and what we don't know about them.

A cluster of high-profile works of narrative nonfiction and fiction published around the end of the twentieth century tell stories about the tension between knowing the brain and living with it—including Sacks's *The Man Who Mistook His Wife for a Hat* (1985) and *An Anthropologist on Mars* (1995), Temple Grandin's *Thinking in Pictures: My Life with Autism* (1995), Kay Redfield Jamison's *An Unquiet Mind: A Memoir of Moods and Madness* (1996), Richard Powers's *Galatea 2.2* (1995), and David Lodge's *Thinks . . .* (2001). These are narratives written in dialogue with various forms of brain research, but otherwise in relative isolation, without the benefits or burdens of a full-fledged cultural neuromania to make them legible as contributions to a debate or trend. By the 1990s, these narratives had come to represent an embryonic form of neuromania—enthusiastic, searching, and perhaps naive to social or political implications that would fuel debates about the relations between brain and self a decade later. Before neuromania, Grandin, Jamison, Powers, and Lodge published narratives that offer detailed descriptions of a phenomenological experience that strays from cognitive norms, link that experience to brain physiology, and tell stories built on the principle that phenomenology and physiology become meaningful through concrete material realities and particular social relations.

I'm using the term *"phenomenology"* here, in lieu of *"interiority,"* because all of these writers emphasize the dynamism—rather than containment—of mental experience. Grandin, for example, insists on the biology of autistic experience, but she narrates herself as a work in progress, with her self-designed squeeze chute as a major force in her cognitive and social development. Similarly, Jamison is a dogmatic advocate of pharmacological treatment of manic depression, but she describes love as an equally powerful force in making it possible to live with mania and depression. In *Galatea 2.2,* Powers dramatizes the creation of Helen, a computer whose capacity to think and feel is measured by her ability to interpret literary texts. In *Thinks . . .,* a brain-shaped university research center is the setting for a novelist and a cognitive scientist to flirt and fuck their way through a series of debates about consciousness—stymied by the screens of language and representation that separate the protagonists from any direct experience of the phenomenologies they argue about. All these texts make mind or consciousness a primary theme; they revel in speculative knowledge about the role of the brain in making consciousness, and they demonstrate—through example—that the material specificities and social complexities required to build a narrative are also necessary components of mental experience. While they may have been conceived and published in isolation, with the exception of collaboration between Sacks and Grandin, their influence is collective. They popularized narrative patterns and ideological dispositions that shaped the emergence of literary neuromania a decade later.

The Case of Oliver Sacks

Oliver Sacks may not have invented neuromania, but he was certainly the Western world's most influential neuromaniac—in literature as much as in other cultural spheres. He made a career of writing more prolifically about the brain and identity than any other writer of the late twentieth century. He made Temple Grandin famous; he inspired novels by Jonathan Lethem and Mark Haddon; Richard Powers based a character on him in *The Echo Maker.* From *Awakenings* (1973) to his autobiography *On the Move* (2015), Sacks emphasizes varieties of tension that arise between knowing brains and living with them. His recurring arguments are all linked to these tensions: The neurodiversity of the human species is wondrous; suffering and insight comingle; when brains stray from the norm, they challenge conventional assumptions about identity; and, perhaps most insistently, while brain damage, disease, and injury create serious challenges and much suffering, they can also lead to valuable modes of perceiving and experiencing the world. Sacks developed a *literary* persona over the course of his career—defined by his curiosity, his refusal of disciplinary boundaries, his clinical and ethical abandon (which sometimes becomes reckless), and his personal bonding with the people, or characters, whose experiences he chronicles.

For Sacks, relations between brain physiology and identity raise serious ethical implications. As he writes in the preface to *An Anthropologist on Mars* (1996), "These are tales of survival, survival under altered, sometimes radically altered, conditions—survival made possible by the wonderful (but sometimes dangerous) powers of reconstruction and adaptation we have. In earlier books I wrote of the 'preservation' of self, and (more rarely) of the 'loss' of self, in neurological disorders. I have come to think these terms too simple—and that there is neither loss nor preservation of identity in such situations, but, rather, its adaptation, even its transmutation, given a radically altered brain and 'reality.'"[2] Sacks's case histories tend to follow a narrative pattern. A person experiences brain illness or injury that alters identity; Sacks's interactions with his suffering subjects raise perplexing questions about the brain, and these send him off on tours of the neurological literature; together, he and his subjects collaborate on a process of discovery that involves resurrecting insights lost in the history of neurology or creating new ones; those insights lead to new ways of being that draw on strengths left intact or created by the subjects' altered brain physiology. To sustain those new ways of being, the other people in the subjects' social spheres—physicians, caretakers, loved ones—must learn to adapt. They must create an environment that enables and encourages the expression and agency that emerge from a particular person's neurological eccentricities—what many now call *neurodivergence*.

In "Witty Ticcy Ray," a case history that appears in the "Excesses" section of *The Man Who Mistook His Wife for a Hat,* Sacks unfolds the pattern—Tourette's syndrome, an apparent disability, becomes ability through creative reorientation of the material and the social—in a single paragraph. Sacks met Ray when he was a twenty-four-year-old man

> almost incapacitated by multiple tics of extreme violence coming in volleys every few seconds. He had been subject to these since the age of four and severely stigmatized by the attention they aroused, though his high intelligence, his wit, and his strength of character and sense of reality enabled him to pass successfully through school and college, and to be valued by a few friends and his wife. Since leaving college, however, he had been fired from a dozen jobs—always because of tics, never for incompetence—was continually in crises of one sort or another, usually caused by his impatience, his pugnacity, and his coarse, brilliant "chutzpah" and found his marriage threatened by involuntary cries of "Fuck!" "Shit!," and so on, which would burst from him at times of sexual excitement.

Ray consults Sacks because he is suffering, but that's not the whole story. He also values his Tourette's, crediting his symptoms with making him a better drummer and enabling his quick wit.[3] Just as significantly, Ray's Tourettic traits vary with context. Sometimes, just after sex, hard exercise, or a performance, he experiences no tics. Ray's story is analogous to one Sacks would publish ten years later, in *An Anthropologist on Mars*—"A Surgeon's Life"—about Dr. Carl Bennett, a surgeon with Tourette's whose tics are quieted while he performs the delicate act of surgery. The fact that certain actions or contexts provide outlets for or respite from the symptoms of Tourette's is a clue for Sacks, potentially illuminating mysterious relations between physiology, phenomenology, and behavior.

In both cases, Sacks emphasizes the idea that Tourette's "has an organic neurological basis," a fact denied by medicine for much of the twentieth century, partly because it varied so much from person to person and partly because, as Sacks writes, "Charcot and his pupils, who included Freud ... as well as Tourette, were among the last of their profession with a combined vision of body and soul, 'It,' and 'I,' neurology and psychiatry."[4] Gilles de la Tourette named and described the syndrome that would come to bear his name late in the nineteenth century, but people like Ray and Bennett were treated with psychoanalysis or psychotherapy, if at all, for a so-called " 'moral disease'—an expression of mischievousness or weakness of the will."[5] Two things changed: In the mid-1960s psychiatrist Arthur Shapiro popularized the treatment of Tourette's with the drug Haldol (haloperidol) and the establishment of the advocacy organization the Tourette Syndrome Association (TSA). The TSA's activism led to increased medical research and more effective treatments. In other words, the physiological and the social converged. When Sacks writes about "body and soul," he means something equivalent to physiology and identity. In the stories he tells, identity is both material and social, even when he doesn't name it as such.

With the cases of Ray and Dr. Bennett, Sacks emphasizes the blurry line between symptom and personality. As Sacks writes, "The Tourette's and the self shape each to the other, come more and more to complement each other, until finally, like a long-married couple, they become a single, compound being."[6] Sacks's phrasing makes it seem as though becoming a "compound being" is unique to Tourette's, but his body of work, including his autobiographical writing, makes it clear that we're all compound beings. He certainly was—with his prosopagnosia, or face blindness, his prolific drug use, his hallucinations, his uneasy relationship to sexuality, and his liminal professional position as a clinical neurologist with a series of unofficial and loose affiliations with the institutions that grant professional credibility. But, of course, every person's compound being takes particular forms, and with regard to Sacks's two famous Tourettic subjects, the material and social elements of identity are as particular as they are explicit. In Dr. Bennett's words, "It's all a question of space. Where I am now, I have no impulse to reach over to that brick wall, but if I were in range I'd have to touch it perhaps a hundred times."[7]

Space is fundamental to the expression of Dr. Bennett's tics. There is no divorcing them from the material world he moves through, and that has everything to do with his decision to become a surgeon—as it does with Ray's decision to become a drummer. As Sacks describes Bennett: "He was always good with his hands and loved the structure of natural things—the way rocks formed, the way plants grew, the way animals moved, the way muscles balanced and pulled against each other, the way the body was put together. He decided very early he wanted to become a surgeon."[8] Surgery, though clinical, is an intensely social act. Sacks observes Bennett at work, as he makes incisions in people's bodies. He removes a melanoma "along with a Brazil-nut-shaped wedge of fat" from one patient's "buttock" or "great flaps of brownish flesh in the groins and armpits" of another. When Sacks describes these details, he emphasizes the intimacy of one person cutting into another's body. Through this process, Sacks observes, Bennett's "whole personality and demeanor—sometimes nervous and diffident—change when he puts on his surgical mantle, takes on the quiet assurance, the identity, of one who is a master of his work." Yet, the details of Sacks's narratives suggest a more complex picture. Bennett's tics do sometimes emerge during breaks in the rhythm of surgery. Some of his actions can't be classified as belonging to his Tourettic self or his "transformed" professional one, as when he shows a patient the lump of flesh he excised from her body, to which she replies, "Ugh! . . . Don't show me. But thanks anyway."[9]

As a narrator, Sacks occupies two epistemological roles: the witness who confidently describes the transformation of his subject's "whole personality," and the commentator who muddies this same distinction and emphasizes the idea that neurology—as a window into the relationship between brain and self—makes it impossible to "have everything locked and understood." He occupies the second position when he generalizes from Tourette's to other neurological identities: "Such identity transformations, reorganizations, occur in us all as we move, in the course of the day, from one role, one persona, to another—the parental to the professional, to the political, to the erotic, or whatever. But they are especially dramatic in those who move in and out of neurological or psychiatric syndromes."[10] And therein lies Sacks's moral: The drama of neurological anomalies can help us see the relationship between brain and self in new ways—and it's a moral dramatized in enormous variety in literary works that respond to the neuromania he played a big role in popularizing.

But the brain's relation to self risks becoming an abstract philosophical subject—one distant from the empirical evidence of scientific research or the lived experience of actual people. Sacks's abstraction, though it's far from his primary mode, is central to two types of critique that trail his legacy. In 2005, *The Guardian* quoted neuroscientist Ray Dolan expressing characteristic skepticism about "Whether Dr. Sacks has provided any scientific insights into the neurological condition he has written about."[11] Dolan is particularly disturbed by "the tendency for Dr. Sacks to be an ever present dramatis persona" in his cases. Of course, Dolan's critique centers on Sacks's critique of medical neurology and empirical neuroscience: Where are the people? The lives? The phenomenology? Surely the brain's intricacy, combined with the documented differences between one brain and another, means the details of every person's neurology are a little different. Luminary Eric Kandel wrote about Sacks with more admiration in 2015, linking him to "a great descriptive tradition in neurology whereby studies of the neurological defects in single patients gave us some of our initial insights into how the brain gives rise to mind." Kandel emphasizes Sacks's contribution to questions about brain-mind relations, rather than making a scientific contribution to the study of particular "defects"—a word that runs directly against the grain of Sacks's efforts to change attitudes about neurological difference. Kandel touches on those efforts when he describes Sacks's "belief that disease often brings out a particular courage and beauty in the afflicted person and a determination to overcome their handicap."[12] Again, the language here represents a fundamental difference between Sacks and the neuroscience mainstream. For Sacks, Ray's virtuosity as a drummer isn't about overcoming a handicap; it's a talent made possible by his neurological difference.

Kandel's use of the word "handicap" would be outrageous to another camp of Sacks's critics—scholars and activists in disability studies. In an oft-cited review of *An Anthropologist on Mars,* sociologist Tom Shakespeare called the book a "high-brow freakshow" and Sacks "the man who mistook his patients for a literary career."[13] At least two scholars of disability and literature—Leonard Cassuto and G. Thomas Couser—have taken Shakespeare's accusations seriously and responded with careful analyses of the ethics of Sacks's writing. Cassuto describes Sacks as "a one-man countertrend" who combines elements of both the freak show and medical case study. Cassuto emphasizes Sacks's "evolving methodology," suggesting that Sacks's work (like Freud's) changed so much over time that it's a mistake to cite any particular work as a representative of his career. He argues that Sacks's "wonder narratives wind up creating a uniquely collaborative space within which disabled people can express themselves." Acknowledging elements of the freak show in Sacks's work, Cassuto concludes that "Sacks's work argues that people will want to stare, and the best way to counter this desire is not to forbid it but to shape and direct it, to make the gaze into a mutual look."[14] Couser evaluates Sacks on two grounds: the ethics of biomedicine and biography, comparing and differentiating two sets of standards. He argues that what's "most problematic from an ethical perspective is Sacks's practice of asking his subjects—particularly children—to perform certain tasks in order to illustrate their neurological difference," particularly when the medium is film or television. But he also argues that Sacks "deviates from, and occasionally challenges, the medical model of disability." In his analysis of "Witty Ticcy Ray," Couser concludes that Sacks portrays his own evolving understanding toward the idea that Tourette's "could be a valid modus vivendi—disability as a matter of identity rather than disorder." Ultimately, he argues that Sacks "points the way toward" but doesn't achieve a form of neuroanthropology characterized by the "dialogism and self-awareness of contemporary ethnography"—what he calls *postcolonial neuroanthropology* and others have called *neurocosmopolitanism*.[15]

In literary terms, there's another kind of critique that might be made about Sacks, one focused on a false naïveté in his narration style. In a *New York Times* review, neuropsychologist John C. Marshall complains, "Dr. Sacks's admirable presentation of seemingly bizarre phenomena and difficult concepts is marred by only one weakness. It is stylistic, but nonetheless extremely annoying. He constantly plays naive about the neurological literature."[16] Marshall is annoyed that Sacks seems to play dumb with the neurological literature in order to create narrative tension. If he doesn't know something any neurologist would, he can represent himself in the act of discovery, as he does, in case after case. This faux naïveté is not limited to the neurological literature. Sacks adopts the stance frequently, whenever he wants to represent discovery. He's describing past events, and like any life writer, he may choose how to sequence events and how to balance a voice that occupies the present and past of the writer simultaneously. When he chooses to represent himself as naive, his narratives start to expose themselves as constructed tales—or, using the language of post-structuralist literary theory, they reveal their gaps.

Sacks's faux-naive narration is central to Couser's critique of the documentary film "Don't Be Shy, Mr. Sacks"—about Heidi Comfort, "an eight-year-old girl with Williams syndrome, a genetic anomaly that renders individuals unusually verbal and sociable while limiting their cognitive abilities." Sacks plays a game with Heidi, covering a plate of muffins and asking her to tell him how many are concealed, then uncovering it and asking her to count again. She gets it wrong both times. Sacks reveals the game's inauthenticity, and Heidi responds with anger. In a related scene, he comments on Heidi's "difficulty with numbers" while shopping with her for a calculator. Heidi rebukes him for his cruelty. As Couser observes, "As Sacks narrates this episode (retrospectively, of course), he disarms her criticism by saying that he had provoked her into revealing further aspects of her condition—acute hearing, emotional sensitivity and "alarming directness."[17] This provocation represents a pattern in Sacks's work, not an anomaly. In "The Lost Mariner" (from *The Man Who Mistook His Wife for a Hat*), Sacks provokes Jimmie G., a man whose retrograde amnesia prevents him from making new memories, with similar faux naïveté. "A sudden, improbable suspicion seized me," Sacks writes. "What year is this, Mr. G.?"[18] It's 1975, but Jimmie G. answers that it's 1945. Sacks asks his age, and he tells him he's nineteen. Then Sacks makes an alarming move:

> Looking at the grey-haired man before me, I had an impulse for which I have never forgiven myself—it was, or would have been, the height of cruelty had there been any possibility of Jimmie's remembering it.
>
> "Here," I said, and thrust a mirror toward him. "Look in the mirror and tell me what you see. Is that a nineteen-year-old looking out from the mirror?"
>
> He suddenly turned ashen and gripped the sides of the chair. "Jesus Christ," he whispered. "Christ, what's going on? What's happened to me? Is this a nightmare?"[19]

As with Heidi Comfort, Sacks represents himself committing an act of cruelty and being rebuked by his subject. Because this is a written case history rather than a film, he also reports precise dialogue whose veracity no reader can verify. As with Heidi Comfort, Sacks defends his actions, this time by pointing out that Jimmie G. won't remember them. However, his argument, by the end of the case, is that Jimmie's "neurological devastation" was by no means complete. He was able to find peace and express his identity through acts of spiritual contemplation: "Memory, mental activity, mind alone, could not hold him; but moral attention and action could hold him completely."[20] With this in mind, Sacks's dismissal of his own cruelty is less than fully convincing. In both cases, Sacks becomes a foil for his own narration. He represents himself mistreating his subjects and then defends his actions. In the process, he creates conflict that provokes his subjects to speak for themselves. In the process, viewers and readers become privy to a relationship—an imperfect one, between a doctor who refuses to conceal himself behind a cloak of objectivity and a patient whose self-representation is imperative to Sacks's mission.

Sacks's lapses are integral to his method—and his portrayal of himself as a literary character. As a writer, Sacks represents himself as fallible, as capable of cruelty and ethical mistakes as anybody. As Couser points out, "One of the problems that Sacks's work presents is that its status isn't altogether clear. It's not medical practice, nor is it medical research producing generalizable knowledge, but it does involve vulnerable subjects."[21] Shakespeare's accusation about "the man who mistook his patients for a literary career" is extreme, and, I would argue, unfair. As Couser observes, Shakespeare is "charging Sacks with commodifying his patients as a means of self-aggrandizement."[22] The key word in Shakespeare's accusation is "literary." Like any writer, Sacks does appropriate his subjects' experience, for the sake of telling stories that enable him to consider questions about neurology and identity. But all life writing—and, really, all literary writing—appropriates the experience of others and subsumes it under the dominant voice of a writer. As an autobiographer, Sacks emphasizes curiosity over mastery. He tells stories about his own fallibility—from the violations in "Don't Be Shy, Mr. Sacks" and "The Lost Mariner" to the extreme amphetamine use, reckless motorcycle driving, or sexual confusion in *On the Move* (2015). As a writer, he represents himself as a fallible physician, researcher, and human being. He may be coy about it, but he's also strategic. When Sacks fails, readers witness the conflicts that ensue, conflicts that demonstrate relational qualities that tend to be occluded by conventional medical practice or scientific research.

When Ray Dolan complains that Sacks makes himself a "dramatis persona," he may or may not be alluding to the mess of human relations that ensues from Dr. Sacks's adoption of a literary technique. But that's exactly what Sacks's techniques achieve, or reveal. As he makes clear in *On the Move,* he was never good at following protocol or minding restrictions. As his mentors at Albert Einstein Medical College tell him, "Sacks, you are a menace in the lab. Why don't you go out and see patients—you'll do less harm."[23] Of course, "do no harm" is shorthand for the guiding principle of medical ethics, nonmaleficence. Sacks is mocking himself *and* critiquing his mentors for their assumption that clinical work is less important than medical research. As a medical writer with no official institutional affiliations for much of his career, Sacks sidesteps the protocols designed to ensure nonmaleficence. In fact, his modus operandi is a critique of those protocols, at least to the degree that they obscure messy subjec-tivity and human relations—or emphasize *knowing* the brain over *living with* it. Sacks's mission was to reveal medicine as a living discipline, a relational one. By occupying dual roles, as Couser observes, he complicated his ethical position—because living with a brain requires variable and often unresolvable ethical positions.

Temple Grandin and Kay Redfield Jamison

In *An Unquiet Mind: A Memoir of Moods and Madness,* Kay Redfield Jamison stresses a problem with writing about her bipolar disorder central to any memoir about neurological difference: "I have become fundamentally and deeply skeptical that anyone who does not have this illness can truly understand it."[24] Similarly, in *Thinking in Pictures: My Life with Autism,* Temple Grandin asserts, "I am frustrated by the fact that some teachers and therapists still do not recognize the importance of sensory over sensibility. It must be difficult for them to imagine a totally different way of perceiving the world."[25] Sacks tends not to dwell on the impossibility of feeling his subjects' experiences, focusing instead on his ability to imagine and represent their phenomenology and gain insight into the flux of their identities. Early brain memoirists, like Grandin and Jamison, had to devise formal means for representing their own flux, what it feels like for them and how they imagine it's perceived by others. Sacks provided a model.

Even in cases of devastating transformation, Sacks finds elements of what Damasio calls the "autobiographical self" intact—as in Sacks's story "The Last Hippie," about a man named Greg for whom the symptoms of a brain tumor are interpreted as spiritual enlightenment by his Hare Krishna community, or "The

Lost Mariner," about Jimmie G., whose Korsakoff syndrome results in severe amnesia. If asked, Greg will still talk about the genius of Jerry Garcia with ebullience, as he did earlier in his life. Similarly, Jimmie G. can narrate his life story up through 1945. Similar tensions propel Grandin's and Jamison's autobiographies. For Grandin, diagnosed with autism as a child, the tendency of others to dismiss the possibility that she possesses a recognizably continuous identity threatens to prevent her from expressing one. For Jamison, the symptoms of mania and depression scare her into imagining a permanent rupture in the continuity of her own sense of self as well as priming others to respond with fear or suspicion to the extremes of her fluctuating behavior. For both writers, the keys to continuity lie in the interplay of their eccentric phenomenologies with particular elements in their material worlds and particular people in their social lives.

Grandin's and Jamison's titles indicate their focus on phenomenology: Grandin thinks in pictures; Jamison's mind is unquiet. As with Sacks, they emphasize both the suffering and strengths their eccentric phenomenologies make possible. For Grandin and Jamison, those strengths are closely connected to their careers in science and their advocacy for what would, in the twenty-first century, come to be called the "neurodiversity movement." Grandin describes her mental experience with characteristic directness and brevity: "I think in pictures. Words are like a second language to me. . . . Language-based thinkers often find this phenomenon difficult to understand, but in my job as an equipment designer for the livestock industry, visual thinking is a tremendous advantage. Visual thinking has enabled me to build entire systems in my imagination." It would be difficult for people who cannot "translate written words into full-color movies" to conceive of Grandin's design process.[26] Most engineers rely on the tools and methods of their field to compensate for the fact that they can't build entire systems in their imaginations.

Grandin makes herself a case history—acknowledging that autism is an umbrella category that includes people whose minds work very differently from hers, but emphasizing the fact that neurological difference enables possibility. In that sense, her advocacy for the autism community is intimately connected to her autobiographical representation of her unique phenomenology. Grandin is committed to the idea that neurodiversity is important for human culture and evolution. "There is no black-and-white dividing line between normal and abnormal," she writes. "I believe there is a reason that disabilities such as autism, severe manic-depression, and schizophrenia remain in our gene pool even though there is much suffering as a result." That reason is that traits we associate with autism, manic depression, or schizophrenia "may confer advantages in milder forms."[27] The idea is consistent with Sacks's insistence on moving away from a myopic focus on neurological deficit and toward a focus on a model that emphasizes the person as an organism, whose differences from the norm may cause suffering and enable new ways of thinking, specialized ways of working, or illuminating modes of perception.

Jamison's description of her phenomenology is often more harrowing. Grandin describes her suffering with relative distance, but Jamison narrates with visceral urgency:

> One evening I stood in the middle of my living room and I looked out at a blood-red sunset spreading out over the horizon of the Pacific. Suddenly I felt a strange sense of light at the back of my eyes and almost immediately saw a huge black centrifuge inside my head. I saw a tall figure in a floor-length evening gown approach the centrifuge with a vase-sized glass tube of blood in her hand. As the figure turned around I saw to my horror that it was me and that there was blood all over my dress, cape, and long white gloves. I watched as the figure carefully put the tube of blood into one of the holes in the rack of the centrifuge, closed the lid, and pushed a button on the front of the machine. The centrifuge began to whirl.
>
> Then, horrifyingly, the image that previously had been inside my head was not completely outside of it. I was paralyzed by fright. The spinning of the centrifuge and the clanking of the glass tube against the metal became louder and louder, and then the machine splintered into a thousand pieces. Blood was everywhere. It spattered against the windowpanes, against the walls and paintings, and soaked down into the carpets. I looked out toward the ocean and saw that the blood on the window had merged into the sunset; I couldn't tell where one ended and the other began.[28]

Jamison's hallucination externalizes her mental experience. The centrifuge in her head is a powerful image of what Sacks calls "compound being." Jamison witnesses a bloody, gothic vision of herself manipulating the centrifuge—a machine that would have been part of her daily routine analyzing blood in the lab, but one whose force and sensitivity would also require a great deal of care and diligence. The machine becomes a vehicle for rupturing boundaries between Jamison's self and surroundings, the blood ultimately merging with the sunset. Jamison experiences the undoing of the boundaries that ordinarily separate her body from its surroundings. In Damasio's terms, she experiences her own body as an object—as we all do, mostly unconsciously—but an object entangled with the objects that make her world, including the sunset. Like so many psychotic episodes, Jamison's has a cosmic dimension. The phenomenology she describes transports her blood into the sky. In symbolic terms, it's difficult not to read the blood as a symbol of both life and disease, particularly because Jamison both emphasizes the feeling of power her manias enable and ascribes them, emphatically, to a genetic lineage in her father's family. Like Sacks and Grandin, she asks readers to notice the impossibility of disentangling the symptoms of disease and the traits and rhythms that make identity.

Jamison's narrative style is supple enough to represent the intensity of her experience and the pedagogical purpose of her writing. She is careful to connect her phenomenological experience to her writing and advocacy:

> I am fortunate that I have not died from my illness, fortunate in having received the best medical care available, and fortunate in having the friends, colleagues, and family that I do. Because of this, I have in turn tried, as best I could, to use my own experiences of the disease to inform my research, teaching, clinical practice, and advocacy work. Through writing and teaching I have hoped to persuade my colleagues of the paradoxical core of this quicksilver illness that can both kill and create; and, along with many others, have tried to change public attitudes about psychiatric illness in general and manic-depressive illness in particular. It has been difficult at times to weave together the scientific discipline of my intellectual field with the more compelling realities of my own emotional experiences. And yet it has been from this binding of raw emotion to the more distanced eye of clinical science that I feel I have obtained the freedom to live the kind of life I want, and the human experiences necessary to try and make a difference in public awareness and clinical practice.[29]

Like Grandin and Sacks, Jamison's professional identity—as a research psychologist and a writer—is linked fundamentally to her illness. The difficulty she describes, "weaving" the disciplinary methods of science with her emotional experience, is cultural more than intellectual. Throughout her memoir, Jamison demonstrates the many ways the symptoms of mania allow her to approach her research and writing with imagination and energy. She turns to memoir because it allows for the weaving, or integration, of multiple modes of thinking—empirical research and gothic narrative, for example. An Unquiet Mind represents a less sentimentalized version of what Sacks calls "a combined vision of body and soul."

Grandin and Jamison build on and expand Sacks's vision, portraying them-selves as "wide minds," to borrow a phrase from philosopher Andy Clark. In Clark's view, tools and objects in our environments become so integral to the way we think and feel that they should be understood as part of the mind itself.[30] It's a controversial idea, but one that's implicit in Grandin's and Jamison's memoirs, dramatized through descriptions of therapeutic practices that fall outside the purview of medicine: Grandin's famous squeeze chute and Jamison's romantic relationships. The squeeze chute plays a major role, almost becoming a character, in Grandin's narrative (as it is in Sacks's title essay about her in *An Anthropologist on Mars*). As a teenager, Grandin observed squeeze chutes designed to hold cattle at slaughterhouses. In particular, she noticed that cows seemed to be calmed by the pressure exerted by the chutes. Having struggled with anxiety throughout her life, partly because of sensory overload and partly because of her difficulty navigating social relationships, the teenage Grandin built herself a chute in her dorm room during high school, to the bewilderment of administrators and teachers. It worked; it calmed her. Ultimately, Grandin designed commercial versions of the chutes for others to use.

From the start, she describes the chute as a vehicle for new phenomenolog-ical experience—its calming effects, the pleasure she derives from it. It becomes central to her quest to develop her own awareness about social engagement:

> From the time I started using the squeeze machine, I understood that the feeling it gave me was one that I needed to cultivate toward other people. It was clear that the pleasurable feelings were those associated with love for other people. I built a machine that would apply the soothing, comforting contact that I craved as well as the physical affection I couldn't tolerate when I was young. I would have been as hard and as unfeeling as a rock if I had not built my squeeze machine and followed through with its use. The relaxing feeling of being held washes negative thoughts away. I believe that the brain needs to receive comforting sensory input. Gentle touching teaches kindness.[31]

With the invention of a squeeze machine for humans, Grandin transformed her world. In her description, this transformation of her physical environment allowed for the kind of transformation of identity Sacks describes in so many of his cases. Where Sacks hints at the transformative possibilities of environ-mental changes for his neurodivergent subjects, Grandin offers the evidence of her experience: She learns kindness through the gentle touch of the squeeze chute. One implicit message is that people diagnosed with autism are not any more static in terms of identity or physiology than anybody else. A history of institutionalization and neglect during the twentieth century made development like Grandin's impossible for far too many autistic people. Grandin's squeeze machine becomes a symbol for much-needed transformations of social structures and attitudes that would become the ethos of the neurodiversity movement two decades after she wrote her memoir.

Jamison attributes her ability to thrive to three forms of therapy: Lithium (the standard medical treatment for manic depression), psychotherapy, and love. Her descriptions of psychotherapy and love indicate a need for the kind of social transformations Grandin suggests. Jamison describes her "debt" to her psychiatrist: "He taught me that the road from suicide to life is cold and colder still, but—with steely effort, the grace of God, and an inevitable break in the weather—that I could make it." The break in the weather is a metaphor to describe the cyclic quality of manic depression, which for Jamison the psycho-pharmacologist is wholly attributable to physiology. The weather metaphor recalls the bloody sky of her manic hallucination, and in that sense suggests a dynamic and relational model of physiology—a model borne out by her descriptions of psychotherapy and love. Describing her psychiatrist, Jamison writes, "It was all the stupid, desperately optimistic, condescending things he didn't say that kept me alive; all the compassion and warmth I felt from him that could not have been said; all the intelligence, competence, and time he put into it; and his granite belief that mine was a life worth living."[32] The relationship she describes depends on what's unspoken. Her psychiatrist's strategic silence arises from the integration of the science and emotion Jamison describes as the aim of her own work. Her psychiatrist is an experienced medical scientist, with no illusions or false optimism about her symptoms; he is also a person who demonstrates compassion, warmth, intelligence, competence, commitment, and belief—affective qualities that often elude language or are expressed outside it. Jamison's call for social change requires a philosophical reorientation in the medical world and, ultimately, medical practices that acknowledge and work with the contingencies that entail from a conception of herself as patient and doctor, with a body whose brain shapes but doesn't entirely define her experience of a world that thrills and terrifies her.

While Jamison describes her commitment to and faith in medicine, her quest to make peace with her symptoms is not entirely medical. Like psychotherapy, a key component of her coping is love—but a love as unsentimental as her psychiatrist's approach to therapy: "No amount of love can cure madness or unblacken one's dark moods. Love can help, it can make the pain more toler-able, but, always, one is beholden to medication that may or may not always work and may or may not be bearable. Madness, on the other hand, most certainly can, and often does, kill love through its mistrustfulness, unrelenting pessimism, discontents, erratic behavior, and, especially, through its savage moods." Love may not be a cure, but Jamison's many descriptions of romantic love suggest that it does become a structure that changes the world for her, making her life possible. Jamison describes two primary romantic relation-ships, the first with a man named David, who died suddenly and left her single again, and the second with her husband Richard. As she describes David, "Although I was still recovering from a long suicidal depression, and my thoughts were so halting and my feelings so gray I could scarcely bear it, I somehow knew that things would be made better by being with him. They were. Immeasurably."[33] Love, for Jamison, involves concrete activities that make an immeasurable difference: walks, meals, sex, reading poetry, and expe-riencing art. Throughout the memoir, Jamison attributes her feelings to her brain, but she also represents her brain as malleable. It changes on its own, when it cycles through mania and depression. It changes in response to drugs. It changes through her relationship with David. She measures the changes in feelings: "Gradually the exhaustion, wariness, and black faithlessness lifted. I began to enjoy music and poetry again, to laugh again, to write poetry again."[34]

What Difference Does Fiction Make?

The emergence of the neuronovel is a tale of two Helens—protagonists who share a name in Powers's *Galatea 2.2* and David Lodge's *Thinks . . .* As a number of literary critics—including Gary Johnson and Francisco Ortega and Fernando Vidal—have noted, these two novels have a lot in common. They plot late-twentieth-century convergence and divergence between the two cultures. They are neuronovels set on college campuses, structured around intimacies and conflicts between a novelist and a cognitive scientist who attempt collabo-ration and argue about the nature of consciousness, its biological connections, its phenomenological qualities, and its aesthetic implications. As Johnson argues, these two novels "serve two important epistemological functions: they implicitly validate the notion that science produces a certain kind of useful and true knowledge and they artfully disseminate that knowledge to the lay public." But Johnson also notes that "We should not, however, underestimate the importance of the dissolution of the relationships between humanists and scientists that occurs in both *Thinks . . .* and *Galatea 2.2.* This aspect of the plots reveals the paradoxical nature of the problem of epistemology for the humanists."[35] Similarly, Ortega and Vidal observe that these two novels are "the best illustrations" of "a salient feature of neuronovels": "they display, through some of their characters' inner conflicts and interpersonal relations, the challenges of writing a neuronovel."[36] The challenge is both aesthetic and epistemological— how to craft a work of fiction that gives cognitive neuroscience its due without capitulating to the idea that empirical observation somehow trumps aesthetic representation as a way of knowing. As novelists, Powers and Lodge invite readers to get involved in social intrigue that arises when their fictional novelists and scientists attempt to collaborate on finding solutions to some of the key conceptual problems in the history of consciousness studies. In both novels, those collaborations get complicated when their protagonists confront a dimension of consciousness they lack the tools to explain—its relation to human bodies.

There's a facetiousness to the premise of Powers's *Galatea 2.2:* teaching a computer to become a literary critic—as a means of measuring whether computers may become conscious. Its plot offers a speculative fiction, imagining an academic world in which the divide between two cultures dissolves. Its pseudo-autobiographical novelist narrator, Richard Powers, collaborates with Lentz, a cognitive neuroscientist, to develop Helen, a computer that mimics the neural systems of a living brain. But conflicts between the collaborators reveal fissures that revive the two-cultures divide—and, ultimately, Powers comes down on the side of a humanities that emphasizes mystery over mastery. As in the nonfiction I discuss earlier in this chapter, the novel sometimes represents the brain as though it is self-contained—and as though we may know enough about it to mimic it through engineering: "Neural networkers grouped their squads of faked-up cells together in layers. An input layer fronted on the boundless outdoors. Across the connective brambles, an opposite squad formed the door where the ghost in the machine got out. Between these, the tool kit of simulated thought. In the so-called hidden layers lay all the knotted space where the net, and networkers like Lentz, associated."[37] The "tool kit of simulated thought" here is hidden, in layers of tissue, but also in metaphors. Groups of cells are squads, brambles, sediment—metaphors that suggest "the boundless outdoors." Boundlessness suggests epistemological uncertainty, the outdoors a fundamental relation between a brain and its environment. Lentz and Powers can't know what's boundless, and they can't engineer a brain without devising means for it to encompass the world it inhabits.

That's where literary criticism comes in, by way of Shelley's *Frankenstein:* "The creature in *Frankenstein* learned to speak by eavesdropping on an exiled family, the most astonishing act of language acquisition until Taylor's beloved *Tarzan,* the books on which the best reader I ever met grew up. Frankenstein's creature had his chattering family and a knapsack of classics: *Paradise Lost,* Plutarch's *Lives,* Goethe's *Werther.* E, like Tarzan, learned to talk more or less on print alone."[38]

What Powers the narrator doesn't say here is that Frankenstein's creature is abandoned by his maker, and as a result turns on him, with bloody results. The elision is a wily signal from Powers the novelist: Beware certainty; learn the lessons in that knapsack of classics—lessons that range from understanding how other people think and feel, the complex relationship between linguistic signs and their referents, or the shifting horizons of social norms. If Frankenstein's creature struggles with these lessons, Richard P.'s Helen archives and parses them but can't embody them, presumably because she lacks flesh.

Helen is the fifth iteration of the collaborative experiment, ready to be tested for its ability to think—and feel—like a human. The experiment proceeds cumulatively, and Powers describes it by way of an analogy to the intertextuality through which literary history evolves: "Each machine life lived inside the others—nested generations of 'remember this.' We did not start from scratch with each revision. We took what we had and cobbled onto it. We called that first filial generation B, but it would, perhaps, have better been named A2. E's weights and contours lived inside F's lived inside G's, the way Homer lives on in Swift and Joyce, or Job in Candide or the Invisible Man."[39] Helen's "nested generations" seem to be analogous to the layers of neurons hiding the secrets of consciousness. The string of literary references implies elusive subjectivity, a history of literature whose boundlessness is as impossible to model as it is to represent in a university curriculum.

Where *Galatea 2.2* dramatizes the major philosophical implications and scientific challenges of building artificial intelligence, *Thinks . . .* reads like a primer for the major debates in consciousness studies—a multipronged field of inquiry lumbering toward academic recognition during the same period. Consciousness studies is beyond multidisciplinary. It attracts psychics, neuro-biologists, poets, novelists, visual artists, monks, priests, physicists, and critical theorists. The intellectual diversity may be astounding, but just as interesting is the fact that the psychics and physicists don't necessarily read or even speak to each other. In *Thinks . . .*, Lodge uses sex—a sort of analogue to consciousness in terms of the perplexing mind-body relations it raises—as a means of putting his two protagonists into dialogue. Novelist Helen Reed and cognitive scientist Ralph Messenger flirt their way through debates about qualia, biology, and aesthetics, and when they agree to terminate their affair, it's with a philosoph-ical pragmatism that mirrors their truce when it comes to questions about whether or not biology or culture is the key to consciousness. *Perhaps there is no key,* they seem to realize over the course of the novel's development.

Lodge's novel opens with an informal experiment, Messenger speaking into a tape recorder, "the object of the exercise being to record as accurately as possible the thoughts that are passing through my head."[40] Messenger doesn't seem to realize that stream of consciousness had been a mode of literary experimentation for nearly a century before his naive (and failed) attempt to document his own river of qualia in language. Lodge uses three primary narrators—Ralph's experimental dictation, Helen's diary, and a third-person reporter. His novel's form is further complicated by a series of embedded narra-tors, in the form of stories about famous philosophical thought experiments about consciousness written by Helen's creative writing students. The multiple narrators give formal shape to the novel's commitment to exploring the subjec-tivity of consciousness.

The flirtation between Helen and Ralph begins as he gives a tour of his Holt Belling Centre for Cognitive Science, a brain-shaped building whose interior includes a mural that visualizes some of the most famous thought experiments in the history of philosophy of mind: Nagel's What Is It Like to Be a Bat?, Flood and Dresher's The Prisoner's Dilemma, Searle's Chinese Room, Jackson's Mary the Color Scientist, Schrödinger's Cat, and the ubiquitous zombies that date at least to Descartes's discussion of "automata" in his *Discourse on Method* (1637). The bulk of the thought experiments suggest that the driving force of Messenger's career—creating artificial intelligence—is folly. As they look at the image of Searle's Chinese Room, "a picture of a man

seated at a desk which bears an In-tray and Out-tray, and a pile of books."
Messenger explains Searle's adaptation of the famous Turing Test: "The idea is
that this guy is receiving questions in Chinese, a language he doesn't speak or
read, and he has a kind of rule book containing logical procedures that enable
him to answer them in Chinese." Helen asks him, "What was the point of it?"
His reply: "I forget. Another anti-functionalist argument." The point means
little to Messenger, as with most ideas he disagrees with. But Helen adds
another twist: "But the Chinese don't have a common language."[41] Once again,
Messenger doesn't know (or much care).

As Helen picks at the scab of his scientific certainty, Messenger's attraction
for her increases. He wields his functionalist beliefs—if cells can make
consciousness, so may wires—as a rhetorical weapon, to demean and shock.
But Helen resists the idea that cells or wires make consciousness. Her point
about a lack of a common language in Chinese culture is indicative of her view;
to deny or ignore culture is to misunderstand consciousness. After examining
the image of Mary the Color Scientist, a sadistic thought experiment that imagines locking a newborn in a monochrome bunker and raising her there, with the
sole purpose of waiting until she reaches adulthood so her keepers may test
whether or not she will be able to see color, Messenger explains that "It's
another argument for qualia being ineffable and irreducible." When Helen
applauds the idea, he concedes that he and his colleagues in brain research
don't know enough to disprove it: "If Mary knew absolutely *everything* there is
to know about colour—which is much, much more than we know at the
moment—maybe she'd be able to *simulate* the experience of red in her brain.
By taking certain drugs, for example."[42] In the process, he reveals that his career
is based on an epistemological fantasy: "If," he says, then "maybe."

Lodge's dialectal structure doesn't let Helen off the hook, either. Her world-
view is challenged as consistently as Ralph's—and their sexual antics create an
analogy between consciousness and desire, two felt states not easily reducible
to a set of discrete qualia. At the climax of their affair, Helen learns that her
dead husband had his own affair with one of her current students, who documents their relationship in fiction she submits as coursework. As Andrew
Gaedtke observes, Helen becomes suspicious when she notes "an uncanny
resemblance to the central figure in her own most famous work of fiction."
Helen recognizes her husband's "unique sexual style reproduced faithfully" in
her student's fiction, and because of her recent education in the vocabulary of

consciousness studies, she thinks about that sexual style as a particularly trou-
bling form of qualia:

> The revelation of her husband's affair reveals that she knew him far less than she
> had believed; she discovers that the qualia of his internal world were in fact
> opaque to her. She comes to believe that she never really knew him and that she
> was separated from his subjective world of experiences and desires by the intrac-
> table problem posed by qualia—the same problem Ralph defines as the core
> problem of cognitive science. This series of traumatic revelations forces Helen to
> confront the limits of her own powers of consciousness. Such challenges to her
> belief in the singularity of her own discursive and cognitive styles and in her
> capacity to intimately know other minds constitute the final nails in the coffin of
> her naive humanism: "I felt stifled, trapped, like someone being nailed into a
> coffin still alive."[43]

Helen's "naive humanism" amounts to a set of beliefs about herself as a singular,
coherent self, a free will, and reliable knowledge about the "internal world" of
her husband—and those of other people in general. In the end, she revises these
beliefs without adopting Ralph's functionalist and apparently cynical belief that
identity is a biological construction reducible to a set of mechanisms negligibly
different from any other machine.

Lodge challenges the idea that empirical knowledge is the last word on
consciousness, by giving Helen the "Last Word" as final speaker at Ralph's
conference on consciousness. Helen takes the opportunity to express the evolution of her worldview catalyzed by her dissolving affair with a neurocognitive
science luminary. She reads passages from Andrew Marvell's metaphysical
poem "The Garden" and uses them to advance her somewhat revised opinion
about what we might learn about consciousness from literature:

> We have heard a lot about qualia in the last three days. There is a difference of
> opinion, I understand, about whether they are mind events or brain events, whether
> they are first-person phenomena forever inaccessible to the third-person discourse
> of science, or whether they are regular patterns of neurological activity which only
> become problematic when we translate them into verbal language. I am not
> competent to adjudicate on this issue. But let me point to a paradox about Marvell's
> verse, which applies to lyric poetry in general. Although he speaks in the first
> person, Marvell does not speak for himself alone. In reading this stanza we
> enhance our own experience of the qualia of fruit and fruitfulness. We see the fruit,
> we taste it and smell it and savour it with what has been called "the thrill of

recognition" and yet it is not there, it is the virtual reality of the fruit, conjured up by the qualia of the poem itself, its subtle and unique combination of sounds and rhythms and meanings.[44]

It's a theme that percolates in neurological fiction: Aesthetic experience can produce comfort with the explanatory gap by substituting the social power of art for the epistemological power of science. Helen's emphasis on qualia is her key to keeping the explanatory gap open. Her argument is haunted by two infidelities: her dead husband's and hers with Ralph. Once she's come to understand desire and sex as complex forms of qualia, she is willing to admit that biology is involved, but not that her sorrow or desire are reducible to biology, at least not biology anybody knows enough about to parse as deftly as she parses Marvell's poem.

That parsing is, of course, all about the idea that literature is a vehicle for stimulating new qualia in readers. In that sense, Helen's "Last Word" has a great deal in common with Elaine Scarry's arguments in *Dreaming by the Book* (2001), a critical analogue to literary brain narratives that planted the seeds of a cultural neuromania that would grow into fruition during the first two decades of the twenty-first century. Like Sacks's work, Scarry's book was a kind of neuro-inflected voice in the wilderness, offering a self-contained argument that would come to influence the direction of the neurohumanities in fundamental ways. Scarry argues that "the verbal arts" work like a vehicle through which "images somehow acquire the vivacity of perceptual objects."[45] When Marvell provokes readers to imagine the qualia of fruit, he creates a new experience for "fruitfulness"—one that's effective because, as Scarry puts it, it "enhances" what readers already know about fruit, through "its subtle and unique combination of sounds and rhythms and meanings." Scarry offers a more detailed and generalized account of literary perception than Helen's, arguing that "that imaginary vivacity comes about by reproducing the deep structure of perception" and emphasizing "the material conditions that [make] it look, sound, or feel the way it [does]." She argues that writers "instruct" readers to perceive in new ways by creating material conditions that play upon what she calls perception's "deep structure," enabling "vibrant, dense, mobile, and animate" qualia by creating images whose contours are shaped by multiple sensory cues. "Imagine the face of a friend," she writes. "But this time place the person at a table by the window where the shadows of an apple tree play across the person's face and shirt. And look at the precise pattern of the shadows. A leaf floats in the window. Let the friend put the leaf in one hand and a book in the other. Perhaps add a second book to the already weighted hand."[46] The combination of perceptual instructions—a face attached to a body, sitting at a table, with shadows moving across her face—is Scarry's key to understanding how black marks on a page become phenomenological experience for readers.

As it does for Helen, Scarry's argument about literary qualia raises epistemological questions. Like Helen, Scarry personalizes her stance: "I alternate between believing that long centuries of analysis have been devoted to solving the mystery of how vivid image-making comes about and believing instead that we have not yet even begun to provide an answer for this question."[47] It's a mantle that Gabrielle Starr takes up in her more recent book *Feeling Beauty: The Neuroscience of Aesthetic Experience* (2013). Starr argues that "the complex thoughts, sensations, actions and feelings that make up aesthetic experience are best understood first as events" because to do so is to "foreground temporality and dynamism" to account for the "varying durations and changing intensities" of aesthetic experience.[48] Starr's collaboration with neuropsychologists, conducting fMRI studies focused on brain activity correlated with the kinds of aesthetic experiences she describes, leads her to draw more concrete conclusions about the physiology of aesthetics:

> [A]esthetic experience starts with sensations or imagery, which we analyze perceptually and semantically and which engage processes of memory as well as of emotion; these sensations and images also have evolving reward value. The minute sequence of the neural events in aesthetic experience requires further experimental elaboration, but in general anatomical terms, neural activation moves from sensory cortex forward toward the basal ganglia (reward processes) and toward the hippocampus and amygdalae (memory and emotion—though these functions are not exclusively carried out in these structures). Activation in the orbitofrontal cortex follows, but there are interactive loops that reach between these frontal areas and the basal ganglia so that higher-order, complex processes of cognition, and emotional and reward processes, may continually feed into each other.

Scarry writes on the cusp of neuromania. Starr writes during its full flowering. She's confident about the "general anatomical" experience involved in aesthetic perception, but acknowledges that the "minute sequence of the neural events . . . requires further experimental elaboration."[49]

While both *Thinks . . .* and *Galatea 2.2* seem to come down on the side of the humanities—their plots suggesting that artificial intelligence is not possible because the explanatory gap is simply too complex to overcome with chips and wires—they also demonstrate plenty of respect for science in general and cognitive neuroscience in particular. Ralph's epistemological fantasy, like Lentz's, motivates him to conduct and oversee brilliant research. His specialty is "affective modeling," a field that represents the evolution of cognitive science, because it's based on the principle that the mind cannot be understood without including emotion as a fundamental form of cognition, an idea that seems a little quaint in 2016 but that was cutting edge in the cognitive sciences in the 1990s.[50] As Ortega and Vidal observe, Lodge and Powers "display, through some of their characters' inner conflicts and interpersonal relations, the challenges of writing a neuronovel." For them, those challenges lie in "the clash between scientific and humanist worldviews."[51] Both novelists dramatize the clash, but their influence takes place largely outside universities, where such clashes mean less—and certainly pale in relation to the fundamental questions hashed out by their characters, questions about physiology, thought, feeling, embodiment, and identity. Neuromania, by definition, involves the expansion of neuroscientific questions into various disciplines within university cultures, but also into worlds outside the university— including the emergent genres of the brain memoir and the neuronovel.

Nearly every brain memoir begins in crisis—either a physiological one, as when Jill Bolte Taylor describes her stroke in *My Stroke of Insight,* or a social one, as when Tito Mukhopadhyay describes educational systems that harm rather than enable autistic students like him in *How Can I Talk If My Lips Don't Move?* Their narratives become quests for answers and change, quests that demonstrate how physiology and culture shape each other. Nearly every neuronovel is an aesthetic experiment, revising a tradition of the mystery novel to weave questions about physiology and identity through plots driven by quests to uncover secrets or solve crimes. As brain narratives, both genres direct readers' attention to entanglement, rather than binaries like self versus brain, or science versus culture. In fact, many of them resist resolution—of both plots and epistemological questions. Instead, they ask readers to consider the epistemological and social profusions inherent in the representation of the particular phenomenological experiences they plot.

The literary legacies of writers like Sacks, Grandin, Jamison, Lodge, and Powers lie in the ways they've influenced a generation of twenty-first-century writers. Grandin articulates the social and philosophical stakes of that legacy: "There is no black-and-white dividing line between normal and abnormal. I believe there is a reason that disabilities such as autism, severe manic-depression, and schizophrenia remain in our gene pool even though there is much suffering as a result."[52] After Grandin, writers of both fiction and nonfiction will affirm, revise, question, and complicate the premises of her claim. And they will do so with some shared ideals—that investigating relations between brain and self requires models that eschew simple categories like "normal and abnormal," that there is value in neurological difference, but also that we must not forget that when difference involves suffering, this creates a set of social obligations, obligations that require attention to relations between physiology and culture. The source of such suffering may lie in brain injury, anomaly, or disease. It may also lie in the injustices of misunderstanding, stigma, discrimination, medical treatments, and educational paradigms that harm rather than help. Brain narratives of the 1990s began to draw cultural attention to the complex interrelationships between physiological suffering and social injustice—a theme that proliferates with increasing range and sharpening specificity in brain memoirs and neuronovels published in the twenty-first-century world of cultural neuromania and neurodiversity politics.

Interlude: Neurodiversity in the Age of the Brain Atlas

HENRY MARKRAM, SWISS NEUROSCIENTIST AND CODIRECTOR OF the Human Brain Project, the European Union's equivalent to the U.S. BRAIN Initiative, represents an unpredictable collision between the ideals that drive publicly funded brain research and the grassroots neurodiversity movement—two global responses to the ascendance of twenty-first-century brain research that are seldom, if ever, discussed in relation to each other.[1] Markram is controversial for his unbridled enthusiasm for a project that would systematize the funding of brain research toward the goal of creating a functional model of the composite human brain, or "brain atlas."[2] In fact, research institutes and universities all over the world are developing versions of the atlas—fine-grained, multidimensional digital models of brains designed to predict how real brains might respond to various forms of stimulus, disease, or injury. Markram is also the father of Kai Markram, whose autism he cites as a personal motivation for his ambitious (and sometimes bizarre) goals for the project: "To be able to dial up everything, the colours, the sounds—that's what motivates me. . . . To be able to step inside a simulation of my son's brain and see the world as he sees it. At the moment, I can use fMRI and ECG [electrocardiogram] to see how the brain processes information and which regions are activated during different tasks but I can't see what it is perceiving, I can't see what it sees."[3]

Markram's goal begins with a fantasy of overcoming the explanatory gap, in both grand and intimate terms. But it goes further. He wants to perceive from the point of view of other people—his son, but also anybody with a brain.

Speaking as a parent, Markram sounds almost like a neurodiversity activist: "[P]sychiatrists were saying that autistic children had no empathy, that they were unable to form a theory of mind," he told *The Guardian*. "But actually I found that Kai could be intensely emotional about certain things and that he seemed to know things about what you are thinking that most people don't know."[4] Markram expresses admiration for his son's abilities, abilities that so-called neurotypical people lack. He's pursuing a research agenda that might result in a paradigm shift in the biology of autism—focused on what he calls the "intense world syndrome," a hypothesis that various forms of autism may involve "a common molecular syndrome . . . activated in autism that produces hyper-functioning in a coordinated manner by forming hyper-reactive and hyper-plastic microcircuits in different brain areas."[5] The intense-world theory resonates with neurodiversity politics. It's consistent with first-person accounts of autistic experience, which tend to emphasize sensory and cognitive over-load, more than with predominant theories that describe autism as a problem of social functioning. Yet Markram champions a global project to model a composite, neurotypical brain designed to become the standard for all brain research.

By contrast, the neurodiversity movement is emerging through grassroots organization among people interested in social change—and gradually making space for itself in government, research, and education. As Steve Silberman argues in *NeuroTribes: The Legacy of Autism and the Future of Neurodiversity,* "Neurodiversity advocates propose that instead of viewing this gift as an error of nature—a puzzle to be solved and eliminated with techniques like prenatal testing and selective abortion—society should regard it as a valuable part of humanity's genetic legacy while ameliorating aspects of autism that can be profoundly disabling without adequate forms of support."[6] Philosophically, the neurodiversity movement is based on what we might call "cerebral pluralism"—the idea that each brain is different and some are more different than others. Politically, the movement is aligned with dis/ability rights movements and is dedicated to eradicating stigmas associated with neurological difference, or neurodivergence, and in making it clear that a history of medical and social misunderstandings and maltreatment have caused a great deal of suffering and prevented a great deal of thriving among neurodivergent people. While the movement is strongest in the autistic community, it encompasses a wide array of neurological experiences—including epilepsy, Tourette's syndrome, mania,

depression, hallucination, dyslexia, prosopagnosia, migraine, and synesthesia—
and emphasizes the fact that many of these experiences cannot be clearly delin-
eated from one another. No two people with the same diagnosis will experience
the world or their bodies the same way; many people diagnosed with one or
another neurological condition will also experience so-called comorbid conditions. It's common, for example, for a person to experience both epilepsy and
migraine or autism and synesthesia.

Nick Walker, author of the blog *Neurocosmopolitanism,* describes three principles of what he calls the "neurodiversity paradigm":

1. Neurodiversity is a natural and valuable form of human diversity.
2. The idea that there is one "normal" or "healthy" type of brain or mind,
    or one "right" style of neurocognitive functioning, is a culturally
    constructed fiction, no more valid (and no more conducive to a healthy
    society or to the overall well-being of humanity) than the idea that there
    is one "normal" or "right" ethnicity, gender, or culture.
3. The social dynamics that manifest in regard to neurodiversity are similar
    to the social dynamics that manifest in regard to other forms of human
    diversity (e.g., diversity of ethnicity, gender, or culture). These dynamics
    include the dynamics of social power inequalities, and also the dynamics
    by which diversity, when embraced, acts as a source of creative
    potential. [7]

Each of these principles chafes against the values implicit in the BRAIN
Initiative and the Human Brain Project. While these projects share with neurodiversity advocates a goal to improve human lives, they are predicated upon the
idea of restoring brains that stray too far from cognitive or social norms. In fact,
their stated goal is to create a model of a composite brain—a brain that represents a " 'normal or healthy' type of brain."

The National Institutes of Health describes the aspirational aims of the
BRAIN Initiative in precisely these terms on the main page of the project
website (which, it must be said, is as much a public relations tool as an infor-
mational one):

The Brain Research through Advancing Innovative Neurotechnologies® (BRAIN)
Initiative is aimed at revolutionizing our understanding of the human brain. By

accelerating the development and application of innovative technologies, researchers will be able to produce a revolutionary new dynamic picture of the brain that, for the first time, shows how individual cells and complex neural circuits interact in both time and space. Long desired by researchers seeking new ways to treat, cure, and even prevent brain disorders, this picture will fill major gaps in our current knowledge and provide unprecedented opportunities for exploring exactly how the brain enables the human body to record, process, utilize, store, and retrieve vast quantities of information, all at the speed of thought.[8]

Few in science or government believe this "new dynamic picture of the brain" is imminent. At present, the most ambitious research in the project is working on creating models of the relations among individual cells in portions of the brains of mice, worms, and flies or computer models that simulate relations among 10,000 neurons using microchips and cables (of the estimated 86 billion in an actual human brain).[9] Though both initiatives hope to create technologies to model whole brains—of humans and other species—there is no widespread consensus about how to do this or how long it may take.

During the summer of 2014, eight hundred neuroscientists issued an open letter "expressing concern with the course of the Human Brain Project." The letter focuses on the narrow aims and funding plans for the project and calls for greater transparency, more involvement of practicing neuroscientists, and greater representation of the diversity of methods practiced in the field.[10] It doesn't articulate widely held reservations in the neuroscience community on both continents: (1) The projects are premature, based on building a model of a brain in the absence of a coherent theory of what that might mean; (2) They attempt to unify scientific research from the top down, a structure likely to curtail the kinds of idiosyncratic research methods that lead to breakthroughs like Darwin's evolutionary theory or Watson and Crick's modeling of DNA; and (3) The motives and structures for the projects are more political and economic than scientific.[11] The neurodiversity movement suggests a fourth problem: No two brains are alike, so a composite model will require adjustments and interpretations in practice.

New York University psychologist Gary Marcus has made a journalistic beat out of both initiatives, publishing most notably in *The New York Times* and *The New Yorker* on the launching, promises, and critiques of the project from within the neuroscientific community. Marcus is cautiously optimistic that the initiatives will yield useful knowledge, but he's also careful to emphasize the fact that the messiness of biology is fundamentally at odds with most of the stream-lined technologies developed to model biological symptoms:

> Biology isn't elegant the way physics appears to be. The living world is bursting with variety and unpredictable complexity, because biology is the product of historical accidents, with species solving problems based on happenstance that leads them down one evolutionary road rather than another. No overarching theory of neuroscience could predict, for example, that the cerebellum (which is involved in timing and motor control) would have vastly more neurons than the prefrontal cortex (the part of the brain most associated with our advanced intelligence).
>
> But biological complexity is only part of the challenge in figuring out what kind of theory of the brain we're seeking. What we are really looking for is a *bridge*, some way of connecting two separate scientific languages—those of neuroscience and psychology. . . . We know that there must be some lawful relation between assemblies of neurons and the elements of thought, but we are currently at a loss to describe those laws. We don't know, for example, whether our memories for individual words inhere in individual neurons or in sets of neurons, or in what way sets of neurons might underwrite our memories for words, if in fact they do.[12]

The hypothetical bridge Marcus describes, between neuroscience and psychology, is really multiple bridges, connecting the phenomenology and physiology of the explanatory gap, laboratory research and the embrained experience of living organisms, and the study of composite models of the brain and the vast diversity of human brains. Despite the emphasis on coordinated effort, it seems unlikely that the Human Brain Project and the BRAIN Initiative will do much to mitigate the messy relationship between the laboratory and life. It does seem likely that they will lead to the collection of massive amounts of data and a variety of methods for modeling human brains—both worthy enterprises that will require revisiting Marcus's bridge, or "chasm," between neurobiology and psychological experience in order to become meaningful.

In the meantime, people living with those actual brains are advocating for themselves. Voices of the neurodiversity movement are proliferating— advocating, debating, insisting, decrying, lobbying, influencing policy, and designing research. It seems inevitable that neuroscience research will face increasing pressure from neurodiversity activists. These activists, after all, are living people who embody the impetus for the research. As a movement, neuro-diversity is largely focused on autism, and while the near future is unpredict-able, it seems likely that it will continue to expand its affiliations. Advocacy organizations of various kinds predate the coining of the term neurodiversity or its emergence as a culture and form of political organizing—including, to name just a few, the Tourette Association of America, the Epilepsy Foundation, and the American Dyslexia Association. While by no means uniform or unified in their ethos or aims, these organizations have advocated for valuing neurological difference and accommodating neurological disability for decades. The neurodiversity movement has emerged as a powerful cultural and political force over the last decade. The amplification of its message in that short time would seem to signal its influence in the coming decade, as its proponents continue to lobby researchers, physicians, and policy makers to develop methods that acknowledge the explanatory gap, value difference, avoid normalizing or pathologizing particular brains, and conceive health care as a means of helping people rather than correcting them—lobbying that will take both grassroots and institutionalized forms.

Video blogger Amethyst Schaber is one of the grassroots proponents. She's the author of the blog *neurowonderful* and the creator of the YouTube channel "Ask an Autistic."[13] Her YouTube channel contains relatively short videos—actually ranging from under a minute to ninety minutes—focused on particular topics relevant to the lives of autistic people, their families or friends, and anybody else who may be interested. Episodes include "What Is Autism?," "What Is Stimming?," "What Is a Central Auditory Disorder?," and "What's Wrong with Autism Speaks?" As their titles suggest, each episode addresses a question. Schaber's answers are clear and direct, her delivery friendly and inviting, her topics ranging from intricate aspects of physiology to social controversies. The first episode was "What Is Stimming?" In it, she articulates her motives: "Right now we're going into a time where people are realizing that maybe what we thought we knew about autism was the observations, sometimes the inaccurate observations, of neurotypical scientists, doctors, and researchers." She explains that "stimming is also known as stereotyped behavior and can be sometimes known as tics." She offers three reasons an autistic person may stim: self-regulation, sensory seeking, and expression. She describes several types of stimming, including hand flapping, rocking, rubbing a surface, smelling a substance, looking at flashing lights, or spinning in a chair. She explains two little known senses—proprioception (sense of the body in space) and the vestibular sense (associated with the inner ear, balance, and motion). In addition, she describes "sensory processing disorder" associated with autism, particularly the fact that sensory input may be experienced as intense and painful to an autistic person. Stimming, she explains, is a means of controlling or reframing sensory input in ways that "regulate" what's painful so that it may become pleasurable, or at least tolerable. In addition to all this, she addresses stigmas associated with stimming. "When it comes to looking normal versus being able to live and function and be a happy, healthy autistic adult who stims," she declares, "I would definitely take the latter." The power of the message is palpable: The assumption of neurotypicality and the stigmatization of neurological difference curtails her health and happiness.

Eleanor Longden is both a grassroots proponent and a professional research psychologist, representing the International Hearing Voices Network, an organization most influential in the United Kingdom and the Netherlands but with international reach. The HVN (also known by its affiliate names the Hearing Voices Movement and Intervoice) is perhaps the neurodiversity movement's closest—and most astonishingly effective—cousin. The Hearing Voices Network was founded in 1990, on the idea that hearing voices is not necessarily a pathological phenomenon or a sign of psychosis. Its mission involves creating community, changing policy, and transforming psychiatric practice. Longden, a psychologist and a person who hears voices, presented a high-profile TED Talk in 2012, recounting her harrowing experience with psychiatric medicine— and medication. She articulates the HVN's guiding philosophy in terms that demonstrate the tension between a neurodiversity perspective and the assumptions underlying the race to produce a composite brain atlas. Longden explains that the HVN objects "to reductionist biomedical mindsets; especially in our approach to voice-hearing. While we acknowledge that hearing voices can cause extreme distress, we consider it a meaningful experience that can be explored and understood (an opportunity for learning and psychological growth, even if the lessons are painful and difficult) rather than just a pathological symptom devoid of context."[14] The lobbying of the Hearing Voices Network, along with the movement of people like Longden into the psychology professions, has resulted in a radical revision of diagnostic practices in the United Kingdom. In 2015 the British Psychological Association published a report, "Understanding Psychosis and Schizophrenia," which shifts practices in a direction very much in synch with the HVN's recommendations: As medical anthropologist Tanya Luhrmann explains, the reports' authors "say that hearing voices and feeling paranoid are common experiences"; "there is no strict

dividing line between psychosis and normal experience"; "antipsychotic medications are sometimes helpful, but that 'there is no evidence that it corrects an
underlying biological abnormality' "; and "that it is 'vital' that those who suffer
with distressing symptoms be given an opportunity to 'talk in detail about their
experiences and to make sense of what has happened to them.' "[15]

These are just two among thousands of notable neurodiversity advocates. Ari
Ne'eman is the founder of the Autistic Self Advocacy Network, appointed by
Barack Obama to the U.S. National Council on Disability. John Elder Robison
is an autobiographer, policy consultant for the national Interagency Autism
Coordinating Committee, and visiting faculty member in the College of William
and Mary's Neurodiversity Initiative, the first university program of its kind.
Carly Fleischmann is the nonverbal host of "Speechless," a comedic YouTube
talk show, and coauthor (with her father, Arthur Fleischmann) of *Carly's Voice:
Breaking through Autism.* Filmmaker Amanda Baggs challenged and inspired
more than a million viewers to reexamine assumptions about autistic identity
with her viral video "In My Language." Neurodiversity bloggers include Erin
Human, author of a blog called *Writing, Cartooning, and Neurodiversity Designs*
(formerly titled *The E Is for Erin*); Nick Walker, author of *Neurocosmopolitanism;*
Cas Faulds, author of *Un-Boxed Brain;* and Dani Alexis Ryskamp, editor of
NeuroQueer, a collective blog for multiple authors "queering our neurodivergence" and "neurodiversifying our queer."[16]

Neurodiversity activism, whether it's grassroots, institutional, or a combination, begins with a premise articulated by Gary Marcus in his critique of the
Human Brain Project and BRAIN Initiative: "The living world is bursting with
variety and unpredictable complexity, because biology is the product of historical accidents, with species solving problems based on happenstance that leads
them down one evolutionary road rather than another."[17] Of course, the idea of
neurodiversity is founded on an assumption—that the root of experience is
neurological. But as neurodiversity writers and activists stress, that assumption
is not the end of the story. Stigma is social, rooted in assumptions that every
human in the living world should burst with a narrow range of "variety and
complexity." These writers and activists are calling for—demanding, really—
to be included in the design of research protocols and the making of policy.

When it comes to the building of a brain atlas, as the project's critics have
pointed out, it may be too ambitious even to imagine a model that captures the
bursting complexity of the composite brain, one that presumes a narrow range

of normal function. In pragmatic and epistemological terms, it's certainly too early to expect a brain atlas that could represent the full "variety and unpredictable complexity" of neurodiversity in humans. Francisco Ortega argues that the neurodiversity movement and neuroscience are both rooted in the idea of the "cerebral subject"—the idea that *you are your brain.* He argues that "the combination of 'neuro' and 'diversity' is by no means self-evident." In his view, the idea of neurodiversity "brings about a paradoxical situation: while neuroplasticity helps account for neurodiversity, neurodiversity advocates tend to homogenize neurodiverse brains and minimize their differences so as to support their claims for the existence of a brain-based autistic identity. Thus, the 'autistic brain' is displayed as ontologically homogeneous and radically different from the also homogeneous 'NT [neurotypical] brain.' "[18]

Conceptually, Ortega is probably right. To speak of neurological identity, as I do throughout this book, is to make a leap across the explanatory gap, attributing neurological meaning to subjective experience. The fact is we are living through a time when humans are bursting with complex ideas about how our brains shape our experience. We don't know what causes autism, but we are sure the brain is involved—and pretty sure most of our theories about *how* it is involved are incomplete or misguided. We don't know why some people experience auditory hallucinations, but we are beginning to recognize the brutality of some of our medical responses to their distress. Given the stakes and the reality of what we know and what we don't, we can live with contradiction and paradox. Henry Markram will pursue his research on the neurobiology of the "intense world syndrome" that may revolutionize understandings of autistic experience and wage political battles in his race to promote the building of the brain atlas. But it's unlikely that Markram will "step inside a simulation of [his] son's brain and see the world as he sees it" anytime soon. Eleanor Longden will work as a psychologist, providing people who hear voices, as she does, a choice about whether or not to ingest antipsychotic medications with severe side effects. Gary Marcus will continue to conduct research and write polemics in pursuit of "bridges" between "assemblies of neurons and the elements of thought."

2

Brain Memoirs

IN 1960, TWELVE-YEAR-OLD HOWARD DULLY endured a transorbital lobotomy, involving the insertion of a surgical instrument through his eye socket to sever connections between his frontal cortex and the rest of his brain. In 1996, Jill Bolte Taylor, a brain anatomist, witnessed her own disorientation when she suffered a stroke one morning as she prepared to go to work. In 2004, Alix Kates Shulman awoke in the middle of the night to find her husband unconscious after having fallen from the loft bed in the remote coastal cabin she used as a writing retreat. In 2006, Siri Hustvedt felt and watched her body convulse, her arms flail, and her skin discolor while she delivered a eulogy at a memorial for her father. These shocking experiences frightened Dully, Taylor, Shulman, and Hustvedt—but they also fascinated them, because they made philosophical or abstract questions about the connections between body, mind, self, and world physically and experientially concrete. All four have written brain memoirs that document their suffering and fascination in response to the physiological changes they've experienced. Their memoirs are chronicles of the push-pull between their selves and their brains. In the case of all four writers, the relations between self and brain they chronicle aren't simply changed by brain disease or injury, but are continuously changing in reaction to altered brain function *and* the writers' living responses to their physiological conditions—including, crucially, writing about them.

Of course, there is a long tradition of autobiographical writing that chronicles mind-body relationships and their implications for selfhood, including the work of Augustine, Montaigne, Thomas De Quincey, Marcel Proust, and Virginia Woolf. Brain memoirs can be understood as the most recent incarnation of this long-standing tradition, though their explicit focus on the brain—and on the writer as organism—is more pointed than that of their predecessors. Brain memoirs do not let their writers—or readers—forget that they are organisms whose lives are shaped to a large degree by accidents of physiology, culture, family, and circumstance. They confront accidents by crafting a sense of agency that's nuanced enough to account for what's beyond their control. This is where their distinctive cultural work begins.

Brain memoirs come in a broad spectrum of forms, and their authors articulate a wide variety of aims. Nonetheless, they share some common features and effects. Broadly speaking, brain memoirs make at least five significant contributions to culture—in varying degrees for each particular memoir: (1) they enable their writers to gain a sense of agency or control in the face of the *accidents* that shape lives, including the accidents of genes, disease, or physical injury; (2) they offer much-needed solace and information to readers who suffer in ways similar to the writer as well as the loved ones and caretakers who support them; (3) they provide detailed, first-person accounts of neurological difference that have the potential to inform and influence brain research and clinical practice; (4) they renew and invigorate philosophical debates about mind and body, qualia, memory, and relationships between self and narrative; and (5) they develop narrative strategies for representing the complexities of the minds and bodies of their authors.

Although the ostensible subject of brain memoirs is the writer's particular subjective experience of an illness, difference, disorder, or injury, very often these memoirs become vehicles for large questions about the relationship between brain and self. If Kay Redfield Jamison and Temple Grandin have written memoirs that are classics in the genre, Oliver Sacks is its most influential progenitor. Since the publication of *The Man Who Mistook His Wife for a Hat* more than three decades ago—a period that coincided with rapid advances in brain research and the widespread cultural ascendance of the neurosciences—numerous memoirists have emerged to tell stories about how their anomalous brains have shaped their lives and selves. These memoirists all share Sacks's penchant for using narrative to approximate the impossible: the revelation of another person's conscious experience. If I can riff on the title of Thomas Nagel's 1974 thought experiment, "What Is It Like to Be a Bat?," these memoirs ask, "What is it like to be epileptic or 'locked in,' to experience profound amnesia or addiction—or, for that matter, to be neurotypical?" Some form of this question drives all brain memoirs, even when their authors are reflective about the impossibility of overcoming the gap between one mind—or mind style—and another. Despite that impossibility, brain memoirists simulate their phenomenologies in language and narrative, inviting readers to imagine their experience. In the process, they involve readers in a kind of experiment in developing a metacognitive awareness about relations between the mind styles they've brought to the text and those the text simulates. Where many traditional memoirs take selfhood for granted, brain memoirs investigate how mind, brain, body, and culture interact to create or perform selfhood, and that investigation has social, scientific, and philosophical implications. In fact, recent brain memoirs may have a thing or two to teach neuroscientists about the self, and they certainly have quite a bit to teach the rest of us about the functional and theoretical promises and limits of current brain research.

In their influential work of criticism on the genre, *Reading Autobiography,* Sidonie Smith and Julia Watson emphasize a paradox of memory that underlies autobiographical writing: "Memory, apparently so immaterial, personal, and elusive, is always implicated in materiality, whether it be the materiality of sound, stone, text, garment, integrated circuits and circuit boards, or the materiality of our very bodies—the synapses and electrons of our brains and our nervous systems. Memory is evoked by the senses—smell, taste, touch, sight, sound—and encoded in objects or events with particular meaning for the narrator."[1] A brain memoirist narrates memories about the force of her material body in the making of her identity, particularly when that body's brain plays an explicit role in the evolution of the writer's understanding of self. In his book *Living Autobiographically: How We Create Identity in Narrative* (2008), Paul John Eakin draws on both Oliver Sacks and Antonio Damasio to argue that autobiography is not simply a genre of literature, but fundamental to the making of identity. We tell stories about ourselves on a daily basis, in writing, in conversation, and silently through personal dialogues with ourselves. As Eakin suggests, "we perform a work of self-construction" when we talk about ourselves. He also acknowledges "there are many modes of self and self-experience, many more than could possibly be represented in the kind of self-narration Sacks refers to, more than any autobiographer could relate." Because self-narration doesn't encompass the totality of experience, Eakin argues, "narrative is especially suited for registering the effects of time and change."[2] In other words, autobiographical acts narrate continuous changes—obvious ones and subtle ones—in identity and experience. In that sense, autobiography itself is fundamentally about the flux of identity. In brain memoirs, that flux is pronounced during moments of injury or diagnosis, the emergence of new symptoms, or dramatic moments of recovery, but it's more often subtle, almost impossible to detect.

Most of these neurological narratives take the form of a quest—for new knowledge, understanding, healing, adaptation, and for reconciliation between scientific theory, medical practice, and the lived experience of patients (and writers). Hustvedt, who wrote *The Shaking Woman,* and Shulman, author of *To Love What Is,* are novelists, so it's no surprise that their accounts are highly literary in their structures, their care with language, their allusions, and their attention to matters of style and voice. At the same time, their aims are every bit as social and pedagogical as those of Dully in *My Lobotomy* and Taylor in *My Stroke of Insight.* All four writers recount their searches to make sense of and live with the profound changes to their lives that arise from disorders, injuries, or anomalies in the brain or the nervous system as a whole. But they also emphasize the fact that they continue to change—and that writing becomes a powerful factor in their evolving identities.

To write *My Lobotomy,* Dully tracked down the files of his surgeon, Walter Freeman, with the help of cowriter Charles Fleming. "The great mystery of my life was inside," he writes. "The question that haunted me for more than forty years was about to be answered." According to the records, Dully's stepmother, Lou, fabricated a diagnostic history so that the stepson it seems she always hated would appear to be a candidate for Freeman's transorbital lobotomy. As a result, Dully is haunted by the question of who he would have been if his brain had not been violated by the crude surgical procedure known as an "ice pick lobotomy." He learns quite a bit from his file about exactly what happened and how. Toward the end of the book, he writes, "Ever since my lobotomy I've felt like a freak—ashamed. But . . . I know that my suffering is over. I know my lobotomy didn't touch my soul. For the first time, I feel no shame. I am, at last, at peace."[3] Dully seems to use *soul* as a synonym for self, and while his story is convincing on the grounds of the peace he has found and the shame he has overcome, it does not offer persuasive evidence that his *self* is untouched by the lobotomy. In that sense, the "great mystery" of his life remains, though he learns to live with it.

Because Taylor is a brain anatomist, it may seem surprising that she is more pointedly concerned than Dully with the matters of the soul and self, or at least with spiritual dimensions of the self and their expression through the brain.[4] Taylor awakens to "a sharp pain piercing [her] brain directly behind [her] left eye" and "stumble[s] into the world with the ambivalence of a wounded soldier." Not yet fully conscious, she makes a characteristically idiosyncratic decision, to hop on her "cardio-glider" and start "jamming away to Shania Twain." Then, it happens: "I felt a powerful and unusual sense of dissociation roll over me. I felt so peculiar that I questioned my well-being. Even though my thoughts seemed lucid, my body felt irregular. As I watched my hands and arms rocking forward and back, forward and back, in opposing synchrony with my torso, I felt strangely detached from my normal cognitive functions. It was as if the integrity of my mind-body connection had somehow become compromised."[5] This detachment persists and increases. Taylor "felt bizarre, as if [her] conscious mind was suspended somewhere between [her] normal reality and some esoteric space." She becomes increasingly interested in this esoteric space because it offers her a view of the world she hasn't seen before. Her book is primarily about her changed relationship to her brain and the implications of that change with regard to how we understand reality. She credits the stroke with rejuvenating her "neurocircuits of innocence and inner joy."[6]

In *To Love What Is,* Shulman offers a sharp and moving account of her search to learn how to live with her husband, Scott, after a brain injury that left his memory severely impaired but other aspects of his self intact. Shulman intercuts the story of Scott's accident and the life it creates for the couple with flashbacks to the history of this unusual marriage. The two were high school sweethearts, separated for decades before uniting in midlife to form an unexpected bond for two people whose lives had diverged pretty sharply. From the beginning, Shulman felt a strong admiration and attraction to Scott's physicality, which she linked to his reserved, masculine, and trustworthy character. Her account makes it clear that memory and identity are not the same thing. Memory gives us a sense of autobiography, provides an ongoing narrative for the self, but Shulman lives with a man whose reserve, masculinity, and compassion outlive his capacity to remember what he's done, where he's been, and who he knows.

The quest Hustvedt recounts in *The Shaking Woman or A History of My Nerves* is even more confounding (if slightly less alarming) than Dully's, Shulman's, or Taylor's because Hustvedt's symptoms are less clear-cut. Hustvedt is determined to find out what role her brain might play in her body's startling behavior: the sudden onset of a condition that caused her to convulse when she spoke in public (which she did often). The first incident occurred at a memorial service for her father:

> I looked out at the fifty or so friends and colleagues of my father's who had gathered around the memorial Norway spruce, launched into my first sentence, and began to shudder violently from the neck down. My arms flapped. My knees knocked. I shook as if I were having a seizure. Weirdly, my voice wasn't affected. It didn't change at all. Astounded by what was happening to me and terrified that I would fall over, I managed to keep my balance and continue, despite the fact that the cards in my hands were flying back and forth in front of me. When the speech ended, the shaking stopped. I looked down at my legs. They had turned a deep red with a bluish cast.[7]

With that glance at her deep red legs, Hustvedt begins her quest to understand what her body did that day—and on so many subsequent days when she spoke in public. As she writes, "I decided to go in search of the shaking woman."[8] Brain memoirists write around, outside, and beyond debates about so-called brainhood. In general, the quests these memoirs chronicle prompt their authors to confront philosophical questions about the relationship between brain, body, self, and culture on just about every page. The insights they offer about these relationships, however, tend to be local and personal, rather than grand or totalizing. Nearly all of them are concerned with how our brains contribute to *particular* aspects of self in the context of a life and an environment. The experience of the memoirists, navigating science and medicine in order to craft lives (and books) that help them cope with their brains, leads to an organic acceptance that we do not know much about the relationship between brain and self. These books offer the theorists a lesson in humility: The neuroscience of the self should be approached only hypothetically, with an emphasis on the experiences of the organisms it studies. Too often, these questions are addressed with premature reductivism, overlooking what we don't know or pretending we know more than we do. For the memoirists, the questions, the hypothetical data, the fluctuating diagnoses, and the grand theories provide a new context in which to explore ancient questions about selfhood. Dully's lobotomy, Hustvedt's convulsions, Shulman's husband's accident, and Taylor's stroke all prompt them to go searching for the relationship between the brain and the self—to seek understanding that will help them live with their altered circumstances. These writers, apropos of Alva Noë, may not *be* their brains, but their brains shape their experiences in ways that are fundamental and undeniable.

Living with Brains

Living with uncertainty is a fundamental theme in brain memoirs, a theme about which the memoirists have something to teach the scientists who study brains and the doctors who treat them. It seems inevitable that the writers' lived experiences will sometimes contradict the advice, doctrine, treatment, and data offered by professionals. The contradictions tend to bewilder patients, even those with the wherewithal to write memoirs at least partly designed to reveal the contradictions and improve the science of medicine in ways that will help future patients.

Howard Dully's neurosurgeon, Dr. Walter Freeman, is the most egregious physician portrayed in any of these memoirs. He was an enthusiastic proponent of the transorbital lobotomy, a procedure so brutal it was sometimes performed with an ice pick. The results were highly variable, from death to miniscule changes in behavior. Freeman's notes about Dully are detailed and frank, so much so that they reveal his stepmother Lou's manipulation of his "symptoms" and Freeman's doubts about his young patient's candidacy and his outcome. Dully learns that Lou visited six psychiatrists before finding Freeman; four of these diagnosed *her* as the problem. Dully learns that Freeman was concerned about his professional status and that his lobotomies had already fallen out of favor by the time he treated Dully. In short, he learns quite a bit, but he does not get his central question answered. He does not learn who he'd have been with a different brain. He doesn't even learn how dramatically his brain may have been altered. At this stage in medical history, nobody can tell him that.

The discoveries Siri Hustvedt makes in *The Shaking Woman* are also about adaptation and living with uncertainty more than hard facts or cures. When Hustvedt goes looking for the woman who shakes, she consults neurologists and psychiatrists, reads philosophy and the history of medicine, and seeks to understand the relationship between mind and body by looking at fMRI images of her brain and practicing biofeedback techniques. In the process, she manages to make philosophy, neurology, and history seem like the stuff of mystery novels. Her book is a page-turner. As in so many brain memoirs, Hustvedt's physicians are flummoxed. They disagree with and contradict each other. Some offer answers that seem too easy; others deny the reality of her experience alto-gether. Finally, she gets a drug in place of a diagnosis. Neurology, psychology, and psychoanalysis can't explain why Hustvedt shakes, but propranolol (or the placebo effect) forestalls the shaking. The chemistry of the shaking woman's brain is at play in making her who she is, but how and why remain vague.

In the absence of answers, Hustvedt finds intellectual stimulation and emotional solace in the philosophical implications of contemporary neuro-science. Her reading ranges freely over William James and Antonio Damasio, Maurice Merleau-Ponty and Jaak Panksepp. The arc of her narrative traces the development of her relationship to the shaking. Early on, she describes her condition almost as a visitation: "It appeared that some unknown force had suddenly taken over my body and decided I needed a good, sustained jolting." Sentiments like this are common in autobiographical works about the brain, which tend to an implicit, though unstable, dualism. They characterize the brain as an entity or force that is both part of and separate from the self or organism writing the story. Illness tends to throw this unstable dualism into relief, to make apparent a kind of alienation between brain and self that haunts everyday life. In Hustvedt's words, "Every sickness has an alien quality, a feeling of invasion and loss of control that is evident in the language we use about it." The condition feels alien partly because its onset is so sudden and partly because it seems willful. But the will in question doesn't feel like her own conscious will. If Hustvedt were writing in the nineteenth century, or if she were a devout Christian, she might see this will as either divine or evil. From Hustvedt's secular position, it seems as though there is a hidden force with a will of its own somewhere inside her body or brain. A friend who witnesses one of her episodes reinforces the split when she tells Hustvedt, "it [was] like watching a doctor and a patient in the same body."[9] In fact, Hustvedt takes on this dual role as doctor and patient, taking a far more active role in her search for a diagnosis than the medical establishment generally encourages or even allows.

Toward the end of the book, still without a firm diagnosis, Hustvedt asks, "Can I say that the shaking woman is a repeatedly activated pattern of firing neurons and stress hormones released in an involuntary response, which is then dampened as I keep my cool, continue to talk, convinced that I'm not really in any danger? Is that all there is to the story?"[10] If the answers to these questions are yes, then the origins of the shaking are beyond the will, arising from the body's ongoing, involuntary processes that maintain homeostasis and keep our systems operating. Keeping her cool, however, is a willful act whereby Hustvedt dampens the impulse to resist or fight what's happening to her. It feels to her as if keeping her cool may have a therapeutic effect, somehow shifting the neuronal and hormonal patterns that drive her body to convulse, her arms to flail, and her legs to turn a deep red. Hustvedt is speculating here. Her "cool" is not a medically recognized treatment. But it is one of the keys to the philosophical questions her book explores, questions about how the conscious and the unconscious impinge on each other as they respond to stimuli (or what Damasio calls "objects") in an organism's world—and how a sense of self is produced in the process.

Damasio could almost be describing Hustvedt's relationship to her shaking body when he argues that we must understand two integrated aspects of self in order to understand biology's role in the formation of identity. He calls these the "self-as-object" and the "self-as-subject." The shaking woman is Hustvedt's object self; the tireless diagnostician is her subject self. According to Damasio, the object self is "a dynamic collection of integrated neural processes, centered on the representation of the living body, that finds expression in a dynamic collection of integrated mental processes." By contrast, "the self-as-subject, as knower, as the 'I,' is a more elusive presence."[11] In other words, research is beginning to reveal how the brain maps the body, making an "object self" out of it, for the purpose of maintaining the preconscious activities necessary for a body to live. At the same time, Damasio could almost be describing the dynamics of narrating autobiography with his theory of the self as both subject and object. Smith and Watson describe autobiographers in language quite similar to Damasio's: "the teller of his or her own story becomes, in the act of narration, both the observing subject and the object of investigation, remembrance, and contemplation. We might best approach life narrative, then, as a moving target, a set of shifting self-referential practices that, in engaging the past, reflect on identity in the present."[12] The autobiographer, as a writer, weaves through subject and object positions, often occupying both simultaneously, but sometimes emphasizing one more than another. With Damasio's argument in mind, a self works much like an autobiographer in this sense. Both are dynamic and evolving. Brain memoirists embody and integrate biological and literary theories of the self as a dynamic work in progress.

In biological terms, the self is "dispersed," meaning that it involves a vast array of brain processes, cognitive traits, and mental functions: perception, memory, thought, emotion, and so on. Brain research is not currently in a position to imagine offering an account of the physiology involved in Hustvedt's evolving feelings and knowledge about her condition, not to mention the ways that condition changes her sense of self as she evolves into "the shaking woman." Damasio would like his readers to "imagine that the self-as-subject-and-knower is stacked, so to speak, on top of the self-as-object, as an additional layer of neural processes that gives rise to yet another layer of mental processing." This layering, he says, reveals that "there is no dichotomy between self-as-object and self-as-knower; there is, rather, a continuity and progression." So the shaking someone may be a product of what Damasio calls the "stacked" relation between Hustvedt "the observing subject and the object of investigation."[13] But of course, this *stacking* is a metaphor, not a concrete description of physiology. Often, metaphors mask the limits of knowledge in science. A memoir like Hustvedt's challenges brain science to acknowledge its current limitations. Like Enlightenment science, today's neuroscience sometimes represents itself on the verge of offering the key to all knowledge—something like Casaubon's "Key to all Mythologies" in George Eliot's *Middlemarch*.[14] But if neither the practitioners nor the theorists can explain Hustvedt's shaking, or tell Dully just how his transorbital lobotomy changed his personality, then those keys are far from unlocking the answers philosophers have been seeking for millennia.

Philosopher Alva Noë offers a different window onto Hustvedt's shaking and Dully's lobotomy. He proposes "that the brain's job is that of facilitating a dynamic pattern of interaction among brain, body, and world. Experience is enacted by conscious beings with the help of the world."[15] The implication is that we should take Hustvedt's grief (and the collective grief of the audience for her eulogy) and the rage in Dully's family (and the abuse it suggests) more seriously as actors in the making of these writers' suffering and searching selves. It seems to me that Damasio believes something very similar, but Noë is making the point that emphasis matters. It's fine for Damasio to believe that body and world are integral to the making of consciousness, but if he spends hundreds of pages on neural mechanisms and just a few paragraphs on the objects that comprise an organism's world, he contributes to the misleading hype that we are our brains, end of story. Disciplinary divides and rhetoric conceal underlying agreements about brain, body, self, and culture—agreements that might offer memoirists like Hustvedt and Dully more insight, more effective treatments, and more humane medical practices if they were to become the focus of the theorists' work.

Because no general theory can encompass the particular experience of an individual, brain memoirists have to find a narrative form that can capture and sustain the complexities of the questions generated by brain anomalies whose symptoms alter identity. Shulman's *To Love What Is,* the testimony of a caretaker rather than a patient, is an illuminating example of the necessity of devising a form to meet the demands of the problem at hand. Her narrative is layered, with alternating descriptions of a youthful fling, a midlife reunion and enduring commitment, Scott's devastating accident, and after that, the couple's learning how to live and love in his eternal present. The layers give the voice a developmental quality. The naive young lover becomes the outspoken feminist novelist who becomes the philosophically minded caretaker determined to protect her own fierce independence and Scott's quality of life. The book is tough and tender. It is wise in its response to what many would call tragedy, and brilliant in its ability to sift through the uncertain knowledge of brain science to develop a set of strategies tailored to living with, rather than diagnosing, Scott's damaged brain.

Shulman isn't suggesting that Scott's injury hasn't changed him, just that it hasn't changed him entirely. The degree to which he's changed varies from day to day, hour to hour, and sometimes minute to minute. Shortly after the accident, he exhibits what is to be the most uncharacteristic behavior that will become, off and on, a new dimension of his personality:

> The dignified, courtly man I love has emerged from his enforced silence a loquacious stranger—sometimes a clown, full of wild flights of wordplay that keep Heather and Norm and me howling with laughter, sometimes a garrulous, nonsensical, even dirty old man hitting on the nurses. *Fluent aphasia* is the name the doctors give to this uncontrollable verbal pandemonium, a result of damage to the brain's speech centers, by which, in place of the elusive, sought-after words, the lips spew forth a circuitous approximation that usually sounds like babble but sometimes hints at wisdom. Are the myriad substitute words arbitrary or telling?

Since aphasia, of both the fluent and non-fluent varieties, is caused by bodily injury or disease and often disappears with time, it would seem purely physical, not psychological. Yet overlaying my modest husband there appears to be another man with multiple alien personalities—now outgoing and entertaining, now authoritative and managerial—and all of them named Scott York. Can his injury have transformed his very self, stricken deep into his identity? Or revealed a buried self I never knew?[16]

Shulman tells us what can be known—that aphasia is associated with "damage to the brain's speech centers." But from there, she offers questions that cannot be answered with what is known about the brain mechanisms involved with language. Like so many brain memoirs, Shulman offers narrative in the absence of answers.

Toward the end of the book, Shulman describes a calculated risk she decided to take: accepting an offer from friends Heather and Norm to accompany them on a trip to Tuscany. At first, Scott is disoriented, asking repeatedly if they are in "The *real* Italy? The *real* Tuscany?" When they arrive at their villa, where the driveway is lined with blooming acacia trees, Scott's perspective shifts: "'Will you just look at that yellow!' cries Scott. . . . He grins with incredulous joy. Beginning with the Cleveland arboretum, where he first kissed me in 1950 beneath the spreading branches of that Ohio buckeye, and on to the renowned botanical gardens of Miami, Sydney, Honolulu, Tucson, and Brooklyn . . . to the famous bo trees and banyans of India, Scott and I, ardent arbor enthusiasts, have basked in and under distinguished trees."[17] Scott's response to the acacia trees, like so many of his sensory responses, is inflected with emotions both familiar and characteristic from the time before his accident. Upon their return from Italy, Scott tells his wife that they "forgot to bring something home from Tuscany." When she asks him what that is, he responds, "A yellow tree!"[18] Shulman's risk has paid off. She has given Scott an experience that becomes a new memory, even if it's a halting and unstable one. Scott doesn't recover substantially more than this; in fact, over time, his memory and health decline. But he does make some successful art; he does express love and rage, disappointment and joy.

Shulman follows the narration of the Tuscany trip with some reflections on the science of memory. "Little is known," she writes, "about the way information in your short-term memory . . . is converted into long-term memory for retrieval whenever you want it." She goes on to explain the well-accepted hypotheses that emotion is crucial to the conversion; that the hippocampi, "important structures deep inside the temporal lobes," are crucial to the process; that "experiments on slugs, rats, and monkeys . . . have established connections between memory retention and, variously, a certain gene, a particular enzyme, REM sleep patterns, a molecular pathway, a habit state." Ultimately, though, these are fragments of a process that still eludes science. In Shulman's words, again, "how memories are actually laid down and stored in the brain—what the process of becoming electrochemically hardwired consists of—remains a mystery."[19] There is no doubt that memory is crucial to the creation of the fully realized autobiographical selves most of us take for granted. There is little doubt that the experiments Shulman lists have identified fundamental aspects of the process by which long-term memory enables us to experience autobiographical selves. But Scott's accident puts Shulman in the position of experiencing, daily, that memory is not all there is to identity.

In *My Stroke of Insight,* Taylor comes to understand her own identity—as an organism—to be a multifarious enterprise that sounds a lot like Damasio's "dispersed" self: "I do believe that the consciousness we exhibit is the collective consciousness of whatever cells are functioning, and that both of our hemispheres complement one another as they create a single seamless perception of the world."[20] Without attempting a comprehensive theory, Taylor suggests that the cellular self is a local expression of a metaphysical reality. With her interest in esoteric aspects of consciousness, Taylor verges on the mystical much more than Hustvedt, Shulman, or Dully.[21] In her account of her stroke, this interest only intensifies as the symptoms become more severe, until she finally loses consciousness and with it the ability to reflect. She notices that her movements "are no longer fluid"; that they are "jerky"; she gains an awareness of "automatic body responses"; she feels "momentarily privy to a precise and experiential understanding of how hard the fifty trillion cells in [her] brain and body were working in perfect unison to maintain the flexibility and integrity of [her] physical form." She feels increasingly isolated, losing awareness of the world around her. The more disoriented she becomes, the more she feels a "growing sense of peace." Her amygdala, she surmises, had not "reacted with alarm," and she feels fortunate. She loses awareness of physical reality, even as she tries to dial her phone for help. But her sheer interest in her experience outweighs alarm. Taylor "felt truly at one with [her] body as a complex construction of living, thriving organisms."[22]

Taylor's optimism makes her book distinctive. She's had a stroke and she's happy about the insight she's gained from the experience. Her book is explicitly pedagogical, as was her TED Talk, which went viral and led to Taylor's minor celebrity. As a form of advocacy, her heroic story of recovery cannot encompass the variety of experiences—many of them much more devastating than Taylor's—of people who suffer from strokes. Nonetheless, Taylor's use of the plural to describe herself as a conglomerate of "living, thriving organisms" contains a hidden thesis. It would be easy to celebrate Taylor's optimism and stop there, but her argument about the plurality of organisms and systems that make us feel like singular, unified selves is just as significant. While her upbeat response to her stroke has received a great deal of attention, her more philosophical point about the neurology of self threatens to go unnoticed.[23]

The neurological experience that motivates brain memoirists to write ensures that they cannot take selfhood for granted, just as the research of a neuroscientist or philosopher of mind cannot. As a result, the memoirists and the theorists draw some consistent conclusions, many of which run against the grain of widespread cultural assumptions and of popular accounts of brain research. The self, they suggest, is by no means a single entity. It's an experience of unity that emerges from conglomerates of neurological, physiological, mental, familial, and social elements. The complexity of this conglomerate is humbling and awe-inspiring. While hasty or reductive claims that we're on the brink of understanding how the brain generates selfhood abound, the real implication of the last few decades of brain research is the spectacular complexity of the brain's collaborative role in generating self.

Writing and the Making of Self

In his essay "The Stream of Consciousness," William James argues that "the object before the mind always has a 'Fringe.'" In other words, we are conscious of the objects we're paying attention to—for these memoirists, the relations between their brains, bodies, selves, and worlds—but our minds also vaguely sense meanings and associations of which we're not quite conscious. Writing, these memoirists suggest, shifts this fringe into the center of attention. Through the process of putting words to page, we become conscious of what we didn't quite know beforehand. James argues that "a good third of psychic life consists in these rapid premonitory perspective views of schemes of thought not yet articulate."[24] The writing of a brain memoir could be seen as an exercise in premonitory thinking, living, and being, ushering not-quite-felt aspects of bodily experience into awareness.

Of course, as James also notes, the making of art is a selective process. Even artists whose intention is to represent something like James's fringe—the surrealists, for example—do so by a careful process of selection and arrangement of the tools of their medium. In James's words, "The artist notoriously selects his items, rejecting all tones, colors, shapes, which do not harmonize with each other and with the main purpose of his work. That unity, harmony, 'convergence of characters,' . . . is wholly due to elimination. Any natural subject will do, if the artist has wit enough to pounce upon some one feature of it as characteristic, and suppress all merely accidental items which do not harmonize with this."[25] It's remarkable how often brain memoirists articulate these two elements of composition—bringing the fringe into awareness and synthesizing new thoughts—as fundamental to integrating their changed neurological experience into their sense of their own identities.

Eakin makes a twenty-first-century form of James's argument, focused directly on autobiography. Drawing on Damasio's theory of the *proto-self* and *core consciousness,* he illuminates the relationship between literary autobiography and bodily, preverbal—or fringe—aspects of self. As Eakin observes, Damasio's proto-self is "a collection of neural patterns which map, moment by moment, the state of the physical structure of the organism in its many dimensions."[26] In Damasio's model, the proto-self precedes conscious awareness but makes core consciousness—the consciousness of being, outside autobiographical time—possible. Building on that idea, Eakin argues that "Individual first-person perspective, ownership, agency—these primary attributes of core consciousness are also key features of the literary form of self, the 'I' of autobiographical discourse."[27] The proposition leads Eakin into the explanatory gap, through the so-called binding problem—a big question in neurobiology, about how varied stimuli come to be experienced as a unified whole by a self that feels whole and real: "Consciousness seems inevitably to generate a sense of some central, perceiving entity distinct from the experience perceived. Damasio stresses, however, that there is no neurological evidence to support such a distinction, for despite the illusion of unified perception that 'binding' miraculously creates, multiple centers of the activity in the brain produce it."[28] Eakin concludes that the self in autobiography "is not only reported but performed, certainly by the autobiographer as she writes and perhaps to a surprising degree by the reader as he reads."[29] The words "miraculously" and "perhaps" are telling signs of Eakin's stance as a literary critic writing from the explanatory gap, trying to articulate how inarticulate aspects of selfhood might manifest themselves both in the forms of autobiography we use in daily life, to build and rebuild identity, and the literary forms that engage readers in a relational process of making identity through narrative.

Like the memoirists, Eakin is interested in how writing and reading, as forms of embodied cognition, contribute to what's already the ongoing making and remaking of self. Shulman "hadn't expected to write about so private and raw a subject" but decided to do so because "there was the possibility that writing about it could help me understand it."[30] She writes her way through a quest to learn to live with her husband, Scott, in the continuous present his damaged memory creates for him. Hustvedt articulates the daily process of writing as a vehicle for synthesizing her sense of self with the "alien" force in her body that makes her shake.[31] Dully comes to peace with his lobotomy by way of his research and writing. Through writing about her stroke, Taylor comes to the conclusion that "this story-teller portion of our left mind's language center is specifically designed to make sense of the world outside us, based on minimal amounts of information."[32] Taylor finds her own hasty "left mind" conclusions "comical" at first, but she comes to a realization that speaks to the role of writing and the evolution of identity dramatized in many brain memoirs: "It has been extremely important that I retain the understanding that my left brain is doing the best job it can with the information it has to work with. I need to remember, however, that there are enormous gaps between what I know and what I think I know. I learned that I need to be very wary of my story-teller's potential for stirring up drama and trauma."[33] The gap between "what I know" and "what I think I know" is vivid in all these brain memoirs. In addition to offering the rest of us some lessons about living with uncertainty, this gap— which sounds a lot like James's fringe—signals the potential for writing to mediate the accidents and agency involved in the making of identity.

By now, it's a consensus of autobiography theory that writing about the self is a social, or relational, enterprise. When memoirists describe the highly personal process of writing as a dynamic trafficking between conscious and unconscious experience that results in the remaking of self, their accounts inevitably involve other people. As Smith and Watson argue, other people—like

James's fringe—reveal contours of self: "This concept of relationality, implying that one's story is bound up with that of another, suggests that the boundaries of an 'I' are often shifting and permeable. Relationality invites us to think about the different kinds of textual others—historical, contingent, or significant—through which an 'I' narrates the formation or modification of self-consciousness."[34] With their focus on the physiology of living and *writing,* brain memoirs are emphatic about the continuous formation and modification of self—and it's a process that includes others. For Dully, writing reconstitutes his relationship to his parents and to Freeman, the villainous lobotomist whose culturally sanctioned malpractice defined his life. For Hustvedt, these others include an enormous cast with a long reach: the audiences before whom she speaks, her husband and daughter, her deceased father, her mother and sisters, centuries of women diagnosed as hysterics, the doctors who diagnosed those women, and health professionals, both real and imaginary, that she consults in her quest to understand her shaking. For Taylor, the most solitary and metaphysical of these brain memoirists, the primary other is "the universe," as she describes her basic reorientation to life itself and everybody in her orbit. Shulman's primary other is Scott, but his professional caregivers also profoundly shape the evolution of her identity.

Shulman describes the process of writing as mediation with characteristic grace: "So it happens that at nine o'clock each morning I banish the real Scott in order to entertain the virtual one, who stays with me on the page until two, when the real one opens our door, exclaiming, 'Look who it is! It's my beautiful wife!' and hugs me like a returning warrior."[35] Her juxtaposition of "the real Scott" and "the virtual one" is incisive: It speaks to *how* memoir might generate agency. By creating a virtual portrait of Scott, a companion to the self-portrait that emerges from Shulman's compassionate and articulate voice, she recreates the life she and Scott are struggling with. In the process, she reorients herself in relation to that life. "Writing," she continues, "takes me out of my sometimes beleaguered self into the trancelike realm of alpha waves, where, like Scott, I live in the moment." The act of writing and the habits of mind it requires shape Shulman's consciousness profoundly. She describes her time in the "alpha waves" as a therapeutic practice that enables her to live: "With five focused hours a day of aesthetic relief, I have my life again, with enough satisfaction to carry me through the entire day, and in the evenings back to the world, no longer alien."[36] The word "trancelike" suggests a liminal state between the conscious and the unconscious, one that, like dreams, promises to put the two aspects of mind into closer contact than they are under ordinary circumstances. The phrase "in the moment" suggests that writing involves the suspension of full-scale autobiographical awareness in favor of what neurologist Antonio Damasio calls alternately "core consciousness" and "core self," whereby an organism interacts with—and is changed by—the objects perceived in its immediate environment. The ironies here are productive: To achieve agency through writing, Shulman suspends conscious intention; to reflect on the story of her life with Scott, she suspends autobiographical awareness; to claim her own agency, she submits to the gaps in Scott's.

Analogously, Hustvedt becomes the shaking woman through writing: She articulates the daily process of writing as a vehicle for synthesizing her sense of self with the "alien" force in her body that makes her shake. "[W]hen I'm writing," she says, "much is generated unconsciously": "I feel beneath my words a preconscious world from which I draw them, thoughts not yet articulated but potentially there, and when I find them, I believe in their rightness or wrongness. Yes, that's what I wanted to say. Against what do I measure this? It is not *outside* me. I don't have some externalized notion of the perfect sentence that best expresses what I want to say. The knowledge lives inside me, and yet, isn't that verbal interior made from the exterior, from all the books I've read, the conversations I've had and their mnemic traces?"[37] Again, the preconscious world Hustvedt relies on—which she calls "that half-remembered underground"—sounds an awful lot like James's fringe, or the blurry line between Damasio's proto-self and core consciousness. Like Shulman, she draws on what's unconscious to craft a sense of control—or agency—through writing. She understands that "the exterior" is part of the equation, too, the social forces shaping her internal sense of self: "all the books [she's] read, the conversations [she's] had."[38] She represents her identity as permeable to her own unconscious cognition and her relations with others.

For Hustvedt, mediating between accident and agency is a process of selection (and dismissal) like the one James describes. Turning perceptual objects into art makes them objects of attention, excluding other objects in the process. Writing foregrounds the dynamic interplay between fringe and intention, and this is why the brain memoir can be such a powerful tool for people forced by neurological circumstances into crafting an identity. Through writing they find ways to accommodate changes in their brains and bodies that can't be ignored.

The memoir is a chronicle of the intricate entanglements so complex they exceed the purview of neuroscience's most advanced technologies of neuroscience as well as human cognitive capacities. Dully's story entangles his parents' neglect of him with the culturally sanctioned medical abuses performed by Freeman and intractable questions about the development of his brain after the transorbital lobotomy. Taylor's story entangles the phenomenology of disorientation and euphoria with her renewed ethical commitments, her international fame, and her personal take on theories about the brain's two hemispheres. Shulman's story entangles the past and present of her relationship with Scott with her own research on neurological theories of memory and her convictions about identity, dementia, and care. Hustvedt's story entangles the medical history of hysteria, in all its brutality, with her experience of shaking in the present; multiple diagnoses (migraine, conversion disorder, mirror-touch synesthesia); and multiple disciplines (neurology, theoretical neuroscience, psychoanalysis). All these memoirs entangle identity and writing. If brain memoirs have a thesis, it's this: The interconnections of brain, body, self, and world require us to learn how to think, how to conduct research, how to write, and how to live in the world of Taylor's gaps, Shulman's alpha waves, Hustvedt's "half-remembered underground," Damasio's proto-self, or James's fringe. These writers are organisms who have learned the wisdom of epistemological humility by making their brains and bodies the objects of their narrative attention.

3

Three Autistic Autobiographers

NAOKI HIGASHIDA WAS FIFTEEN YEARS OLD WHEN he published his memoir *The Reason I Jump: The Inner Voice of a Thirteen-Year-Old Boy with Autism* in Japan (2007) and twenty-one when it was translated into English (2013). Tito Rajarshi Mukhopadhyay was eleven when he published his first two memoirs, *Beyond the Silence: My Life, the World, and Autism* (with Lorna Wing, 2000) and its expanded U.S. edition, *The Mind Tree: A Miraculous Child Breaks the Silence of Autism* (2000); sixteen when he published his short story collection, *The Gold of the Sunbeams* (2005); and nineteen when he published his next memoir, *How Can I Talk If My Lips Don't Move? Inside My Autistic Mind* (2008). John Elder Robison was fifty when he published the first of four memoirs written in less than a decade, each exploring a distinct angle on his autistic experience: *Look Me in the Eye: My Life with Asperger's* (2007); *Be Different: My Adventures with Asperger's and My Advice for Fellow Aspergerians, Misfits, Families, and Teachers* (2011); *Raising Cubby: A Father and Son's Adventures with Asperger's, Trains, Tractors, and High Explosives* (2013); and *Switched On: A Memoir of Brain Change and Emotional Awakening* (2016). The ages of these authors indicate their generational relationship to the culture's rapidly evolving response to autism—and the very public debates about *the brain and identity* it has raised. Whereas many brain memoirists write to emphasize the particularity or idiosyncrasies of their experiences, autistic memoirists write as representatives of a community and a set of political and philosophical debates particular to autism's brutal history and its broadening and splintering definitions. Autistic autobiographers are rhetoricians shaping relations between this community, this history, these definitions, and the culture at large.

Publishing a book at age eleven or fifteen is a remarkable achievement, but that's not the primary reason age matters when it comes to Mukhopadhyay's and Higashida's memoirs. Their youth is significant because it represents both the development of the culture's response to autism *and* a first-person childhood perspective on autistic experience. Robison's age matters because he was diagnosed at the age of forty, a common experience for people born before the increasingly inclusive and public diagnostic practices of the American Psychiatric Association's *Diagnostic and Statistical Manual of Mental Disorders* (*DSM*) influenced a generation of medical and educational professionals to identify autistic traits in children. In that sense, Robison's age represents the rapid ascent of autism as a category of identity *and* a first-person adult perspective on autistic experience. Higashida, Mukhopadhyay, and Robison are memoirists *and* public advocates for autistic experience and culture—roles that involve a range of rhetorical work: public speaking, media appearances, interviews, and consulting on educational, governmental, and medical policy. Like other brain memoirists, they write to craft agency in response to the accidents of physiology and culture that shape their identities. But they also write more explicitly as rhetoricians, makers of emergent and rapidly evolving autistic culture and neurodiversity politics. The marketing of their books, as with most autistic autobiographers, tends to focus on the power of the writing to take readers "inside" autistic minds or worlds. In their writing, though, they emphasize writing as the power to challenge stereotypes about autism, assert their authority, and shape cultural debate.

In his book *Representing Autism: Culture, Narrative, Fascination* (2008), cultural critic Stuart Murray argues that "autistic presence contains its own logic and methods," and "preference, and the pleasure which can come from it, allows for a series of moments when those with autism show us how they determine the tenor of their lives, and in so doing ignore and escape the many narratives that would contain and combine them." Murray demonstrates that mainstream autism narratives, in both popular culture and medicine, have tended to propagate assumptions and stereotypes—that autistic people are absent, that their experience represents a series of deficits or defects, that autistic behaviors (say counting train schedules or flapping hands) represent suffering or social disengagement. He argues that autistic autobiography tells a very different set of stories. Murray bases his concept of autistic presence on the earliest clinical writing on autism, by Leo Kanner and Hans Asperger. Writing in the early 1940s, on two different continents, Kanner and Asperger published clinical descriptions of children they labeled autistic—children who experienced difficulty with communication, prone to repetitive behaviors and movements, with little apparent interest in social interaction. As Murray argues, these clinical descriptions are limited by their perspective: They describe autistic children from the outside. However, Murray repurposes some uncannily similar language in Kanner's and Asperger's publications to suggest more intimate and humane ways of understanding the behavior they describe. "He just is there," Kanner wrote, describing a composite of autistic children. "The autist is only himself," Asperger wrote.[1]

Murray interprets these phrases to encompass multiple and conflicting rhetorical valences:

> If the "just" or "only" is seen in a pejorative way, then the character is barely present, a prosthetic figure in the margins used only to make other aspects of the narrative work. As we shall see, such usage is common in many recent novels and films featuring autistic characters. If the emphasis in Kanner's and Asperger's observations is different, however, with a stress on the last words—"is there," "himself"—then we have the possibility of centrality and agency, of the occupation of the narrative foreground and—potentially—that the person with autism might have some say in the definition of terms through which he or she is seen. It is the kind of presence we see in the many life accounts of those with autism.[2]

For Murray, the representation of autistic *preferences* and *pleasures* is key to the making of narratives—and cultural possibilities—that resist stereotypes by representing agency in concrete terms. In their published life accounts, Higashida, Mukhopadhyay, and Robison assert their presence through the act of writing, but also through continuous descriptions of their phenomenological experiences in relation to preferences and pleasures—emphasizing the logic of their choices and the complexities of their pleasures.

If writing makes the presence of autistic autobiographers visible, the similarities and differences among their preferences and pleasures demonstrate the diversity of their experience. Higashida is a poet, essayist, fiction writer, and blogger who has published more than twenty books in Japan, where he is a well-known figure. After husband and wife David Mitchell and KA Yoshida translated *The Reason I Jump,* it became an international phenomenon. Mukhopadhyay is also a poet and fiction writer, who regularly makes media appearances, along with his mother, director of HALO (Helping Autism through Learning and Outreach), who promotes a controversial educational technique for autistic children, the Rapid Prompting Method (RPM). Robison, who identifies as a person with Asperger's, has been a scholar-in-residence at the College of William and Mary, whose Neurodiversity Initiative is the first university program of its kind. He teaches courses at William and Mary, is a member of the federal government's Interagency Autism Coordinating Committee, and makes regular media appearances. All three writers are makers of autistic culture *and* ambassadors for it, invested in improving the lives and prospects of autistic people, but also aware of the complexity of acting as a representative for an emerging culture built around a broad medical diagnosis that can't possibly describe the variety or range of autistic experience. Higashida and Mukhopadhyay are largely nonverbal poets with lyrical sensibilities who have been prolific writers since childhood. Higashida communicates through typing and communication boards, Mukhopadhyay through writing by hand. Robison is a highly verbal, blunt, and exuberant noncomformist who began writing in middle age (after successful careers as an auto mechanic, toy designer, and sound engineer). Their differences from each other are generational, cultural, and personal. It's important to note that while Murray's preferences and pleasures are central to these writers' rhetorics, they articulate their presence in other ways too—through intellectual engagement with scientific research and theory, through (often-playful) rebellion against or careful analysis of neurotypical norms, through exploration of feelings that include pleasure but range through frustration, shame, concern, and hope.

The role of autistic autobiographers as makers and ambassadors of autistic culture offers some clues to untangling theoretical tensions raised by their memoirs. As portraits of autistic phenomenology, their books seem to promise new insight about what it feels like to be autistic—to take readers "inside" autistic minds. As with all memoirs, though, memory, language, and narrative conventions mediate the experience they narrate. Brain memoirists tend to emphasize identity in transition, exploring how neurological experience catalyzes new experiences or attitudes about the self. All brain memoirists are makers of culture by virtue of being writers with an implicit relation to the neurodiversity movement. In the current moment, the making of culture is more central and more emphatic for autistic autobiographers than for most brain memoirists. Their memoirs navigate and drive the rapid evolution of autistic culture in direct response to institutionalized marginalization, misapprehension, and abuse that prevailed for half a century after autism was defined as a distinct neurological condition. At the very least, reading autistic autobiography rhetorically illuminates the emergence and evolution of autistic culture in the twenty-first century—an ascent so rapid and divergent it can be very difficult to make sense of. It also has the potential to make new meanings of autism, meanings that challenge assumptions about neurological experience and that demand social change.

As Douwe Draaisma observes, "Well into the 1980s it was the specialists—paediatricians, psychiatrists, clinical psychologists—who shaped the public image of autism. Today, the general understanding of autism is shaped from many different sides, such as education, literature, film and news media."[3] Increasingly, the public image of autism is being reframed by advocates of autistic culture and activism—whose first wave was dominated by parents but whose current momentum is channeled by autistic people who demand a defining role in the shaping of autism's "public image." While the power dynamics are shifting—so quickly they elude fixed descriptions—the forces shaping the public image of autism have not displaced one another. Rather, they have made for a crowded, and often rowdy, conversation. Medical models align and compete with educational ones; parents and their autistic children argue and collaborate; advocacy groups coalesce and splinter; bloggers and memoirists exploit the tools of different (though overlapping) media and genres to garner multifarious audiences.

In other words, an autistic autobiographer contends with particularly charged forms of questions that haunt any memoir: What's the relationship between experience and truth? Individual and culture? Phenomenology and experience? Identity and rhetoric? In the author's note to *Look Me in the Eye,* Robison makes a typical move in contemporary memoir, articulating his self-consciousness about the vexed relationship between narration and truth: "In this book I have done my very best to express my thoughts and feelings as accurately as possible. I have tried to do the same when it comes to people, places, and events, although that is sometimes more challenging. When writing of my time as a small child, it is obvious that there is no way for me to remember exact words of conversations. But I do have a lifetime of experience with how my parents talked and acted, how I talk, and how I have reconstructed scenes over the years. Armed with that, I have reconstructed scenes and conversations that accurately describe how I thought, felt, and behaved at key times."[4] The truth matters less than how it felt—*for Robison.* Phenomenology trumps accuracy. But what does the phenomenology mean? What kinds of work does it perform?

Paul Heilker and Melanie Yergeau argue that "autism itself is a rhetoric, a way of being in the world through language." What definitions of autism and rhetoric "have in common is a focus on language use in the social realm, a focus on communication in social interaction."[5] Autistic memoirists are major contributors to the evolution of that rhetoric. They don't simply describe autistic presence; they create it. Ian Hacking contends that these "autobiographies do not so much describe the mental life of their autistic authors, as constitute it by choosing words from ordinary language to be applied in connection with their behaviour." In other words, autistic autobiographers make rhetoric. In the process, he argues, we should "think of the descriptions as constituting autistic experience."[6] According to Heilker and Yergeau's argument, autism is already rhetoric. According to Hacker's, autistic autobiographers make identity through that rhetoric. Though I don't believe it's their intention, these arguments risk suggesting that autism is only or simply rhetoric—socially constructed, end of story. But like other brain memoirists, autistic autobiographers are intensely interested in the role of their biology in the making of identity. Murray's concept of presence is made of both rhetoric and physiology.

The rhetorical situation autistic autobiographers face starts with a set of epistemological questions, articulated elegantly by Heilker and Yergeau:

> We do not yet know what causes autism. In addition, there is considerable argument about what, exactly, autism is, how we should think about it, and how we should respond to it. Is it a disease? A disorder? A disability? A diversity issue? All these things, and more? How meaningful—and to whom—is the concept of autism spectrum disorders (ASD) (and all that such a rainbow metaphor entails)? How meaningful—and to whom—are the distinctions among autism, high-functioning autism, Asperger syndrome, and pervasive development disorder-not otherwise specified (PDD-NOS)? And how meaningful—and to whom—are the distinctions between people on the autism spectrum and those who are often presented as their polar (and more desirable) opposites, the neurologically typical?[7]

We don't know what autism is—or even whether it's "meaningful" to consider the range of experience and behavior associated with its types and subtypes as a single or unified phenomenon. Autism is *medical,* sometimes. It is almost certainly *neurological.* There can be no doubt that it's *phenomenological.* The emergence of autism politics and culture demonstrate that it's *social.* Many people still believe it's *environmental,* caused by toxins or vaccines (though the evidence to discredit the vaccine theory is by now definitive). There is a preponderance of evidence to suggest autism is primarily rooted in *genetics,* though as Steve Silberman observes in his book *NeuroTribes,* by 2010 "molecular biologists had identified more than a thousand candidate genes and hundreds of de novo mutations associated with autism." As Silberman reports, "The authors of a major study published in *Nature* admitted that even those most common genetic factors brought to light in their research were found in less than 1 percent of the children in their sample."[8] In response to all this uncertainty, autism proliferates meaning. Autistic memoirists are rhetoricians of its competing meanings.

Higashida, Mukhopadhyay, and Robison write within a tradition of autism memoirs, a tradition that has tended to reiterate the promise to take readers "into" the minds or worlds of autistic people—a tendency often signaled in titles or subtitles. When Clara Claiborne Park published *The Siege: A Family's Journey into the World of an Autistic Child* (1967), it was widely assumed that an autistic person could not write autobiography. Famously, Donna Williams and Temple Grandin disproved that preconception with memoirs they published during the 1990s. Williams's *Nobody Nowhere* (1992) and *Somebody Somewhere* (1994) demonstrated her sophistication with language and her acute social insight, two qualities unavailable to an autistic person, according to its medical definitions and cultural stereotypes. With *Emergence: Labeled Autistic* (1986), which Grandin coauthored with Margaret Scariano, and with *Thinking in Pictures: My Life with Autism* (1995), along with Oliver Sacks's biographical portrait of Grandin in *An Anthropologist on Mars* (1995), Grandin asserted the value of a specifically autistic intelligence, in her case an intelligence she attributes to her Asperger traits. Grandin's emphasis on the relation between "classic" autism and Asperger syndrome also challenge the idea that autism was a singular phenomenon. In the years since the publication of Grandin's and Sacks's famously influential books, the number of memoirs written and published by autistic people has become too big to count. Notable examples include Daniel Tammet's *Born on a Blue Day: Inside the Extraordinary Mind of an Autistic Savant* (2007), Elizabeth Bonker and Virginia Breen's *I Am in Here: The Journey of a Child with Autism Who Cannot Speak but Finds Her*

Voice (2011), Jeannie Davide-Rivera's *Twirling Naked in the Streets and No One Noticed: Growing Up with Undiagnosed Autism* (2013), and Austin Shinn's *A Flickering Life: A Memoir of Autism* (2016). Of course, memoirs by parents or family members of autistic children continue to be published in droves. Ralph Savarese's *Reasonable People: A Memoir of Autism and Adoption* (2007) and Jenny McCarthy's *Louder than Words: A Mother's Journey in Healing Autism* (2007) represent extremely different approaches to the autism family memoir. Savarese documents his adaptation to his son's differences, his process of learning to collaborate with him to find outlets for his strengths and accommodations for his difficulties; McCarthy recounts a pat story of heroism, whereby she "saves" her son from autism—in a book that is widely reviled among autism activists. Even this short list demonstrates the diversity of autism memoirs, hundreds of which have been published in the last two decades. Higashida's, Mukhopadhyay's, and Robison's contributions represent the evolution of the genre as it expands to represent more varieties of experience as well as emergent ideas about what autism is or means. They build on the rhetoric of their predecessors, most of whom assert what Murray calls "autistic presence," whereby the act of writing challenges the presumption that they are absent—somehow lacking mental experience. But this new generation of autobiographers goes further, emphasizing a proliferation of possibilities for what autistic presence might mean, to envision autistic culture on terms that allow both its autonomy and the utility of its blending with the culture at large.

Phenomenology as Rhetoric

At first glance it might seem that Higashida, Mukhopadhyay, and Robison write primarily to educate neurotypical audiences about autism. That is certainly part of the story. As Murray argues, autistic autobiography—like other "disability life stories"—seeks to expand the range of possible meanings and narratives that "surround" autistic experience: "Those who come to disability life stories as interested readers of autobiographical writing, or who want to engage with the rising profile of such narratives on the web, probably see in these stories the possibility of an engagement with disabled difference. But there is more to such accounts than the straightforward notion of their being a window on to autistic lives. In the ways in which we read these narratives there is the real potential to form a conception of autism that extends beyond the ways in which the condition is labeled in medical and other institutional contexts."[9] Murray's emphasis on "the ways in which we read" is fundamental to the enterprise of expanding the meanings of autism beyond clinical definitions and cultural stereotypes. For autistic writers, the "we" of the audience Murray describes is anything but simple.

All three writers address so-called neurotypical readers with the aim of offering detailed accounts of the phenomenology that motivates autistic behaviors these readers are likely to find perplexing—stimming, repetitive actions, unusual vocal patterns, unexpected responses in social situations. This might seem to suggest a firm divide—or fixed binary—between autistic and neurotypical experience. But as rhetoricians, they write for multiple audiences, without presuming fixed or static distinctions among readers. In their representation of the interplay of physiology and phenomenology, Higashida, Mukhopadhyay, and Robison call on all readers to examine the particularity of their mind styles, blurring lines between neurotypical and neurodivergent experience.

In a wry early chapter of *How Can I Talk If My Lips Don't Move?*, entitled "The Color of Basic Words," Mukhopadhyay describes a memory of his mother urging him to speak, despite the judgments of onlookers. He describes the synesthesia of his language development and as a rhetorical response to the social judgment his mother struggled with:

Mother had to be careful no one was around because she did not want those women to smile at her for trying to explain things to a boy who had not even learned how to talk yet. Their smiles were the color of jaundice yellow, and that yellow was so dense, every color could be choked by its strength. I believed that Mother saw what I saw. And I believed that she was careful because she did not want to be choked by jaundice yellow either.

"You need to talk basic words to him first," those voices would tell Mother. Basic words included a series of *dada, mama, kaka, baba,* and so on.

"Only after he masters those words, will he be able to follow explanations like "Try hard to talk." I would hear their words in their voices of jaundice yellow.

I wondered which colors would go with basic words like *dada, mama, kaka,* and *baba.* So I would stand in front of the mirror and mentally say those basic words and wait for the mirror to show me their colors reflected in it. I soon realized that the mirror could not reflect the colors of those basic words.

"Only after it masters how to reflect basic words, will it be able to follow other explanations like, "Try hard to reflect," I concluded.[10]

Mukhopadhyay's narration is puckishly rebellious—describing his sophisticated, multimodal phenomenology in response to the voices of women who tell
his mother he lacks all understanding of language. His account is both a translation of his experience and a social critique. His synesthesia represents the
smug smiles of the women in jaundice yellow "so dense, every color could be
choked by its strength." The lyrical description of the "choking" yellow blends
cognitive perception with an emotional response to painful social interaction.
The implication is clear: Synesthetic perception is a cognitive experience integrated with the other variables of mental life.

Mukhopadhyay offers an equally complicated counter to the idea that autistic
people lack "theory of mind"—or an awareness of other people's mental states.
He describes his belief that his "Mother saw what I saw" and that "she did not
want to be choked by jaundice yellow either." Narrating with hindsight, he
makes it clear that he now knows he was wrong about his mother's cognition.
She wasn't experiencing the social shaming they shared synesthetically. But he
was making guesses about her mental state, guesses he revised over time. As
narrator, he controls a portrait of himself making a mistaken supposition. He
may have been wrong, but he was present, and he was exploring his evolving
preferences. He describes his desire to avoid the jaundiced smiles he describes,
but his writing represents another desire, to revisit—and skewer—the smug
assumptions behind the smiles. The mirror is a recurring figure in the book. The
mirror was silent, like him, and he attributed agency to it, telling it stories and
expecting it to return the favor. When the mirror doesn't reflect the synesthetic
colors of the "basic words," he comes to the conclusion that it must first "master
the basic words" before it will be able to follow the more complex instructions
he gives it: "Try hard to reflect." Mukhopadhyay represents the phenomenology
of his understanding not only of his mother's instruction, "Try hard to talk," but
of the more abstract idea of "reflecting." His irony emphasizes the sophistication of Mukhopadhyay's thinking, a form of presence invisible to those who
presume his absence.

Mukhopadhyay was a young adult reflecting on his childhood experience
when he wrote *How Can I Talk If My Lips Don't Move?* He crafts a wry voice that
can encompass layers of experience, a point of view that blends the past and
present. These rhetorical choices are the ingredients of a counternarrative to
many standard autism narratives. Murray argues that "Tito's writing presents
a highly complex account of autistic subjectivity and presence, and one that . . .

does not fall within orthodox boundaries of what autistic production is often seen to be. Tito's 'special ability' as a writer cannot properly parallel the work of other child figures . . . whose talents when they were young existed within certain understood and defined ideas of autistic creativity. . . . Indeed, in his literary ability to work with imaginative creativity and metaphor, Tito is producing the kind of material that is commonly believed to be outside the scope of any individual with autism."[11] Lyricism doesn't make many appearances in standard definitions of autism, but it's fundamental to Mukhopadhyay's writing (as well as Higashida's). His lyrical description of his synesthetic experience demonstrates that he already understood language well beyond the basics—and that as a nineteen-year-old writer of considerable talent he is now able to reflect both on his own childhood development and widely held misconceptions that equate difficulty with verbal communication with an absence of mind. It's a sly demonstration that the inability of others to understand him is at least as much of a problem as his difficulty learning to speak or to develop according to neurotypical assumptions. In fact, the autistic child understands much more about neurotypical culture than most people understand about autism.

Though his tone couldn't be more different, Robison makes a similar rhetorical move early in *Look Me in the Eye,* when he explains his book's title: "To this day, when I speak, I find visual input to be distracting. When I was younger, if I saw something interesting I might begin to watch it and stop speaking entirely. As a grown-up, I don't usually come to a complete stop, but I may still pause if something catches my eye. That's why I usually look somewhere neutral—at the ground or off into the distance—when I'm talking to someone. . . . And now I know it is perfectly natural for me not to look at someone when I talk. Those of us with Asperger's are just not comfortable doing it. In fact, I don't really understand why it's considered normal to stare at someone's eyeballs."[12] Where Mukhopadhyay's mode is lyricism, Robison's is a playful social satire in which he often celebrates his own brash disavowal of social norms—ranging from looking a person in the eye to telling the truth or not experimenting with explosives in domestic settings. In this particular case, Robison describes his phenomenology to demonstrate the disparity of a relatively mundane difference—visual input distracts him—and its social consequences. When he doesn't look others in the eye, they often reprimand him, express bewilderment, and suggest it's a sign of flawed character or even a sign of evilness. He turns the tables on his interlocutors who assume not looking them in the eye is a sign of his absence. He asserts his presence with signature humor, defamiliarizing a social commonplace by questioning "why it's considered normal to stare at someone's eyeballs." The humor comes with the physicalization of the eyeball—and almost approaches something like Mukhopadhyay's lyricism. The move from "eye" to "eyeball" transforms its significance, from a symbol of self to a wet, globular sense organ with a direct connection to visual areas of the brain. Robison *prefers* not to look at other people's gooey organs.

As a rhetorical move, humor like this expands and multiplies Robison's presumed audience. Throughout his memoirs, he is a roving narrator, addressing multiple audiences. He tends to link his humor to an Aspergian mind style, but in a multidimensional way. In *Look Me in the Eye,* he informs readers that "humor and sarcasm often go right over my head." Nonetheless, he's a relentless practical joker. In one pivotal chapter entitled "Collecting the Trash," he reluctantly attends a garden party hosted by friends of his parents, Annette and Walter. He fabricates a series of stories about working as a garbage collector—which he's never done—to shock a bewildered group of university professors at the party. They listen attentively as he describes a life of gun violence, gang affiliations, and extortion. His mother and Annette reprimand him, and he responds with more jokes. He promises to apologize to the professors he duped, but he gets in one more joke, this one addressed to readers: "I walked back to the group of garbage aficionados I had collected. 'I'm sorry I've got to go. They just called from work. Emergency. One of the other garbage companies firebombed our truck.' "[13] Robison describes the scene to illustrate his discomfort socializing in a neurotypical world. But his parents' world is far from typical—neurologically or otherwise. His mother is prone to depression and psychosis, his father a severe and often delusional alcoholic, many of their friends and associates eccentric in the extreme. Robison associates his socially inappropriate humor with what he calls "Aspergian" traits, but its audiences and effects are promiscuous. His presumed audience is anybody willing or able to get in on the joke, whether or not that willingness indicates anything about neurological disposition.

By contrast, the structure of Higashida's book seems to imply a strictly neurotypical audience. He titles his chapters with questions he imagines neurotypical readers might ask: "Why don't you make eye-contact when you're talking?" "Is it true you hate being touched?" "Do you have a sense of time?" "Why can you never stay still?" In a chapter entitled "Why do you ask the same questions over and over?," Higashida offers a simple answer: "Because I very quickly forget what I've just heard." But he follows that explanation with a reflection on memory, play, sound, and rhythm: "So I do understand things, but my way of remembering is different from everybody else's. I imagine a normal person's memory is arranged continuously, like a line. My memory, however, is more like a pool of dots. I'm always 'picking up' these dots—by asking my questions—so I can arrive back at the memory that the dots represent." The "normal person" here is presumably neurotypical. While the label "normal" generally reinforces a binary between typical and atypical, it may also perform a very different kind of narrative inclusion here, inviting all those who don't identify as normal to reflect, with Higashida, on what a so-called normal memory might work like. In his description, a typical memory, "arranged continuously," isn't just an accurate description. It also sounds much duller than one comprised of a "pool of dots" that can be "picked up" with questions. The lyricism of Higashida's dot metaphor, contrasted with the mundanity of "normal" memory, turns the rhetorical tables on neurotypical norms—a common move in neurodiversity discourse. The implication, offered playfully, is that to be neurotypical is to be boring.

As he continues, Higashida makes it clear that the pleasure he takes in repetition is multidimensional, partly rooted in the utility of memory but also in the pleasures of language: "But there's another reason for our repeated questioning: it lets us play with words. We aren't good at conversation, and however hard we try, we'll never speak as effortlessly as you do. The big exception, however, is words or phrases we're very familiar with. Repeating these is great fun. It's like a game of catch with a ball. Unlike words we're ordered to say, repeating questions we already know the answers to can be a pleasure—it's playing with sound and rhythm."[14] The repetition of language is an expression of preference and a source of pleasure. Higashida makes his point through another complex rhetorical move when he alternates first-person singular and plural descriptions of his own phenomenology. The move has a double effect. It positions readers in opposition to the "we": *You* are like this, but *we* are like this. But it also has the potential to invite readers to become or feel included in the *we* category. Rhetorically, the move is similar to Robison's, destabilizing assumptions about who belongs to which category—or whether it matters. Higashida describes a relationship to language that may be characteristically autistic but that is shared by anybody with a lyrical sensibility (and certainly by any child at various developmental stages of language learning). Simply put, he blends the categories of the autistic and the neurotypical.

In "Autism and Rhetoric," Heilker and Yergeau emphasize the entanglement of questions about rhetoric, audience, and neurological difference by interrupting the structure of standard academic argument with italicized sections entitled "Paul Speaks" or "Melanie Speaks." In one of these sections, Yergeau reflects on the kinds of reframing autistic autobiographers perform when they represent their phenomenology in rhetorical terms: *"Understanding autism as a rhetoric brings a certain level of legitimacy to what I might consider my commonplaces—repetitive hand movements, rocking, literal interpretation, brazen honesty, long silences, long monologues, variations in voice modulation—each its own reaction, or a potentially autistic argument, to a discrete set of circumstances."* Autistic autobiographers demonstrate "the legitimacy" of their "commonplaces" through the forms they choose—one might say prefer— to portray their phenomenology, as presence, preference, and pleasure. Higashida describes his pleasure in repeating questions; Robison, his preference to avoid eye contact and the pleasure of using humor to destabilize the norms of social engagement; and Mukhopadhyay, the presence of silent, lyrical engagement with language. In the process, they make implicit arguments about the meanings of their circumstances. The results are potentially transformative. As Yergeau argues, *"Coming to autism rhetorically recasts items such as a 'difficulty smiling'—from pitiful disease symptom into autistic discourse convention, from a neurological screwup into an autistic confluence of structure and style. So too has understanding neurotypicality as a rhetoric legitimized my autistic ways of communicating: such an understanding involves calling attention to normalized discourse patterns frequently portrayed as desirable and ideal, involves calling attention to ways of being that are not the ways of being."*[15] If autism and neurotypicality are both rhetorics, they are both subject to continuous revision and recasting. Neither is a stable category. When autistic autobiographers blur or combine these categories in their address to readers, they invite the kinds of recasting Yergeau celebrates.

The Pleasures of Rhetorical Neuroscience

Heilker and Yergeau observe that "human neurology itself, autistic or other, is likewise a profoundly rhetorical phenomenon."[16] *Are you your brain?* is a rhetorical question, generally asked by somebody who believes strongly in an affirmative or negative answer. When autistic autobiographers explore the question, it's rhetorical in a more productive sense—leading pretty swiftly to nuanced reflections on the tension between neurobiology and rhetoric, tensions at the heart of any literary representation of physiological identity. Most neuroscience research comes in one of two modes: research that investigates the functions of a composite, or so-called normal brain, and research that focuses on brain anomalies resulting from injury, disease, development, or difference. Plenty of research focuses on investigating anomalies in order to understand standard brain physiology—for example, studying relationships between brain lesions and particular disruptions in function. Any neuroscientist will tell you that individual brains vary and that a damaged brain may adapt to surprising and unpredictable functional differences. But research on what I'll call the "composite brain"—the digital modeling, or composition, of a so-called normal brain based on data collected from the brains of many subjects—aims for statistical averages that reduce differences among the various brains that are the data sources for a particular study. Stanislas Dehaene, one of the most influential neuroscientists working today, has conducted extensive studies looking for "signatures of consciousness": brain activity associated with consciousness and only consciousness, including synaptic patterns, the synchronization of particular frequencies of synaptic activity, and the electrical amplitudes they produce. The goal is to identify signatures that may one day lead to an explanation for the hard problem of consciousness, the explanatory gap between neural correlates and phenomenology.

In his book *Consciousness and the Brain: Deciphering How the Brain Codes Our Thoughts* (2014), Dehaene asserts the necessity of subjective reports in his research: "introspection provides shaky ground for a science of psychology, because no amount of introspection will tell us how the mind works. However, as a measure, introspection still constitutes the perfect, indeed the only, platform on which to build a science of consciousness, because it supplies a crucial half of the equation—namely, how subjects feel about some experience (however wrong they are about the ground truth). To attain a scientific understanding of consciousness, we cognitive neuroscientists 'just' have to determine the other half of the equation: Which objective neurobiological events systematically underlie a person's subjective experience?"[17] Brain memoirs have emerged as a significant and growing literary genre devoted to the shaky ground of introspection about the relationship between mind and brain—though much more than Dehaene does, they emphasize other variables, like the body as a whole, social relations, and the environment.

Any writer of a brain memoir is likely to have developed relationships with neurologists and sometimes research neuroscientists—and as such to have gained a certain amount of professionalization, more than most of the research subjects Dehaene describes. Autistic brain memoirists write at the cusp of cultural and medical conversations about brain differences, whose focus is not on investigating anomalies for their own sake—to understand brain difference as a phenomenon. As a rhetorician, Dehaene writes from a perspective that presumes commonality, though of course he's well aware that brain physiology varies. Autistic autobiographers are different kinds of rhetoricians, writing from a perspective that presumes—and values—difference. Dehaene is a supple thinker, an inventive researcher who asserts a strong stance: We are our brains, and we're going to prove it. When autistic autobiographers theorize about their own brains, they change the terms of the debate, from a focus on whether we are our brains to how to live with them. As rhetoricians, they represent difference in a world that presumes a commonality as a norm, a value, even a necessity for living. With their responses to published brain research, autistic autobiographers make a hybrid of Dehaene's two categories, "introspection" and "objective neurobiological events." They fill the explanatory gap with a combination of research data and lived experience.

In his book *Autism* (2011), Stuart Murray summarizes current theories about the physiology of autism, including both neurobiology and genetics. As he observes, "studies show that the brains of those with autism sometimes work in ways that are noticeably different from those who are non-autistic." That word "sometimes" indicates the contingency of the theories. It's important to note that contingency does not imply illegitimacy, but it does imply a need for both interpretation and a focus on the utility of theory. "After all," as Murray writes, "autism is only of interest because of the fact that it affects people, and if we cannot extend what we know about it to make a real difference then there is not much point to any research on the condition." When Murray surveys the research—including studies on "underactive connections in the 'social brain,'" the shape and size of "autistic brains," "cell density," "noticeable increase in connections between neurons" in brain regions including the hippocampus, amygdala, and cerebellum, or the development of brain-scanning techniques or genetic profiles that might predict autism—he does so with both interpretation and utility in mind.[18] As he points out, "there are no biological markers for autism, neurological or otherwise." An autism diagnosis "is an evaluative process that nearly always requires the work of more than one specialist."[19] It is not surprising, then, that autistic autobiographers claim their role among the specialists, offering theories about the physiology of autism conceived to improve the quality of their own lives.

For example, Higashida refers to his brain routinely in his descriptions of daily experience, often theorizing about its role. In a chapter entitled "Why do you repeat actions again and again?," Higashida's answer offers a characteristic account of his general portrayal of the relationship between physiology—specifically, the brain—and personhood: "I do some action or other that I'm not allowed to do; then I get told off for it; and last, my impulse to re-create this sequence trumps the knowledge that I've been told not to do it, and I end up doing it again. The next thing I know, I feel a sort of electrical buzz in my brain, which is very pleasant—no other sensation is quite the same. Perhaps the closest thing is watching your favorite scene on a DVD, looping on auto-repeat, over and over."[20] That electrical buzz "trumps" social norms. It's worth the risk of "getting told off"—an act of rebellion that mixes intention and unconscious desire. Higashida is seeking a phenomenological pleasure he describes as "a sort of electrical buzz in my brain." Repetitive actions—rocking, lining up toys or objects, a certain sequence of movements—induce feelings. Higashida's electrical buzz may be a metaphor, or he may feel it as located in his brain. Either way, he represents his brain as a vehicle for manipulating consciousness—or mediating the relationship between environmental stimuli and subjective feelings.

Higashida introduces questions about the brain's role in autistic experience but quickly moves from physiology to phenomenology—a pattern repeated throughout the book. For example, he writes,

So is there something wrong with the circuitry of our brains? Life's been tough for people with autism, pretty much forever, yet nobody's been able to identify the causes of autism. For sure, it takes us ages to respond to what the other person has just said. The reason we need so much time isn't necessarily because we haven't understood, but because by the time it's our turn to speak, the reply we wanted to make has often upped and vanished from our heads.

I don't know if this is making a lot of sense to you. Once our reply has disappeared, we can never get it back again. *What did he say again? How was I going to answer her question?* . . . Search me! And all the while, we're being bombarded by yet more questions. I end up thinking, *This is just hopeless.* It's as if I'm drowning in a flood of words.[21]

Higashida's physiological question quickly becomes a phenomenological one. When he writes, "For sure, it takes us ages to respond to what the other person has just said," he is addressing his own question about the brain circuitry of autistic people. Science can't explain what the link between that circuitry and autistic conversational styles is, but Higashida offers an account that's consistent with most autobiographical writing about autism. What seems like simple conversation to neurotypicals involves a flood of sensory and cognitive stimuli for him. He's "drowning in a flood of words." The delays he describes are rhetorical responses to that flood.

Mukhopadhyay's account of obsessions resonates with Higashida's reflections of repetitive behavior, but with more detailed emphasis on brain physiology: "An obsession begins in the caudate nucleus in the brain. From the caudate nucleus, the impulse passes to the prefrontal cortex. From the prefrontal cortex, the impulse goes to the cingulate cortex. The impulse from the cingulate cortex goes back to the caudate nucleus, then completing a cycle. The cycle repeats again and again inside the mind. So an obsessive impulse is not easy to distract. Why does it bring an extreme manifestation of behavior? That is because the caudate nucleus is so close to the amygdala region of the brain, which is responsible for all our primeval emotions, like fear and anger. When the caudate nucleus is stimulated, the amygdala is also affected."[22] Mukhopadhyay presents hypotheses about the brain as fact—for example, "the amygdala . . . is responsible for all our primeval emotions" and he reduces complex behaviors to a fairly simple account of brain physiology—for example, "An obsession begins in the caudate nucleus."

At moments like these, Mukhopadhyay seems to equate personhood with what historian Fernando Vidal has called "brainhood." Those first couple of paragraphs suggest that Mukhopadhyay *is* his brain. But such a reading oversimplifies the relationship between physiology and personhood depicted in *How Can I Talk If My Lips Don't Move?*—and in many other brain memoirs. Mukhopadhyay elaborates his account of the brain physiology involved in obsession with the social and phenomenological contexts that give it meaning: "My extreme obsession with train rides was beyond my reason and control, although I understood that I was being irrational about it. It is the same process that goes on in the mind of perhaps a chain-smoker, who, although he knows and understands completely well that he is not supposed to smoke, is still compelled to."[23] When Mukhopadhyay compares his obsessive behavior to the "process that goes on in the mind of . . . a chain-smoker," he is offering a pretty similar explanation to Higashida's. The obsessive behavior changes his state of mind. It allows him to manipulate environmental stimuli in order to change the way the world makes him feel.

Mukhopadhyay is more emphatic about the brain's role in the process, engaging both neurological medicine and theoretical neuroscience in detail. In a chapter entitled "Exposure Helps Shape Visual Perception," he tells the story of an encounter with Bill Hirnstein, "one of the scientists who first tested me when I came to the United States." Hirnstein showed him a picture and said, "Tito, name this object." In Mukhopadhyay's words, "I began to search all the names that were associated with that object, like *carnivore, stripe, ferocious, forest, hunt,* etc. All those names appeared in my mind except the word *tiger.* I was getting desperate because I felt trapped in the focal points of the waiting eyes of those scientists who were ready to prove 'Who knows what.'" Mukhopadhyay aces the test when he realizes that if he starts with a definition—"a striped animal, which is not a zebra, is a TIGER," he can name the objects Hirnstein shows him.[24] The meaning of the tiger is physiological, cognitive, and social. Mukhopadhyay's ability to match a word with an image is shaped by the stress of the clinical encounter, his metacognitive response to that stress and the demands of the test, and the brain physiology involved in the emotional and cognitive demands of the situation.

Mukhopadhyay turns to neurologist and theoretical neuroscientist Antonio Damasio's theory of "convergence zones" to speculate about the physiology involved in the cognitive experience he describes:

In his book Damasio mentions two types of converging zones, the lower converging zone and the higher converging zone. The lower converging zone is responsible for storing a general image of faces, with two eyes, a nose, and a mouth below the nose. The higher converging zone is responsible for storing images of one particular face and recalling that face at the right moment from some past experience.

After reading that, I made my own hypothesis. I might have trouble with the higher converging zone regions of my brain. That may lead me to find it difficult to recall a person's name based on his face, although I can recognize who he is from his voice or his personality traits, which are usually stored as a symbolic representation or combination of different sensory stories. That is my hypothesis.[25]

Mukhopadhyay's hypothesis is untested—and perhaps untestable. Damasio's convergence zones involve multiple systems of brain physiology through which neural connections proceed via what he calls "feed forward loops" that enable "knowledge retrieval" through "relatively simultaneous, attended activity in many early cortical regions, engendered over several iterations of such reactivation cycles."[26]

Using a different set of terms, Dehaene describes a similar phenomenon when he explains the "global neuronal workspace" theory he's developed in collaboration with Jean-Pierre Changeux. Dehaene reframes Damasio's convergence zones as a "global assembly" designed to "send and receive numerous projections to and from a broad variety of distant brain regions, allowing the neurons there to integrate information over space and time. Multiple sensory modules can therefore converge onto a single coherent interpretation ('a seductive Italian woman'). This global interpretation may, in turn, be broadcast back to the areas from which the sensory signals originally arose. The outcome is an integrated whole."[27] *Convergence zones* and *global assemblies* are metaphors for brain activity, as is Mukhopadhyay's tiger. Dehaene's "seductive Italian woman" is one kind of sensory story—one that presumes, reflects, and reinforces a dense set of social norms. Mukhopadhyay's tiger is a sensory story that represents a mode of consciousness operating outside these norms. His theory appropriates Damasio's metaphor—and, implicitly, Dehaene's—to suggest how his own brain might tell a neurological story about consciousness that's consistent with the theories of professional neuroscientists even while it demands an expansion of their terms that would more readily accommodate both physiological and phenomenological difference.

In *Switched On,* Robison asserts his own theories about the brain and consciousness. In fact, he reflects on brain physiology continuously as he reflects on his experience as a research subject participating in studies on the use of transcranial magnetic stimulation (TMS) as a therapy for particular symptoms of autism—in particular, the ability to notice and interpret social cues. As a narrator, he is highly aware of the hypothetical quality of the research he's engaged in—and that his phenomenological input is valuable to the people who design and conduct the research. He becomes an avid reader of neurological literature, determined to understand the physiological details, medical applications, and philosophical implications of the research:

> Stimulation of the frontal lobe . . . often has no visible effects because you're not stimulating brain cells with simple direct connections to the outside world. It had been easy for the scientists to figure out where to fire the TMS to make my index finger twitch. But knowing how to fire TMS into my frontal lobe to make me *want* to twitch my finger . . . that is infinitely more complex. There's just one set of neurons that actually moves my fingers, and their general location is well known to neurologists. There are a million sequences of thought that could set those cells into action, some of which are under my conscious control and others not.
>
> Yet that's in essence what the scientists hoped to accomplish by beaming electromagnetic energy into the heart of my consciousness. The frontal lobe connections they targeted are thought to be unique to humans, and if that's true, these higher functions are part of what sets us apart from other animals. But the complexity of the frontal lobe meant that isolating what particular connections do is difficult. Any area they might stimulate would be connected to thousands of other brain areas, with most of those connections unknown except in the most general sense. So they could hope to guess correctly about the function of an area, but what else stimulating that area might do would have to be discovered by observation. That was my job, and I took it seriously.[28]

Robison describes his role—or "job"—in the research process as that of observer, but in a very particular sense, an observer whose experience might shed light on both what's not known about the "complexity" of frontal lobe activity and connections, and the particularity of his own experience. His rhetorical strategy circumvents polarizing debates about brainhood, by putting heavy emphasis on words that signal hypothesis and contingency: "if," "hope," "but," "might." This rhetorical stance makes room for Robison's presence as an active participant in the research and the conclusions that might be drawn from it. He may be a cerebral subject, but nobody can explain how stimulating his brain changes his experience of selfhood. By writing a best-selling autobiography about the experience, Robison gives his interpretations more cultural purchase than the research itself. He owns the rhetoric. He represents himself through a series of hypotheses, more a contingent subject than a simply cerebral one.

Robison is acutely conscious of the potential for his involvement in TMS research to be interpreted as an attempt to cure his autism, but he's a deft rhetorician, careful to articulate his commitment to the value of what Murray calls "autistic presence," articulating his involvement in the research as an evolution of his identity rather than a cure for a disease: "In my writing and my speaking I had said that my autism was a way of being, that it was part of who I was. That it wasn't a disease and there was no need for a cure. I still believed that, but I also believed in being the best I could be, particularly by addressing the social blindness that had caused me the most pain throughout my life." Robison addresses controversies about curing autism more directly than either Higashida or Mukhopadhyay. He believes his "social blindness" is linked to his particular neurological signatures, and he sees his engagement with TMS as a matter of preference. He describes it with considerable pleasure—but also with a range of emotional responses that reflect his attitude about his Asperger's diagnosis:

> Should I be happy? Should I be sad? Should I be relieved? I felt all those things and more. Learning about autism and Asperger's was a huge deal for me, because it gave me a legitimate explanation for why I was different. Hearing that I was different and not defective was certainly inspiring, though it took years to fully sink in. Reading about how folks with Asperger's typically act helped me to see some of my own behaviors in a new light. With that insight it became clear why some people reacted negatively to things I said or did.
>
> Having a neurological explanation does not change the fact that I often acted like a jerk. That's one of the problems with growing more self-aware—you have a lot more moments where you think back on things you said and did and cringe in shame.[29]

As a critic, Murray emphasizes preference and pleasure as signs of what he calls "autistic presence"; he makes a rhetorical choice to emphasize details that are obscured by standard autism narratives. In his self-representation, Robison expands what counts as presence. His preference to avoid eye contact and the pleasures he finds in machines are signs of his presence, but so are cringing in shame, relief, sadness, and inspiration. Robison finds a new measure for his experience, in relation to "how folks with Asperger's typically act," rather than how people in general are supposed to act. The observation that "a neurological explanation does not change the fact that I often acted like a jerk" is a version of the relationship between "introspection" and "objective neurological events" that Dehaene describes as the necessary halves of consciousness research. But in this case, neither is clear-cut.

When Dehaene measures what he calls "conscious access," he does it primarily through isolated sensory experience—for example, displaying images for durations that allow subjects to perceive them, and alternating them with shorter durations too quick to perceive. "Acting like a jerk" is a much more complicated form of subjective experience that only makes sense in a social context, involving particular people and actions that are comprised of language, gestures, emotions, time, information, and beliefs. Similarly, it makes little sense to describe Asperger's as a "neurological event," and an Asperger's diagnosis is only loosely correlated with a few hypothetical "neurological signatures"—ones we might, using Dehaene's description of introspection, describe as "shaky." In addition to all this, TMS remains an experimental technology whose precise effects are not well understood. Dehaene describes TMS's power to stimulate phenomenological experiences through electrical stimulation of brain areas associated with them—say, motion, sound, or sight. From his rhetorical perspective, as a researcher and theorist, the power and precision of the technology are impressive, because they demonstrate a clear correlation between brain events and subjective experience: "A battery of accumulators suddenly delivers a strong electrical current to a coil placed atop the head. This current induces a magnetic field that penetrates the head and generates a discharge at a precise 'sweet spot' in the underlying cortex. Safety guidelines ensure that the technique is harmless: only an audible click and, occasionally, an unpleasant muscle twitch occur."[30]

Robison is equally enthusiastic about TMS technology, but, unsurprisingly, he's both more introspective (and more circumspect) about the teleology of its effects. Where Dehaene describes the TMS experience as "an audible click" and the occasional "unpleasant muscle twitch," Robison devotes eight paragraphs to describing a single session—that felt, to him, to pass in an instant. Robison begins his description of the session by naming the clinician—Shirley—who runs it. They've formed a relationship through his preparation. The experience is social. It's also perceptual, intellectual, emotional, durational, and embodied. Dehaene's click becomes a thirty-minute series of pops:

> My proto-terror faded with the first pulses. Nothing awful was happening. . . . I felt a jolt of electricity that hit my head with every pulse—not enough to hurt me, but enough that I knew for absolute certain what it was. Anyone who's been shocked knows the feeling—it's unmistakable.

Is that electromagnetic induction? That thought passed through my head, but almost as quickly as it arrived, it was gone. All that remained was the march of time, as defined by the coil. *Pop. Pop. Pop.* My head twitched with every pulse, but oddly enough, it wasn't uncomfortable. It wasn't really anything at all."[31]

His face twitches, he becomes tranquil, his "internal dialogue" is "somehow subdued." The clock on the wall becomes the objective counternarrative to his phenomenological experience of time stopping. His presence, in Murray's terms, is diminished—and he likes it. By contrast, he experiences aftereffects that are, by his account, more extreme than anything the technology or its practitioners promise. First, he experiences auditory hallucinations, memories of live concerts he worked on as a sound engineer, as though they are happening in the present. For a few days, he feels like he can read other people's minds, an experience that dims with time into what he describes as "sensing and feeling emotion" in ways he hadn't previously. Correspondingly, his "speech became more expressive, with more tonal range and more change in rhythm or prosody."[32] His marriage deteriorates as he becomes highly sensitive to his wife's emotions. But he doesn't regret the changes. In a dramatic statement, he proclaims, "Before TMS I was a car mechanic in a small New England town. After TMS I emerged on an international stage, sought out for my thoughts on autism and neurodiversity."[33]

Introspection and data analysis involve very different—but complementary—epistemologies. In order to collect data to demonstrate the complexity of his global neuronal workspace theory, Dehaene must limit and decontextualize the conscious experience of his subjects. In order to reflect on neurological theories that might help him understand his own autistic presence, Robison expands the phenomenological dimension of his experience. The paradox is one more version of the push-pull between neuroscience and literary responses to it. It's common for brain memoirists to express frustration with the medical establishment or aims of brain research that are too far removed from the experience of living people's needs. As Robison makes clear, though, he finds considerable pleasure in his engagements with TMS research—and theoretical accounts of the brain. The pleasures are far from idle. Like so many brain memoirists, he makes it clear that he doesn't have the luxury of eschewing neuroscience on philosophical grounds. His brain matters. It interests him. Like Higashida and Mukhopadhyay, he makes direct appeals to medical researchers, practicing physicians, and educators—asking these professionals to attend to the details of the phenomenological experiences that shape his autistic experience.

Rhetorics of Change

As they engage neuroscience research, autistic autobiographers craft rhetorical styles that are closely aligned with their mind styles, strategically designed as an implicit corrective to the most controversial aspect of medical rhetoric about autism: the "search" for a cure. The organization Autism Speaks is at the center of the controversy. Both Mukhopadhyay and Robison were formerly affiliated with the organization and broke with it publicly because of the rhetoric it uses in its campaigns, rhetoric shared by other parent-focused organizations like Cure Autism Now (CAN), which has merged with Autism Speaks, and Defeat Autism Now! (DAN!). Another set of advocacy groups—for example, the Autistic Self Advocacy Network and Aspies for Freedom— challenges the rhetoric of cure. In fact, these groups point out that arguments about cure rely on metaphors rather than the (often experimental and untested) medical approaches they tend to advocate. The debate reveals the complexity of the rhetorical situation. As Murray argues, "All serious research into autism acknowledges that it is a lifelong condition, and that it is built into the fabric of the person who has it. It is . . . not an illness. As such, it cannot be cured." But that's not the whole story. A more accurate understanding of autism requires rhetoric that can encompass "one straightforward fact . . . often forgotten in these various accounts of progress. The condition is one of developmental delay. Autism is not some kind of static state into which an individual regresses, never to change. Children with autism might not develop speech when two years old, but a number will do so before they are ten; they may avoid all eye contact when they are three, but will happily hold the gaze of a parent, and clearly respond to emotions, when they are twelve." Murray argues that dominant narratives of autism fail to account for the complexity of autism as a developmental condition—and all that implies about the fluidity of identity, or presence. Too often, "stories of curing and healing autism are indicative of a belief that change is possible and that, when it comes it is somehow 'miraculous.' The idea that the change being witnessed may well just be normal, part of a process of development that may not be that of children who are not autistic, appears to be somehow too ordinary to warrant comment, even if it happens all the time. That some forget this is indicative of the extent to which the idea of the condition being 'tragic' is still ingrained in contemporary culture."[34]

If Higashida, Mukhopadhyay, and Robison write as representatives of autistic culture, they do it to show that individuals express traits associated with the condition in personal, distinctive ways, that autism is intrinsic to their identities without defining them entirely or fixing them to a set of static behaviors. In his essay "Autism as Culture," Joseph Straus identifies three qualities of autistic thinking that become characteristic of autistic writing: "a propensity to perceive the world in parts rather than as a connected whole"; "a preference for orderliness, system, and ritual"; and the development of a system "of private meanings" composed of "rich networks of association" rather than "a chain of logical coherence."[35] In other words, he describes qualities of autistic rhetoric. These rhetorical qualities in Higashida's, Mukhopadhyay's, and Robison's writing result in some formal similarities, all of which play with time in ways that enable their writers to portray their intellectual development without capitulating to standard narrative tropes that equate development with normalization.

Higashida's structure is crafted to focus on parts of his experience: Each chapter addresses a question about sensory or cognitive experience, resulting in an anti-chronological narrative. In *How Can I Talk If My Lips Don't Move?*, Mukhopadhyay's chapters are similar, each addressing an aspect of his mental experience, but they build chronologically geographically, beginning with childhood in Mysore and Bangalore, India, and moving through adolescence in Los Angeles and Austin, Texas. In *The Mind Tree,* the central metaphor of the tree as Mukhopadhyay's mind, along with the integration of prose memoir and lyric poetry, create a particularly strong effect of an associational network of meanings whose coherence depends on readers' willingness to think on the author's terms. Each of Robison's books is episodic, revisiting and reframing aspects of the same expanding story. Many of the episodes he recounts emphasize the ways he personalizes his work, family, and social lives by asserting his idiosyncratic preferences. Two running themes—his preference for nicknames and his love for machines—reflect his rhetorical style. When Robison asserts his preference for nicknames (and his refusal to use given names), he describes a subtle ongoing practice of playfully insisting that people interact with him on his terms. His relationship with machines is a means of describing his social disconnection, but over time it becomes a metaphor for his evolution toward his goal of greater awareness and ease with social interaction.

The formal choices all three writers make reject the idea that autism is a disease that may be cured while making room to represent their evolving identities in relation to autism as a developmental condition. In an essay on his blog, explaining his break with Autism Speaks, Robison offers an alternative vision, designed to account for the complexity and range of autistic experience, rather than reducing it to a simple narrative:

> I celebrate the gifts autism brings us, and I have discussed at length the emerging realization that autism—as a neurological difference—confers both gift and disability on everyone it touches. It's the fire that moves humanity forward, while simultaneously being a fire that can burn us individuals as we try to make our way.
>
> Many autistic people are aware of this dichotomy. Some of us feel "totally disabled" and others feel "totally gifted." Most of us—I'd venture to say—feel both ways, at different times, depending on what we're doing at that particular moment.
>
> Consequently, I support the idea of changing society to make it more accommodating for people who are different. I also support the idea of developing therapies, treatments, and tools to relieve suffering and disability from both autism and the conditions that accompany it for some people. I know how hard life is for some on the spectrum, but I also see the gifts other autistics bring. Both are touched by autism, and it's part and parcel of who we are. That's why we face such a difficult challenge, to keep the gifts while relieving the suffering. It's immeasurably harder than simple disease fighting.[36]

Similarly, Higashida asks, "*What am I going to be, if my autism isn't cured?*" He acknowledges that "When I was little, this question was always a big, big worry"—but swiftly turns the tables:

> I hope that by reading my explanations about autism and its mysteries, you can come to understand all the obstacles that present themselves don't come from self- ishness or from ego. If all of you can grasp this truth about us, we are handed a ray of hope. However hard an autistic life is, however sad it can be, so long as there's hope we can stick at it.
>
> And when the light of hope shines on this world, then our future will be connected with your future. That's what I want, above all.[37]

Higashida's question about a cure implies his autism is a disease, a belief he's revised over time. His older self, the writer, imagines a world when "our future will be connected with your future." Higashida's vision of neurodiversity asks readers to think about "the obstacles" he describes in both physiological and social terms. Some obstacles proceed from neurological development and some from social attitudes that misunderstand difference, resort to stigma, or inhibit personal development through ill-conceived medical or educational models— from the bald dismissal of autistic ability that resulted in half a century of insti- tutionalization and neglect, to the cure-based rhetoric of organizations like Autism Speaks (an organization both Mukhopadhyay and Robison once supported and both broke with in public ways). In their writing, Robison, Higashida, and Mukhopadhyay respond to the damaging history of medical and political rhetoric that defined their lives—their selves—as impossibilities. In its place, they offer rhetorics supple enough to unite the complexity of autistic presence with a demand for concrete social changes that account for the range of autistic experience.

Interlude: If You've Met One Autistic Reviewer . . .

AUTISM AND ASPERGER COMMUNITIES HAVE BECOME THE model for the neurodiversity movement as a whole (along with activist groups like the Hearing Voices Network, whose ethos is similar but with a focus on diagnoses historically associated with psychosis or delusion). It's not surprising that autism memoirs and novels have gained so much public recognition. If Temple Grandin's *Thinking in Pictures* (1995/2010) is our era's most influential autism memoir, Mark Haddon's *The Curious Incident of the Dog in the Night-Time* (2003) is its most influential work of autism fiction—and possibly the single most widely read and influential neuronovel published to date. Haddon's novel has won numerous awards, including the Whitbread Award for novel of the year in 2003. It has become a common text in high school curricula and in advanced-degree programs for high school literature teachers—as well as becoming the subject of a censorship debate when a Florida high school removed the novel from its summer reading list after parents objected to its use of profanity.[1] The evolving reception of the novel dramatizes tensions between aesthetics and ethics—or form and politics—that ensue when a novelist crafts a voice composed of symptoms of a neurological syndrome.

Initial reviews of Haddon's novel—in *The Guardian, Salon,* and *The New York Times* (twice in a week)—were unanimously positive.[2] In *The New York Times,* novelist Jay McInerney praised the novel for its cognitive effects: "disorienting and reorienting the reader to devastating effect." He describes Christopher John Francis Boone, the novel's narrator, as "a curious hybrid of the reliable and unreliable" and suggests that "Haddon manages to bring us deep inside Christopher's mind and situates us comfortably within his limited, severely logical point of view, to the extent that we begin to question the common sense and the erratic emotionalism of the normal citizens who surround him, as well as our own intuitions and habits of perception." The novel is a formal experiment. Any reader would notice Christopher's cognitive eccentricities—and that Haddon uses them to experiment with form. As McInerney observes, the novel works by inviting readers "inside Christopher's mind" but ultimately emphasizes the "gulf between Christopher . . . and the rest of us," as he puts it later in the review. Though the narrator is never diagnosed in the novel, he attends a school for children with "special needs"—very much like the one where Haddon once taught—and has surely been subject to multiple diagnostic evaluations. Nonetheless, the jacket copy for the U.S. edition describes Christopher as autistic and includes a blurb by Oliver Sacks calling it a "brilliant autism novel." The jacket for the U.K. edition was more specific, diagnosing Christopher with Asperger syndrome. Michiko Kakutani's review in *The New York Times* (published the same week as McInerney's) follows suit: "Christopher emerges as a wonderfully vivid individual. He never for a moment feels like a generic teenager or a composite portrait of someone with Asperger's syndrome (the form of autism that he presumably suffers from)."

Kakutani's review implies that the novel would be an aesthetic failure if Christopher were to feel like a "composite portrait of someone with Asperger's." The sentiment resonates, in a curious way, with the autistic community's most emblematic catchphrase: "If you've met one autistic person, you've met one autistic person."[3] You might just as easily say that if you've met one autistic book reviewer, you've met one autistic book reviewer. And that's where the reception history of Haddon's novel takes some interesting turns. In 2004, William Schofield, a university student diagnosed with Asperger's, published yet another positive review for *The Guardian:* "This book is a good murder mystery story but a better description of how the mind of a different person with some kind of special need looks upon how things work and come about. I think that there are certain characteristics that show Chris's condition is similar to Asperger syndrome." Schofield seems to indicate his identification with Haddon's narrator by calling him "Chris," a designation never used in the novel itself (nor in other reviews). He even lists the characteristics he shares with Haddon's narrator, including liking to keep different foods separate; disliking crowds, new places, and new people; self-soothing by scrolling through a "database of films in [his] head"; and difficulty making himself understood in conversation. Nonetheless, Schofield asks, "Can you, though, diagnose a fictional character?" His answer is confident: "you cannot."[4]

In 2011, Greg Olear, father to a son diagnosed with Asperger's, published a highly critical review in *The Huffington Post,* entitled "When Popular Novels Perpetuate Negative Stereotypes: Mark Haddon, Asperger's and Irresponsible Fiction." Olear accuses Haddon of gimmickry. He objects to inaccuracies he finds in the novel's depiction of Asperger's, pointing out that though Haddon does not diagnose his narrator in the novel itself, he allowed the novel to be published with the diagnostic jacket copy. When he gets specific, Olear makes a powerful observation: "it is telling that many of *Curious Incident*'s 73 one-star Amazon reviews (there are a staggering 1,720 reviews in all, most fours and fives) were submitted by aspies."[5] While the number of reviews is too staggering to parse, it is true that most of the negative reviews on Amazon are written by people who identify as "aspies," or "auties," to use common terminology of the movement and the community. It's also true that people who identify as such have written positive reviews, but nonetheless it is significant that members of the autistic community are so much more likely to write a negative review.

The stakes are high because the novel is so influential. In academic circles, the novel's reception has been similarly mixed, in ways that emphasize these stakes. In her book *Why Do We Care about Literary Characters?,* Blakey Vermeule praises "Haddon's excellent novel" for its portrayal of Christopher's atypical cognition—particularly his difficulty interpreting other characters' emotions.[6] In *Disability Studies Quarterly,* Sarah Jaquette Ray argues that the novel's first-person point of view allows for a direct critique of cognitive norms. In *Literature and Medicine,* Shannon R. Wooden demonstrates the novel's widespread adoption in high school literature courses, arguing that it's a vehicle for pedagogical discussions of ethical questions about disability, parenting, education, and medical diagnosis—despite the fact that it "may not be a perfect representation of any autistic experience."[7] In the *University of Toronto Quarterly,* Ian Hacking surveys autism fiction written in the last decade, expressing concern about the fact that among the wide range of texts published during that time, Haddon's novel alone "has become a staple in teacher-training courses." Hacking observes, "Thus the model furnished by Haddon is transmitted to a generation of teachers. It may in turn be implicitly passed on to their charges. And they, the autistic children, thereby learn how they are expected to be. Role models are important, but not if they make you think you can ace mathematics by the time you are thirteen years of age."[8] Hacking cites an essay by Dutch psychologist Douwe Draaisma, entitled "Who Owns Asperger's Syndrome?" Draaisma argues that because Asperger's is a "fuzzy" category, Haddon's novel participates in a "looping effect," whereby psychiatric theory is "owned," or redefined through its representations in literature, media, the law, and education.[9] Both Hacking and Draaisma are wary of the possible circulation of stereotypes made possible by the novel, rather than directly critical of Haddon's portrayal of Christopher.

In 2015, autistic blogger Elizabeth Bartmess objected to the novel's influence—or looping—in a detailed, angry review for *Disability in Kidlit,* an interactive blog that encourages dialogue and debate among people who share particular diagnoses or disabilities: "this book portrays its autistic protagonist in ways that will give readers negative, incorrect, and in some cases abusive ideas about autistic people. You should not recommend this book to autistic people or their families or friends, or to anyone else, *especially* not as a good representation of autism."[10] Bartmess cites a statement Mark Haddon published on his website in 2009, in response to the numerous invitations he receives "to become involved with organisations who work on behalf of people with asperger's and autism." Haddon admits that he knows "very little about the subject" and that "he did no research" for the novel. In his words, "I'd read oliver sacks's essay about temple grandin and a handful of newspaper or magazine articles about, or by, people with asperger's or autism." Haddon "borrowed" Christopher's traits from people he knows, "none of whom would be labeled as having a disability." Finally, he argues, the novel "is not a book about asperger's . . . it's a novel about difference." Haddon argues that "good literature is always about peeling labels off." He rejects diagnosis and expresses regret about allowing the word "Asperger" to appear on the novel's jacket copy. His intent was to write a novel "standing up for difference and trying to understand outsiders who see the world in surprising and revealing ways."[11] Nonetheless, Bartmess contends—rightly— that Haddon's novel has been received as representative of both autism and Asperger's. In fact, it's the most high-profile and highly lauded text representing autistic experience outside the autistic community. And it's fiction.

In addition to what she sees as Haddon's careless research and the novel's inaccuracies, Bartmess objects to the novel's depiction of Christopher as "elitist, violent, and lacking empathy." As she observes, "In his favorite dream, almost everyone in the world dies, preferably in ways which don't leave bodies everywhere, so that he can do whatever he wants, such as breaking into other people's houses and taking their things. The only people remaining are people like him who are very shy and who he rarely has to see. Wishing everyone you knew was dead (he does not describe anyone else as similar to him) is pretty horrible, and many autistic people would be devastated at losing family members and friends. Christopher is not at all bothered by this."[12] Christopher finds comfort and joy in an apparently sadistic dream. In addition, as Bartmess points out, the novel's neurotypical characters demonstrate empathy while he does not; he is sometimes violent, particularly in response to overwhelming sensory stimuli; Christopher's father abuses him physically once in the novel, and nobody does anything about it; neurotypical characters routinely fail to take Christopher seriously, though he is the only character with any insight into the novel's first mystery: the murder of a dog; and, finally, the only character who seems to offer genuinely helpful support for Christopher—his teacher, Siobhan, is largely absent during the second half of the novel.

Bartmess informs readers that "most autistic people" with whom she's discussed the novel "didn't relate to" Christopher, but acknowledges parenthetically that "some do." The lively conversation in the comments section bears this out. Contributors identify themselves as on the spectrum or parents of children who are; as they debate the representivity and usefulness of the novel, Bartmess joins the discussion, sometimes expanding and even revising her original readings. One reader—Amanda Forest Vivian—suggests an alternative reading: "you could read the book against the obvious intended meaning, as being about a kid who's not empathetic because . . . shocker, everyone abuses him and treats him like he doesn't have any feelings." Bartmess replies, "I think that's a plausible alternative reading—he doesn't exactly have good role models! And it's not difficult to see why he might want to not be around the people he's usually around."[13] Vivian's reading demonstrates a version of its own argument: Autistic people engage in social behavior all the time, even if that social behavior has not always been recognizable as such to neurotypical observers. The dialogue becomes a collaborative—and profoundly social—interpretive endeavor. It reflects the collective spirit of activism in the autistic community and challenges not just stereotypes about, but the very definition of, "autism" (meaning, originally, self-centered). As a result, Christopher's fantasy acquires multiple meanings.

Christopher imagines an apocalypse that transforms the world into one in which neurotypicality is not an assumption, one that won't ostracize him for violating cognitive norms. It's a vision of a bloody revolution that achieves the aims of the neurodiversity movement. I'm arguing that a typical reading presumes an implicit recognition that Christopher is an unreliable narrator, that his pleasure in the dream is a form of fantasy he never entertains in a serious way, and that it is a motivated response to the violence and injustice he experiences—as in the counterreading Vivian offers (though she does not believe the novel itself endorses that reading). But a typical reading is not a definitive one. Bartmess's incisive reading takes the violence of Christopher's fantasy seriously. The violence is in the text, just as it is in unreliably narrated stories by writers like Edgar Allan Poe or Angela Carter.

Linguist Elena Semino argues that novels about autism, including *The Curious Incident,* demonstrate the atypicality of their protagonists through varieties of "pragmatic failure," an unfortunately loaded term used by sociolinguists to describe miscommunication in social contexts. Semino identifies three types of pragmatic failure in the dialogue in these novels: "problems with informativeness and relevance in conversational contributions; problems with face management resulting in unintentional impolite behaviours; and problems with the interpretation of figurative language." She argues that these novels use dialogue full of pragmatic failures in order "to contribute to the projection of distinctive mind styles, and more generally to the characterisation of the protagonists as individuals with communication and socialisation difficulties that are likely to both reflect and reinforce general perceptions of autism-spectrum disorders."[14] The definitions of these "failures" would seem to place all the responsibility for communication on the autistic characters and presumably on autistic people in the world outside the novels. I would argue that *The Curious Incident* asks readers to imagine a world in which Christopher's neurotypical interlocutors share this responsibility (and mostly fail to meet it). Following Semino's lead I would go even further, arguing that the novel asks readers to value a "mind style" characterized by atypical approaches to defining relevance and informativeness, interpreting facial and bodily gestures, and defamiliarizing figurative language so that its literal components become visible. Building on the work of linguist Guy Cook, Semino argues that "in literary discourse, the use of distinctive linguistic patterns typically facilitates the 'refreshment' of readers' existing schemata." In other words, the literary representation of autism might compel readers to reexamine relations between normative and autistic mind styles.[15]

But there's another wrinkle here. What's an autistic mind style? What's a neurotypical one? As Steve Silberman observes, "Most researchers now believe that autism is not a single unified entity but a cluster of underlying conditions."[16] In the dialogue about Bartmess's review, some of her interlocutors suggest that Christopher may not be simply autistic, that he may suffer from "comorbid" symptoms, as so many people on the spectrum do. But as Silberman points out, autism itself may be defined precisely by comorbidity. Despite the ever-evolving taxonomies of the *DSM*, the subjective experience of autism—like that of bipolar disorder, schizophrenia, Tourette's, or any number of neurological anomalies—exceeds attempts to stabilize or unify it as an object of analysis or diagnosis.

When Haddon suggests that his novel is about difference, rather than autism or Asperger's, and that "good literature is about peeling labels off," he acknowledges the social dimension to his aesthetic experiment. More than that, he articulates his aesthetic aims in terms nearly identical to the disability-studies challenge of medical models of neurological difference. In the process, though, he stumbles into a theoretical debate whose material stakes couldn't be more urgent for a community of people fighting for social recognition and integration—in the wake of a very recent history that judged them as incapable, treated them as inscrutable, and locked them in institutions whose design exacerbated their suffering and prevented the expression of their abilities. Haddon's aesthetic experiment is consistent with one of the autistic community's founding principles: *If you've met one autistic* narrator, *you've met one autistic* narrator. But it ignores another: *"Nothing about us without us."*[17] To compound matters, his novel has become representative of the community he doesn't name. As its neurotypical readers make clear, the novel is often received as a stand-in for actual autistic people. As Michael Cohn, one of Bartmess's respondents, observes: "I don't think that readers with no experience or knowledge about autism will be able to read between the lines. If this is being suggested as the *first* book to read on the subject, that means they won't have much to compare it to."[18] Cohn's observation is key. Most readers of Haddon's novel won't have the luxury of reading it through the lens of debates about its merits among autistic reviewers—or scholarly reflections on representations of autism. Most readers will accept the word of the jacket copy and read it from there, as a novel about a boy named Christopher, diagnosed with autism or Asperger's—and standing in, though he doesn't exist, for all people who identify with these diagnoses.

In his essay "Eye on Fiction: Generic Images of Autism," Draaisma argues that best-selling works of fiction like *The Curious Incident* are "a major force in shaping lay understandings of autism"—and that they inevitably deal in stereotypes. In his view, stereotypes are inevitable. Testimonies by self-identified auties and aspies are just as likely to perpetuate them as works of fiction. "Rather than try to expel stereotypes or ask which ones are 'true,'" he suggests, "we should be aware of their origins, the forces that shape them and the agendas they're on."[19] Social movements need representatives, but no single voice can represent a movement fully.

In his book *Beyond the Wall: Personal Experiences with Autism and Asperger Syndrome,* Shore, an education scholar and influential autism advocate, notes two factors that complicate diagnosis: (1) "[I]t is not possible to state unequivocally that a person with autism must have a particular trait or cannot have another trait"; and (2) "[I]t can be difficult to tease out whether certain attributes result from one's personality or from the autism spectrum disorder."[20] The same is true of any form of neurological difference. Shore's insights are fundamental to the neurodiversity movement's aim to replace cognitive norms with a nuanced understanding of the multiplicity of cognitive differences that shape relations between brain and identity. A person is more than a diagnosis. Nonetheless, diagnosis is fundamental to autistic identity. Individual diagnosis is necessary in the pursuit of support services, medical treatment, and education. Collective agreement about the range of diagnoses that define the autistic community is crucial for political organization and collective advocacy, but that's where agreement stops, partly because achieving it means creating a very wide tent. It certainly doesn't promise agreement about the merits of a work of fiction marketed to represent the autistic community.

Haddon's novel dramatizes the destigmatization of neurological difference—and the increased understanding of autistic or Asperger experience. It also perpetuates stereotypes and circulates misinformation when Christopher is read as a singular representative for autistic experience. The novel's emphasis on Christopher's lack of empathy angers Bartmess because she knows this is not a universal characteristic of autistic experience. Responses to the novel, in mainstream publications and among disability communities, demonstrate its cultural relevance. If the novel's publishers have been cavalier in their marketing of the novel, they have an opportunity to reframe it by including links or even the full texts of debates about the novel's representation of autistic experience in future editions. Because this is unlikely, educators should consider integrating these debates into any curriculum designed around the novel. Haddon's novel—as a recasting of detective fiction through the curious mind style of its protagonist— is a considerable aesthetic achievement, but one that risks gimmickry. Its value, in the near future, lies in the debates it has catalyzed, debates that have the potential to propel the key tenet of the neurodiversity movement: Value neurological difference.

4

Narrating Neurological Difference

When I thought about these things, another track in my brain
intoned brainyoctomy brainyalimony bunnymonopoly baileyoctopus
brainyanimal broccopotamus.
—Lionel Essrog, narrator of Jonathan Lethem's *Motherless Brooklyn*

BRAIN MEMOIRS MAKE VOICES OF NEUROLOGICAL DIFFERENCE public. When
Temple Grandin, Kay Redfield Jamison, Naoki Higashida, and Siri Hustvedt
publish accounts of their neurological experience, they write portraits of identity in the process of becoming. If they also become advocates of the neurodiversity movement, they do so partly by demonstrating that they may not be
reduced to a diagnosis. Their relationship to the movement varies, but their
aims are all consistent with its ethos: They ask health practitioners to measure
subjective experiences against diagnostic protocols and treatment regimes; they
provoke readers to reexamine assumptions about cognitive norms; they find
strength in neurological difference; and they strive toward Ralph Savarese's
cosmopolitan ideal—"the feeling of being respectfully at home with all manner
of neurologies."[1]

But what happens when novelists narrate neurological difference in fiction—
translating traits associated with autism, Tourette's, PTSD, amnesia, or Capgras
syndrome into a narrative voice? Symptoms of medically defined neurological
conditions become patterns of narration in novels like these: Tourette's syndrome
in Jonathan Lethem's *Motherless Brooklyn* (1999), autism in Mark Haddon's
The Curious Incident of the Dog in the Night-Time (2003), and post-trauma in

Tom McCarthy's *Remainder* (2005). These novels, like most neuronovels, should also be understood as twenty-first-century heirs to modernist literary experiments. Their authors appropriate neurological difference in order to experiment with novel narration styles, as Faulkner did with Benjy, or Woolf did with Septimus Smith. But modernism didn't invent the narration of neurological difference. Lethem, Haddon, and McCarthy write in a tradition of fiction narrated by or through characters with eccentric cognitive dispositions—many of them in direct dialogue with psychological theories, medical practice, or the philosophy of mind: Cervantes's delusional Don Quixote, Sterne's extravagant-minded Tristram Shandy, Poe's many nervous narrators, James's haunted governess, Gilman's hallucinatory heroine in *The Yellow Wallpaper,* Ellison's disassociated outlaw in *Invisible Man,* Plath's Esther Greenwood, Keyes's Charlie in *Flowers for Algernon,* Morrison's abused Pecola in *The Bluest Eye,* Ishiguro's bewildered Ryder in *The Unconsoled,* and Beatty's manically stoned narrator in *The Sellout* (a product of his father's psychological experiments).

Neuronovels contribute to this lineage—with the key difference that they participate in debates about neurocognitive difference that arise from increasingly detailed diagnostic categories in psychiatry, philosophical questions about embodiment and consciousness emerging from theoretical neuroscience, and the political questions raised by the neurodiversity movement. In the process, they throw ethical questions about representing neurological difference into stark relief *and* demonstrate how questions about representation underlie forms of neuromania both in and outside the arts. To make an argument about the significance of the brain in education or economics, you need a theory of the brain. To conceive a theory of the brain, you need representations of it. Those representations originate in neuroscience or philosophy—for example, in brain-scanning technologies or thought experiments—but are downplayed or erased in most contemporary discussions of the brain's capacity to drive economies or to be trained through neurological self-help programs. Neuronovels retrieve questions about the power of representation, compelling readers to consider not just *what* brains mean, but *how* the tools we use to imagine the mysterious power of the organs in our skulls shape what we think we know.

If brain memoirs are quest narratives, neuronovels are almost always revisionist mysteries that emphasize or expose the formal conventions through which they represent neurological experience. As with Sherlock Holmes, the protagonists of these novels become good detectives because of their neurological difference. They detect details other characters miss. Unlike Sherlock Holmes, they narrate their own stories, which requires their authors to translate a composite of neurological traits into distinctive voices. As Lisa Zunshine observes, detective fiction challenges a reader's capacity to think hypothetically, to collect clues and evaluate them without understanding what they might mean: "they push this ability to its furthest limits, explicitly requiring us to store information under very strong advisement—that is, to 'suspect *everybody*'—for as long as we can possibly take it, to readjust drastically much of what we have been surmising in the process of reading it."[2] Though she doesn't invoke the concept, Zunshine is describing detective fiction's capacity to *afford* particular forms of cognition. In *Thinking with Literature: Towards a Cognitive Literary Criticism* (2016), Terence Cave draws on psychological theories of affordance—a term coined by James J. Gibson to describe "the potential uses an object or feature of the environment offers a living creature."[3] Affordance theory has migrated into a host of disciplines, including design, architecture, technology studies, and philosophy. Its architectural applications make the concept's import particularly clear: A ramp affords access to a building, whereas stairs preclude access. Cave argues that literature affords particular kinds of thinking, and in the process he expands the term's definition "to include not only the uses of an object but also the object itself viewed in light of those uses: the tree is in that sense a multiple affordance [for nesting, perching, nourishment, shade, or play]; the wheel is an affordance for transportation, pulleys and gears, for clockwork, and so forth."[4]

In general, neuronovels build on detective fiction's speculative tendencies, weaving hypothetical questions about the physiological self into the mysteries of their plots; neuronovels narrated by neurodivergent characters plot the social stakes of these questions and give fictional form to tensions between medical diagnosis and identity, without resolving those tensions. In *Motherless Brooklyn,* Lionel Essrog finds out who killed his beloved boss and mentor, but he doesn't put to rest questions about language and embodiment raised by his echolalia and motor tics; in *The Curious Incident*, Christopher Boone identifies the murderer of his neighbor's dog, but he doesn't resolve debates about autistic mind styles or the social stigmas that stick to them; in *Remainder,* the most experimental (or revisionist) of these novels, the unnamed narrator "re-enacts" an elaborate crime that becomes a substitute for understanding the psycho-biology of trauma.

As an aesthetic strategy, narrating neurological difference in fiction is fraught, likely to reinforce cognitive norms in some ways and challenge them in others. I argue that the ethical questions raised by appropriating neurodivergent experience for the sake of aesthetic experiment are unresolvable but important to consider. In fiction, patterns of language perform an illusion of phenomenology, a fictional person. Of course, they also reflect the phenomenology of a shadowy figure, an author, responsible for the patterns. What are the ethical responsibilities of this author to the living people whose experience provides material or inspiration? Haddon, Lethem, and McCarthy write their way into diversity politics from the outside, creating a vexed outsider-insider position for themselves. Narrating neurodivergence risks dealing in caricatures of neurological difference, reinforcing stereotypes, or making readers feel they are gaining genuine knowledge from fictional portraits.

Of course, the cultural effects of any novel are variable and unpredictable, but they are shaped in part by the dynamics in reading established by the writer's formal choices. These particular novels require readers to immerse themselves in their narrators' mind styles, and they create powerful protagonists whose "creative potential" is directly linked with their neurological differences. They may provoke readers to reconsider their relations to cognitive norms, or they may provide a comfortable outlet reaffirming those norms. Nonetheless, they dramatize the social prejudices that shape their protagonists' stories; they root these prejudices in widely held preconceptions about normative minds; and they suggest that a philosophical orientation that conceives the mind as embodied, dynamic, and relational is a necessity for their fictional protagonists to thrive. Aesthetics and politics collide in these neurodivergent narrators. Their fictional experiments are contiguous with the neurodiversity movement, but not of it. The particularity of their experience resonates with the principles of neurodiversity, but it also sometimes exceeds or violates these principles. Lethem's Lionel Essrog is neurodiversity's underbelly; Haddon's Christopher Boone, its poster child; and McCarthy's narrator, its philosophical terrorist.

At the level of plot, the detective narrators of these novels engage in a literary form of *"niche construction"*—a term evolutionary biologists use to describe the remaking of physical environments to meet an organism's needs. A beaver's dam is the classic example. In *Biology Under the Influence,* Richard Lewontin and Richard Levins make an argument about the role of ecology and culture in evolution. They revise evolutionary theories that characterize an "ecological niche" as "a kind of hole in ecological space that may be filled by a species." Instead, they argue, "Organisms do not experience or fit an environment, they construct it."[5] In recent years, anthropologists have adapted the term to consider relationships between human evolution and social behavior. Anthropologist Jeremy Kendal and his colleagues argue that the application of niche-construction theory to human culture can help us recognize the "reciprocal influences" of culture and evolution—what they call "eco-evolutionary feed-backs."[6] Even more recently, the term has begun to migrate into educational theory, to describe how classrooms might be redesigned in ways that enable students' neurocognitive differences to become strengths. Neurodiversity educator Thomas Armstrong adapts the idea for practical use in classrooms. Armstrong proposes seven elements of "positive niche construction" in educational settings: strength awareness, positive role models, assistive technologies, human support networks, strength-based learning strategies, affirmative career aspirations, and environmental modifications.[7] In their fiction, Haddon's, Lethem's, and McCarthy's detectives adapt to and remake their environments in ways that resonate with biological, anthropological, and educational theories of niche construction—shedding the ties to evolution.

Both detection and narration are forms of environmental modification. Detectives use clues to afford rearrangements of a world thrown off balance by crime; narrators invite readers to participate in the development of a fictional world. In their idiosyncratic ways, the neurodivergent narrators of Haddon's, Lethem's, and McCarthy's novels negotiate all seven of Armstrong's elements. They play to their strengths, admire role models, reflect on career aspirations, experiment with technologies, and make the most of human support networks. Because evolution is not the point, though, the "reciprocal influences" they drama-tize take place between the detectives and their local cultures. Because those influ-ences are reciprocal, they're unpredictable and sometimes unruly. Literary detectives both interpret and revise the social worlds they investigate. In the process, they emphasize the expression of their cognitive eccentricities in and through their bodies. Detective work requires a great deal of movement—walking, driving, riding trains, knocking on doors, sneaking into forbidden spaces. As these detectives rove through their environments, they direct readers to become intimate with the ways their eccentric minds manifest through their bodies. As they do, they give narrative shape to what disability scholar Rosemarie Garland-Thomson calls "misfitting"—"a dynamic encounter between flesh and world"—but they also engage in various forms of *refitting* when they require their worlds to bend to their ways of being.[8] In that sense, the novels themselves are affordances that enable readers to engage with questions about neurodiversity.

Narrating Niches

Narrating from a neurodivergent point of view is a kind of formal niche construction, creating a story world built on the cognitive perspective of the narrator. As narrators, these fictional detectives create worlds that require readers to adapt to simulations of neurodivergent ways of being. Cave observes that language itself is an affordance, structuring "our perceptions of sensori-motor experience" and constraining "our ways of reimagining those percep-tions." In literary contexts, he suggests, "the successful affordances are the ones that allow us to grasp multiple phenomena as packages, or as integrated wholes." Broadening his argument, Cave finally offers an ecological perspec-tive on the relationship between literature and culture, arguing that his affordance theory makes it "possible to redescribe the relationship between form and its particular instantiation not as a relationship between vehicle and content, but as an ecological, adaptive, and ultimately innovative interaction."[9] By this account, neurodiversity politics are part of a larger cultural moment that makes Haddon's, Lethem's, and McCarthy's novels possible. Crucially, their publication contributes to that culture, affording new ways to "grasp" the multi-plicity of neurodivergent experience through particular "packages." The neuro-divergence of a detective-narrator is not simply a "vehicle" for aesthetic experiment, but an affordance that enables literary innovation that multiplies possible meanings for neurological difference. If detectives remake their niches, they do it by creating new forms of affordance—by changing the fictional worlds they navigate and by narrating aesthetic experiences for readers.

Fiction communicates its affordances through distinctive styles of narration. As critic James Wood writes, a novel with an unreliable narrator "teaches us how to read its narrator." The novels I'm discussing here don't presume any knowledge about PTSD, autism, or Tourette's—which means they have to teach readers to recognize their symptoms, by creating affordances that make them evident. In *Remainder* and *Motherless Brooklyn,* both of which name their narrators' diagnoses, the instruction is explicit; in *The Curious Incident,* which never names its narrator's diagnosis, it's implicit. Teaching readers how to respond to a narrator built through rhythms of language that translate symptoms of medical diagnosis into a literary style is a socially ambiguous endeavor. For starters, these narrators are unreliable—in ways that are directly related to their symptoms. Wood observes that "we know a narrator is unreliable because the author is alerting us, through reliable manipulation, to that narrator's unreliability."[10] It might seem that teaching readers to judge neurodivergent narrators as unreliable reinforces hierarchies of cognitive difference and stigmas associated with them. However, it's also true that the unreliability of these particular narrators is linked to neurological experience that enables them to become brilliant detectives who narrate the reconstruction of the niches they probe.

The apparent unreliability of these neurodivergent sleuths is trumped by the many ways their cognitive eccentricities make them good detectives. Lionel Essrog exposes cracks in the world's signifiers through his tics and echolalia; Christopher Boone detects minutiae others dismiss and defamiliarizes other people's actions because their social motives mystify him; and the narrator of *Remainder* employs a vast team of collaborators who believe they're exploiting his obsessive re-enactments, missing the fact that he's exposing ruptures in the world they share, ruptures they erase through their easy associations of self and perception. In the language of narratology, implied authors cue readers to recognize clues to their narrator's reliability when other characters respond too simplistically to their apparent unreliability.

Remainder is a mystery novel turned inside out; its brand of affordance involves considerable disorientation. Its unnamed narrator finds himself wealthy after a financial settlement he receives while he's recovering from a traumatic accident he can't remember, except that it involved "something falling from the sky": "I don't even remember the event. It's a blank: a white slate, a black hole. I have vague images, half-impressions: of being, or having been—or, more precisely, being *about* to be—hit; blue light; railings; lights of other colours; being held above some kind of tray or bed. But who's to say that these are genuine memories? Who's to say my traumatized mind didn't just make them up, or pull them out from somewhere else, some other slot, and stick them there to plug the gap—the crater—that the accident had blown?"[11] The symptoms named here involve memory. After his accident, McCarthy's narrator forgets and confabulates; the ordinary vicissitudes of memory become extreme. The apparent mystery involves reconstructing the accident. But the accident becomes incidental to the novel's resolution. Other symptoms—dramatized but not named in this passage—involve heightened sensory perception and a feeling of disassociation from the present. The "vague images and half-impressions" of the accident migrate into everyday life. McCarthy cues readers to mistrust his narrator's memory, but also to enter into his disassociation and to invest in his emotional need to reunite his perceptual experience with his feeling of self-hood, to recapture the sense that his experience belongs to him.

The narrator orchestrates what he calls "re-enactments"—elaborately staged events designed to help him overcome his disassociation and match his heightened perception to the events he's creating. In other words, literal acts of refitting the world to afford him the experience he craves. The goal of the re-enactments is "to be real—to become fluent, natural."[12] *Remainder*'s big crime (a bank heist) happens not in the past but the future. The narrator's secret is that he has been planning a crime, not solving one. In order for readers to invest in this outlandish narrative stunt, they will have to immerse themselves in the novel's aesthetic experiment, at the level of the sentence, to experience a simulation of the link between the narrator's disassociation and his heightened perceptions.

In *Motherless Brooklyn,* Lionel Essrog is more sanguine about his symptoms. He explicates them almost gleefully, and readers learn that the explication itself is a symptom. His tics, for example, afford constant interpretation: "Have you noticed that I relate everything to my Tourette's? Yup, you guessed it, it's a tic. Counting is a symptom, but counting symptoms is also a symptom, a tic *plus ultra.* I've got meta-Tourette's. Thinking about ticking, my mind racing, thoughts reading to touch every possible symptom. Touching touching. Counting counting. Thinking thinking. Mentioning mentioning Tourette's." Lionel's tics are the visible sign of Tourette's, and readers learn to recognize them in the repetitions and wordplay of his echolalia. Essrog routinely ascribes agency to his brain, particularly with regard to the echolalia beyond his control: "When I thought about these things, another track in my brain intoned brainy-octomy brainyalimony bunnymonopoly baileyoctopus brainyanimal brocco-potamus."[13] The "track" in his brain that experiments with novel combinations of words and syllables is an interpreter. Throughout the novel, Lethem suggests that the root of Essrog's symptoms is a compulsion to interpret and reinterpret events—qualities central to detective fiction and to Essrog's agency. Tourette's becomes a vehicle for Lethem to write a meta–detective novel, starring a sleuth whose outlandish behavior leads others to underestimate him, to mistake his dogged pursuit of the truth for meaningless compulsion.

In *The Curious Incident,* Christopher never names his diagnosis, but he does refer to his symptoms throughout the novel. For example, he announces to readers, "My name is Christopher John Francis Boone. I know all the countries of the world and their capital cities and every prime number up to 7,057."[14] He titles his chapters with sequential prime numbers, and he introduces diagrams of facial expressions that his teacher Siobhan uses to help him recognize other people's emotions. As the evidence accumulates, it becomes clear that Christopher is a precocious kid with a genius for mathematics, difficulties interpreting social cues, an acute sensitivity to sensory stimulation, and an extreme literal-mindedness—all symptoms commonly attributed to people diagnosed with Asperger syndrome and autism. Like Lionel Essrog, Christopher becomes a detective, one whose eccentric behavior complicates the mystery plot but also enhances his ability to see what neurotypical characters cannot.

If Lethem, Haddon, and McCarthy teach us how to read their narrators, they do it by drawing on taxonomies of symptoms like those created (and continuously revised) by the *DSM.* The notorious problem with those taxonomies is that they are composites that don't describe any particular person's experience with precision. Individuals exceed diagnosis. Ian Hacking published a critical review of the *DSM-5* (2013) in the *London Review of Books.* "[T]he *DSM* is a work in progress," he observes. Its revisions reflect the evolution of psychology. Its original taxonomic structure is rooted in botanical science; its first two editions reflect the dominance of psychoanalysis in the 1950s and 1960s; the *DSM-III* (1980) reflected the pharmacological directions psychology was taking; *DSM-IV* (1994) and its revision, *DSM-IV-TR* (2000) began to move away from the idea of disorder and toward syndromes, to account for the fact that the cause of most mental illnesses are unknown, or at least widely debated. The *DSM-5* embraces the idea of spectrums, an idea that has gained widespread cultural purchase and is predicated on a paradox that ensues from the *DSM*'s ever-increasing focus on biology and neurology and the failure of psychological or neurological research to make much headway when it comes to the causes or etiologies of given categories of disorder. The result is an increasingly complex set of menus designed to reflect these uncertainties. In Hacking's words, "*DSM-5* owns up to two difficulties that anyone trying to use previous editions quickly experienced: NOS and comorbidity. NOS stands for 'Not Otherwise Specified.'"[15] A person's symptoms may reflect more than one disorder, or they may reflect a general condition that doesn't yield to the specificity of ever-proliferating diagnoses. In the meantime, as Hacking points out, therapists are likely to make diagnoses first and then to turn to the *DSM* to anchor those diagnoses in its criteria second.

As an affordance, the *DSM* enables diagnosis, treatment, prescriptions, insurance coverage. But it's not a simple vehicle. It's used pragmatically, loosely, in context. In fiction, its taxonomies become a different kind of affordance, like a spotlight shining on the gap between the exactitude of diagnostic guidelines and the variability of experience. In fiction, the gap multiplies and mutates. Writers are not beholden to protocols. Their imperative is to create distinctive characters, rather than representative ones. The influence of the *DSM* is evident in most neuronovels, which tend to reflect the tome's evolution toward neurobiological perspectives. But whereas the *DSM* seeks to fix relations between signifiers (diagnosis) and signifieds (symptoms), fiction tends to unhinge these relations. Novels proliferate their own signifiers. If they were to reproduce the schematic and composite impulses of the *DSM,* they would be aesthetic failures. Instead, they create narrators who may be unreliable in various ways but who become reliable through the acts of interpretation that define them as detectives.

To be an unreliable narrator means your author is conspiring with readers, who share knowledge you don't possess. The conspiracy is achieved via rhetorical elements of narrative that afford (largely unconscious) readerly recognition of particular forms of unreliability. Narratologist James Phelan names six types of unreliability: "misreporting, misreading, misevaluating—or what I will call 'misregarding'—and underreporting, underreading, and underregarding."[16] Readers conclude that a narrator is unreliable when they recognize rhetorical moves like these. Like all taxonomies, Phelan's is designed to tame a range of rhetorical techniques through naming; and like all taxonomies, its naming system is incomplete. Phelan designs his system to demonstrate that unreliable narrators are shaped by their rhetorical dispositions. When *The Curious Incident*'s Christopher misreads social cues, or when *Motherless Brooklyn*'s Lionel overreports plot points, readers recognize symptoms of autism or Tourette's. The question that arises is whether the rhetorical dispositions of these narrators also enable forms of knowledge or insight that result from neurological difference. In other words: Do their authors do more than conspire against them? Do they also conspire *with* them to bewilder readers into questioning the reliability of cognitive norms? Does the text establish a reciprocal relationship between narrator and reader, whereby meaning is made through a negotiation of the cognitive differences foregrounded by the experiment?

Though he doesn't use the term "niche construction," Phelan's argument about the ethics of narration emphasizes the idea that writing and reading fiction are real-world activities—and as such they create rhetorical niches whose stakes are not simply aesthetic. He describes "character narration" as "an art of indirection," meaning that when authors narrate from the point of view of characters, they create a rhetorical situation whereby meaning emerges through readers' recognition of what is unsaid. From those meanings, fictional worlds, or niches in which characters pretend to live, emerge. In the process, Phelan argues, ethical questions inhere in the narration of experience:

> Any character's action will typically have an ethical dimension, and any narrator's treatment will inevitably convey certain attitudes toward the subject matter and the audience, attitudes that, among other things, indicate his or her sense of responsibility to and regard for the told and the audience. Similarly, the author's treatment of the narrator and of the authorial audience will indicate something of his or her ethical commitments toward the telling, the told, and the audience. Further, the audience's response to the narrative will indicate their commitments to and attitudes toward the author, the narrator, the narrative situation, and to the values expressed in the narrative.

That rhetorical situation is shaped by "the opportunity it offers to encounter other minds"[17]—including the fictional minds of characters and narrators, the semifictional minds of the figure narratologists call "the implied author," and the real but ultimately inaccessible minds of authors. All narrators are unreliable, even when they pretend omniscience. Every narrator creates a different rhetorical situation, working through varieties of understatement, exaggeration, misinterpretation, and so on. What a narrator tells a reader is not what the author means. It's language designed to afford the interpretation of implicit meaning. The rhetoric of fiction puts readers in the position of evaluating the epistemological relationship between author, narrator, and characters. When a narrator represents some form of neurodivergence, interpretation becomes an exercise in working out relations between neurological difference and neurological norms. In that sense, it calls on readers to engage in imaginative niche construction.

The Curious Incident's Christopher never names his diagnosis, but he does refer to his symptoms throughout the novel—as he does when he tells us "he cannot lie":

> 37. I do not tell lies. Mother used to say that this was because I was a good person. But it is not because I am a good person. It is because I can't tell lies.
>
> Mother was a small person who smelled nice. And she sometimes wore a fleece with a zip down the front which was pink and it had a tiny label which said *Berghaus* on the left bosom.
>
> A lie is when you say something happened which didn't happen. But there is only ever one thing which happened at a particular time and a particular place. And there are an infinite number of things which didn't happen. And if I think about something which didn't happen I start thinking about all the other things which didn't happen.[18]

It's probably not surprising that Christopher's autistic traits, varied as they are, lead to some curious combinations of Phelan's categories of unreliability. When Christopher tells us about the zipper and logo on his mother's fleece, he's over-reporting, but he's also underreporting, in the sense that he's focusing on apparently mundane details rather than offering details about his mother's character. That same rhetorical dynamic is at play when he philosophizes about truth and falsehood: It's true enough that "only ever one thing . . . happened at a particular time and a particular place," depending on how you define time and place. Christopher assumes that times and places can be fixed and that all onlookers— or readers—can or will have access to the absolute truth of a given moment. Haddon conspires with readers, assuming we'll recognize Christopher's rhetorical disposition as signs of autism. At moments like these, his unreliability and his neurological difference seem yoked, in a fairly clear-cut way, though the yoke loosens or even unravels at other moments in the narrative.

Lionel Essrog describes himself as unreliable because his Tourettic interpretation appears misleadingly solipsistic: "Conspiracies are a version of Tourette's Syndrome, the making and tracing of unexpected connections a kind of touchiness, an expression of the yearning to touch the world, kiss it all over with theories, pull it close. Like Tourette's, all conspiracies are ultimately solipsistic, sufferer or conspirator or theorist overrating his centrality and forever rehearsing a traumatic delight in reaction, attachment and causality, in roads out from the Rome of self."[19] But the plot doesn't bear out Essrog's self-described solipsism.

His "making and tracing of unexpected connections" enables him to unravel the complex conspiracy that led to the death of his mentor, Frank Minna. He describes himself as an overregarder, making too much of details, and an overreporter, telling people too much about what he regards. But his unreliability is thin. In the novel's opening paragraph, Lionel describes a dual impulse for his tics, sometimes "smoothing down imperfections" in his environment and sometimes disrupting the world's orderliness because "Reality needs a prick here and there."[20] Lionel's compulsions are a form of agency. He smooths and pricks his phenomenological experience of the world—and, in doing so, he reconstructs other characters' realities. When he does, they spill secrets and lead him to clues.

In the opening lines of *Motherless Brooklyn,* Lionel signals the agency he's gained retrospectively. As a narrator, he's proud to declare himself Tourettic—and to do it in literary language that emphasizes both his difference and his power, even while the story he tells focuses on his struggle with social stigmas and ostracization. "I'm a carnival barker," he writes, "an auctioneer, a downtown performance artist, a speaker in tongues, a senator drunk on filibuster. *I've got Tourette's.*"[21] Unlike Christopher, Lionel diagnoses himself directly:

> My mouth won't quit, though mostly I whisper or subvocalize like I'm reading aloud, my Adam's apple bobbing, jaw muscle beating like a miniature heart under my cheek, the noise suppressed, the words escaping silently, mere ghosts of themselves, ... [like] the surface of the world, tickling reality like fingers on piano keys. Caressing, nudging. They're an invisible army on a peacekeeping mission, a peaceable horde. They mean no harm. They placate, interpret, massage. Everywhere they're smoothing down imperfections, putting hairs in place, putting ducks in a row, replacing divots. Counting and polishing the silver. Patting old ladies gently on the behind, eliciting a giggle. Only—here's the rub—when they find too much perfection, when the surface is already buffed smooth, the ducks already orderly, the old ladies complacent, then my little army rebels, breaks into the stores. Reality needs a prick here and there, the carpet needs a flaw. My words begin plucking at threads nervously, seeking purchase, a weak point, a vulnerable ear. That's when it comes, the urge to shout in church, the nursery, the crowded movie house. It's an itch at first. Inconsequential. But that itch is soon a torrent behind a straining dam. Noah's flood. That itch is my whole life. Here it comes now. Cover your ears. Build an ark.
>
> "Eat me!" I scream.[22]

Lionel's symptoms include verbal outbursts (shouting obscenities, whispering to himself, subvocalization, echolalia), but also a variety of physical tics (patting shoulders, jerky gestures, bobbing Adam's apple) and psychological compulsions (counting and polishing silver). He describes himself as a narrator in search of a perfect story and an itch to disrupt it, which he does routinely through combinations of overreading and overreporting—noticed by other characters, with various degrees of bewilderment and disgust. But these characters are misregarding. Lethem writes over and around their dismissive or hostile interpretations. When Lionel's friends and colleagues give him the nickname "Freakshow," they abuse and alienate him, but they also become his dupes, underestimating the interpretive and investigative acumen afforded by his echolalia and his compulsions. Lionel unravels the novel's mysteries while the other characters flounder.

Lethem describes his novel as an aesthetic enterprise, using Tourette's to revamp detective noir through a figure who embodies "Joycean wordplay," "the need to constantly rearrange and order language." Yet he also claims that Tourettic readers impressed by his impersonation express admiration for its verisimilitude: "Lionel's constant struggle to negotiate his tics, that internal battle to censor them and mete them out only when he's absolutely forced to struck them as so accurate that they were surprised I didn't have Tourette's myself."[23] Lethem reveals the aesthetic ambition behind his choice to experiment with a Tourettic narrator. He's after Joycean wordplay—or, more accurately, a rationale for the wordplay to which he's already prone, so prone that he identifies strongly with his narrator's tics. Of course, wordplay, like echolalia, "rearranges" language, mixing and matching syllables through associations of sound as much as meaning, creating nonsense that might become sense again when readers decipher its resonances: "brainyoctomy brainyalimony bunny-monopoly baileyoctopus brainyanimal broccopotamus." But Lethem doesn't simply adapt Tourette's to suit his experiment. He imbues his narration style with Tourettic traits. As literary critic Ronald Schleifer observes, research on Tourette's reveals "powerful connections between linguistic and motor activity." Schleifer argues that tics combine the verbal and the motor in ways that are distinguishable from poetic experiment only because their context is different. As he argues, "Tourette's inhabits the juncture between biological formations and cultural formations, between the motor tics of Tourette's syndrome—squinting, tapping, arm waving, sticking out the tongue, even licking objects—and its phonic tics—clearing the throat, sniffing, barking, repeating verbal sounds, rhymes, puns, shouting obscenities."[24] Lionel's tics add a physical dimension to Lethem's wordplay. They combine sense and nonsense as well as the verbal and the physical. They cajole readers to detect multiple meanings that arise from their associational interplay of sound and sense. When Lionel invokes Henry James's "The Figure in the Carpet" (1896)—a classic story about the fruitless search for the perfect narrative—without naming that story, readers who spot the reference will detect a telltale disruption: the intrusion of the author into the narrator's voice. Lionel is smart, but he doesn't read Henry James. The allusion is a clue, and a clue is always an affordance: This is another story about imperfect meaning, and Lionel is its perfect narrator.

In *Remainder,* McCarthy's narrator becomes a kind of director—somebody who constructs niches, for effect. After staging several re-enactments, employing film crews, stunt people, actors, and extras, he takes inventory of their result:

> They'd all had the same goal, their only goal: to allow me to be fluent, natural, to merge with actions and with objects until there was nothing separating us—and nothing separating me from the experience that I was having: no understanding, no learning first and emulating second-hand, no self-reflection, nothing: no detour. I'd gone to these extraordinary lengths in order to be real. And yet I'd never stopped and asked myself if it had worked. Naz had kind of asked me after the first building re-enactment—and the question had struck me as odd. The realness I was after wasn't something you could just "do" once and then have "got": it was a state, a mode—one that I needed to return to again and again and again. Opioids, Trevellian had said: endogenous opioids.[25]

In Phelan's terms, McCarthy's narrator underregards the extraordinariness of the actions he's reflecting on, but he's cogent and philosophical in his reflections. He portrays a tension between his character and biomedical perspectives on self-hood. Trevellian is his doctor, who reduces the results of the re-enactments, their capacity to make the narrator feel real, to neurochemistry: "endogenous opioids" (opiatelike chemicals endemic to the brain). The implication is that the re-enactments work like a drug, correcting for chemical imbalances apparently caused by the trauma of the accident. But as the narrator observes, the re-enactments require other people's actions and material objects. When he "merges" with these, he achieves "a state, a mode," though the effects are fleeting. The state he's after may well involve endogenous opiates, but it requires both synchrony with his environment and connection with other people. In that sense, his narration acquires another layer of unreliability: He misregards his similarity to ordinary people, whose identities emerge through social and environmental relations as much as his, whose states of mind are as variable. The narrator conceives himself as unique, cut off from other people, an *Übermensch.* He taxonimizes himself into isolation, but the narration portrays him as a character whose traumatic experience overlaps quite a bit with the experience of other people.

Taxonomies are containers. They parse and separate. Theories of narrative and diagnostic protocols share a taxonomizing impulse. Of course, narratology and medical diagnosis are very different endeavors, but over the past century both have proliferated increasingly complex categories, debated the validity or efficacy of these categories, and revised them, often to the bewilderment of their audiences. But a literary voice will always exceed such taxonomies, as neurological experience will exceed medical ones. The trick is to interpret their rhetorical qualities without reducing them to fixed systems that will never contain them, to identify their patterns in the contexts of the story worlds, worlds that allow, or even demand, that they are fluid, inconsistent, and subject to change—interpretive practices strikingly similar to those that make a good fictional detective.

But literary niche construction brings with it a series of ethical complications. As Garland-Thomson observes, her concept of "misfit emphasizes the particularity of varying lived embodiments and avoids a theoretical disabled body." A neurodivergent narrator cannot help but be both a particular fictional character and a theoretical representative of a diagnosis. Of course, Garland-Thomson emphasizes bodily differences; her argument is easily adapted to encompass neurological ones—which are always physical, phenomenological, and social. If narrating is, as I've been suggesting, a literary form of niche construction, its social implications are even more complicated because of a paradox Garland-Thomson describes: "the concept of misfitting as a shifting spatial and perceptually temporal relationship confers agency and value on disabled subjects at risk of social devaluation by highlighting adaptability, resourcefulness, and subjugated knowledge as potential effects of misfitting."[26] Haddon, Lethem, and McCarthy have crafted resourceful narrators who navigate social obstacles deftly and gain agency through adaptation. If they become representatives of their diagnoses, as Garland-Thomson cautions, they risk undercutting the very real suffering and prejudice experienced of people subject to those diagnoses in the real world. Through the very strength of their agency, they may create the sense that the onus for niche construction is on them alone—rather than a collective social obligation to examine what kinds of experience existing cultural affordances enable and disable. These novels enact these paradoxes without resolving them.

The Detective's *Umwelt*

Cave identifies early-twentieth-century biologist Jakob von Uexküll's *Umwelt* concept as a significant predecessor to affordance theory.[27] Cognitive narratologist David Herman draws on Uexküll's theory to make a complementary argument. In his description, an *Umwelt* is "an animal's environment in the sense of its lived, phenomenal world." The *Umwelt* of a bat and a beaver will be very different, partly because of their differing biologies and partly because of their different environments. As Herman observes, Uexküll stresses the idea that no two individuals in a species will experience the world in identical ways, and uses a human example to illustrate: "The best way to find out that no two human *Umwelten* are the same is to have yourself led through unknown territory by someone familiar with it. Your guide unerringly follows a path you cannot see." Herman's goal is to challenge the assumption that literary modernism is primarily characterized by an "inward turn" that implies a strict dualism between mind and body. Instead, he argues that "the storyworlds through which modernist texts guide readers constitute a staging ground for procedures of *Umwelten* construction." In other words, modernist texts entangle minds, bodies, and worlds. In that sense, he argues that writers like Virginia Woolf or James Joyce "suggest how narrative itself forms part of the cultural equipment by means of which humans seek, with more or less success, to transform unknown territories into negotiable places."[28] In other words, narrative is a form of hypothetical niche construction. As fictional detectives rove through their fictional worlds looking for clues, they defamiliarize the world and audition social norms for signs of contradiction or illogic. When they do so from a neurodivergent point of view, their own bodies become catalysts for subtle but meaningful social change.

Motherless Brooklyn's Lionel describes "the strangeness of having a Tourette's brain" as a difficulty of distinguishing symptoms from personality traits—and as a propensity to defamiliarize ordinary objects, the affordances that comprise his *Umwelt*:

There are days when I get up in the morning and stagger into the bathroom and begin running water and then I look up and I don't even recognize my own toothbrush in the mirror. I mean, the object looks strange, oddly particular in its design, strange tapered handle and slotted miter-cut bristles, and I wonder if I've ever looked at it closely before or whether someone snuck in overnight and substituted this new toothbrush for my old one. I have this relationship to objects in general—they will sometimes become uncontrollably new and vivid to me, and I don't know whether this is a symptom of Tourette's or not. I've never seen it described in the literature. Here's to the strangeness of having a Tourette's brain, then: no control in my personal experiment of self. What might only be strangeness must always be auditioned for relegation to the domain of symptom, just as symptoms always push into other domains, demanding the chance to audition for their moment of acuity or relevance, their brief shot—coulda been a contender!—at centrality. Personalityness. There's a lot of traffic in my head, and it's two-way.[29]

When Essrog observes the blurry line between symptom and trait—or syndrome and personality—he expresses a theme common to brain memoirs and to the neurodiversity movement's critique of medical and educational institutions. The passage is also reminiscent of Oliver Sacks's descriptions of his Tourettic subjects—and of course Lethem decided to experiment with Tourettic narration after reading Sacks. It's a moment when the author emerges from his first-person narrator to reveal a philosophical position with social implications. It's also a moment when Essrog displays his reliability as an interpreter of social conditions. His interpretive talents enable him to reenvision, and sometimes remake, the social and material conditions of his *Umwelt*.

Lionel is defined by the reciprocal relations between the two-way traffic in his head. But his symptoms are not just in his head. They're all over his body; he exchanges them with every character he meets. The metaphor could also be used to describe Lethem's method. He creates a kind of dialectic between the symptoms of Tourette's and the conventions of detective fiction. They're both about interpretation. Symptoms and clues converge in Lionel. His propensity for experiencing a sudden and overwhelming vividness of objects resembles symptoms associated with a variety of neurological conditions, including the sensory sensitivity of autism and the flashbacks of PTSD. The coincidence speaks to the taxonomizing impulse of diagnosis. Lionel's symptoms, like those of Christopher and McCarthy's unnamed narrator, are expressed both through his body, where they're visible to others, and his phenomenological experience, where they're not. Following the lead of medical neurology, all three narrators search for the origins of these symptoms in their brains. If there's any truism that represents contemporary neuroscience, it's that brain systems (like genes) work through their interconnections with each other. Memory systems impinge on emotional systems that impinge on sensory ones, and so on. A trait is a so-called normal expression of such interconnected systems, and a symptom is one that strays from social norms. When these norms are entangled with biological systems, any given trait may "audition" for the status of symptom. Of course, detective fiction involves another kind of quest, to solve a crime or uncover a secret, one that requires its protagonists to move their bodies and minds—or their embodied minds—through the world. In fact, their narrative arcs are structured around quests to reshape their social worlds in ways that transform perceived disability into ability.

As a social practice, niche construction involves reshaping physical environments, institutions, and social relations in ways that enable perceived disabilities to become abilities—for example, ramps for people who use wheelchairs, or eliminating sensory stimuli like loud music or harsh lighting for people prone to overstimulation. Without naming the concept, Lethem, Haddon, and McCarthy have created narrative arcs that dramatize their narrators reconstructing their niches. Their worlds don't bend to them, so they bend their worlds—in small but strategic ways. In experimental fiction, though, niche construction doesn't much resemble its corollaries in the real world. The niche of the story worlds are built through narration. Their narrators are also fictional organisms, whose distinctive points of view create the fictional social worlds they inhabit—worlds populated mostly by more neurotypical characters. Their authors emphasize the misfittings they experience in the pursuit of solving crimes, but the narration itself simulates a fantasy whereby cognitive norms are upended by neurodivergent narrators who control and create their fictional niches. But that fantasy depends on the response of readers whose neurological dispositions, ideological predilections, and variable moods shape the novels' reception.

I described Lionel Essrog as the neurodiversity movement's ironic underbelly because his life works according to premises of the movement. His mentor, Frank Minna—a minor player in organized crime in Brooklyn and New Jersey—gives him a job and defines that job in terms of niche construction: "Minna encouraged me to have a take on everything and to spit it out, as though he thought my verbal disgorgings were only commentary not yet anchored to subject matter."[30] In fact, within the subculture of Minna's operation, Essrog plays a key role made possible by his Tourettic traits: "Coney and the other Minna Agency operatives loved doing stakeouts with me, since my compulsiveness forced me to eyeball the site or mark in question every thirty seconds or so, thereby saving them the trouble of swiveling their necks. A similar logic explained my popularity for wiretap parties—give me a key list of trigger words to listen for in a conversation and I think about nothing else, nearly jumping out of my clothes at hearing the slightest hint of one, while the same task invariably drew anyone else toward blissful sleep."[31] Compulsive monitoring begins for Lionel as a way of inventorying his own consciousness and monitoring its excesses, but he adapts it to fill a professional niche in his world of Brooklyn orphans. *Motherless Brooklyn* is profuse with descriptions of Tourettic traits as ability rather than disability. The novel translates compulsion into focus, tics into attentiveness, and of course, echolalia into the interpretation of clues.

In *The Curious Incident,* Christopher's bluntness becomes a technique for challenging assumptions about neurological difference—and, in particular, defamiliarizing both ability and disability in their social context. When a character tells him he's clever, in a condescending way, he tells readers, "I was noticing how things were, and that wasn't clever. That was just being observant. Being clever was when you looked at how things were and used the evidence to work out something new."[32] While Christopher's bluntness itself is clearly intended to represent an autistic trait—and, at times, seems to do so in a stereotypical way—it also becomes a sign of what Phelan calls the "implied author." Christopher conspires with readers with his sly observation about what it means to be observant. In the niche of Haddon's story world, characters who condescend to Christopher demonstrate their own lack of observation *and* cleverness. Their apparent neurotypicality becomes a form of disability. He considers observation a necessary but insufficient ability. He knows he's good at it, but what he really values is cleverness: the use of evidence to work out something new.

When Christopher cites Sherlock Holmes as his role model, Haddon situates him in a lineage of fictional detectives whose cognitive eccentricities enable them to solve crimes and challenge social norms because their senses detect clues where others see no significant meaning. Holmes is a work of fiction, like Christopher, whose eccentric mind is routinely diagnosed—usually as autistic, addictive, or sociopathic—by readers and adaptors of Conan Doyle's work:

I also like *The Hound of the Baskervilles* because I like Sherlock Holmes and I think that if I were a proper detective he is the kind of detective I would be. He is very intelligent and he solves the mystery and he says

The world is full of obvious things which nobody by any chance ever observes.

But he notices them, like I do. Also it says in the book

Sherlock Holmes had, in a very remarkable degree, the power of detaching his mind at will.

And this is like me, too, because if I get really interested in something, like practicing maths, or reading a book about the Apollo missions or great white sharks, I don't notice anything else and Father can be calling me to come and eat my supper and I won't hear him.[33]

Christopher compares himself to Holmes on two counts, his powers of observation and his concentration on special interests (two commonly described autistic traits). In *Imagining Autism: Fiction and Stereotypes on the Spectrum* (2015), Sonya Freeman Loftis observes that the legacy of Holmes is a host of stereotypically autistic detectives in fiction. Because Watson narrates Holmes's story, his "neurotypical perspective elides the issue of autism as a social construction." Loftis observes that "ultimately no one representation can encapsulate the incredible diversity of the spectrum."[34] While she acknowledges the illogic of the impulse to diagnose a fictional character created nearly a century before autism became a social construction (or even a diagnosis), she objects to Watson's ableist narration, which casts Holmes's intellectual obsessions, his acute observational skills, his sensory sensitivity, his solitary nature, and his pacing as pathological. Loftis interprets *The Curious Incident* as "a humorous parody of the autistic detective tradition."[35] She reads Christopher's struggle to reconstruct his niche—his family, the police force, public transport, relations with neighbors—as reinforcing "the cliché of autism as family tragedy." Despite her conclusion, Loftis acknowledges Haddon's humor and his depiction of "some of the unique difficulties of parenting an autistic child"—two details that, together, represent the relationship between Haddon's narration style and a narrative arc that moves toward a reorientation of neurocognitive norms in the direction of positive niche construction.[36] Christopher outwits neurotypical characters, and in the end his cognitive eccentricities become the key to finding the murderer of the neighbor's dog: his father. He compels his family and community to reexamine their assumptions, a cue to readers to do the same. Nonetheless, if Christopher (or Holmes) is understood to represent all autistic people—or really, any autistic people—then his character becomes a vehicle for reinforcing stereotypes about autism and autistic norms. Understood as a character, a fictional representation of autistic experience, he might instead become an affordance for rethinking assumptions about those norms.

Remainder's experimental form might be described as hyperrealism, designed to follow from or mimic its narrator's post-traumatic phenomenology. McCarthy creates distance between his narrator and implied author through the strategy Phelan calls "underregarding." His narrator's tendency to underregard the outlandishness of his actions may lead to unreliability, but it also leads to a purposeful implausibility. In that sense, McCarthy forestalls the problem of representivity. His narrator isn't likely to be received by readers as an exemplar of a community. The detection skills of the traditional detective novel are translated into an ability to orchestrate crime, rather than solve it.

McCarthy's narrator uses a neurological term—"rerouting"—as a guiding metaphor for the radical and destructive niche construction he is intent to re-enact. He has to learn to move again, through a combination of physical and cognitive therapy:

> Rerouting is exactly what it sounds like: finding a new route through the brain for commands to run along. It's sort of like a government compulsorily purchasing land from farmers to run train tracks over after the terrain the old tracks ran through has been flooded or landslid away. The physiotherapist had to route the circuit that transmits commands to limbs and muscles through another patch of brain—an unused, fallow patch, the part that makes you able to play tiddlywinks, listen to chart music, whatever.
>
> To cut and lay the new circuits, what they do is make you visualize things. Simple things, like lifting a carrot to your mouth. For the first week or so they don't give you a carrot, or even make you try to move your hand at all: they just ask you to visualize taking a carrot in your right hand, wrapping your fingers round it and then levering your whole forearm upwards from the elbow until the carrot reaches your mouth. They make you understand how it all works: which tendon does what, how each joint rotates, how angles, upward force and gravity contend with and counterbalance one another. Understanding this, and picturing yourself lifting the carrot to your mouth, again and again and again, cuts circuits through your brain that will eventually allow you to perform the act itself.[37]

His therapy involves a functional approach to the explanatory gap. Imagination, in the form of visualization, enables the rerouting of synapses; "understanding

. . . cuts circuits through your brain." The metaphor of the train tracks connects the process to the physical world, a world of movement, commerce, catastrophe, and conflict. After he recovers his ability to move and is released from the hospital, the narrator begins his quest to reroute his physical world. He starts wandering, compulsively. At first he's not sure why, but a memory of an ambulance ride during a transfer from one hospital to another suggests an explanation: "I'd been laid flat, and all I'd been able to see was the ambulance's interior, its bars and tubes, a glimpse of the sky. I'd felt I was missing the entire experience: the sight of the ambulance weaving through traffic, cutting onto the wrong side of the road, shooting past lights and islands, that kind of thing. More than that: my failure to get a grip on the space made me nauseous. I'd even thrown up in the ambulance."[38] His body and world are out of synch. The remainder of the novel is a quest to repair their relationship.

Then a moment of déjà vu becomes, as the narrator describes it, "the event that, aside from the accident, was the most significant of my whole life." He remembers a building, in minute detail, except its location: "Right then I knew exactly what I wanted to do with my money. I wanted to reconstruct that space and enter it so I could feel real again."[39] So he wanders London, looking for a building that resembles his memory enough that it might be renovated into it. He employs a team of explorers, who become extensions of him. Despite the team, the narrator finds the building himself. His crew renovates it, and he begins his re-enactments. The narrator starts by rerouting his brain through physiotherapy and ends up rerouting London through the violence of car crashes, gunshots, and a bomb. The novel resists didacticism, so the meaning of this exercise in nihilistic niche construction is difficult to interpret. It may be that the narrator's brain made him do it; that his psychological damage is responsible; that McCarthy is playing with the idea that cultural revolution requires violence and terror; that he's examining the terror and violence of twentieth-century life through the careful representation of the phenomenology that drives his character's violent impulses; or that he's engaging in aesthetic pyrotechnics for sensational effect. As a "package," to use Cave's term, the novel encompasses all these possibilities. As a cultural "laboratory," to return to Heather Houser's term, it's a provocation to debate these same possibilities—a catalyst for interpretation. *Motherless Brooklyn, The Curious Incident,* and *Remainder* are not just experiments in neurodivergent narration. They're also experiments in the pleasures of neurodivergent interpretation. Their protagonists change their worlds through interpretation, which raises questions about whether—or how—their novels change the world through their readers' interpretations.

Christopher Boone, Lionel Essrog, and McCarthy's narrator are all quite explicit about their quests to transform their worlds—their will to craft niches that enable them to thrive, as detectives, but also as social beings. Their quests to solve crimes become quests to find or make "negotiable places" in worlds defined by neurotypical norms. By definition, the solving of mysteries requires them to move their bodies through their worlds, and their experiences emphasize—even stress—the fact that their bodies and minds are thoroughly, if unpredictably, integrated. Lionel Essrog, who had seldom left his familiar Brooklyn neighborhood (Gowanus), is compelled by Minna's death to travel back and forth between there and Manhattan—and finally through Connecticut, throughout New England, and to Maine and back. Christopher Boone had seldom left Swindon, the town where he grew up. His determination to find the dog's killer compels him to walk first in and out of neighbors' homes, conducting interviews, and finally to the train station and into London, where his mother, separated from his father, has moved. McCarthy's narrator becomes a compulsive wanderer, first tracing the routes he traveled leading up to his accident, then searching the whole of London for a particular building he either remembers or imagines into being, and finally all over the city scouting locations for his re-enactments. As they move their bodies through space—feeling combinations of reluctance and compulsion—they face the obstacles of what appears to be nonnegotiable space, but each narrator, in his particular way, transforms the spaces through which he moves. These transformations are consistently portrayed as working in two directions: The narrators change their worlds, and their worlds change them.

Niche construction means transforming affordances, in their many forms, including the physical, cognitive, affective: A ramp enables a person in a wheelchair to move through an environment; a system for learning language through visual and tactile practices enables a nonspeaking child to become a writer; a family or a group of colleagues with a nuanced understanding of an individual's unique set of neurological challenges (say migraine, depression, or seizure) becomes able to make contributions that ignorance about those traits would preclude. Because affordances are about design, they make it clear that the *Umwelt* of a species or an individual is not a static given. Affordances involve a version of what Lionel Essrog calls "two-way traffic"—between those who design the world and those who live in it. In the novels I've been discussing, the narrating detectives make it clear that anybody living in a world is also a designer. These narrators tell stories whose arcs trace the evolution of their own agency as niche makers, as they confront and challenge obstacles and stigmas, using their neurodivergent interpretive practices to reveal what others miss.

That narrative dynamic is partially consonant with the aims of the neurodiversity movement. In an op-ed published in the *American Medical Association Journal of Ethics,* physician Christina Nicolaidis asks, "What Can Physicians Learn from the Neurodiversity Movement?" Nicolaidis writes as a doctor and a mother of an autistic child, and like much neurodiversity discourse, her article focuses on autism but resonates with a variety of neurological differences. She offers several concrete answers—among them some that are relevant in a literary context. Nicolaidis advises physicians to note that autism-awareness campaigns may "inadvertently promote negative stereotypes, diminish our patients' self-worth, or portray them as broken individuals or burdens to others"; she advocates "including autistic individuals and family members [as] equal partners in the research process"; she urges her colleagues "not [to] separate 'the person' from the 'autism,'" to recognize the "social context of disability," and to resist "the fallacy of the linear autism spectrum."[40]

Fictional accounts of neurodivergence entangle and scramble the ideals Nicolaidis describes. Lethem and Haddon were both inspired to write their novels after reading essays by Oliver Sacks and did little in the way of further research.[41] Christopher Boone continuously describes his inability to empathize, duplicating one of the most pervasive stereotypes about autism; but Haddon portrays the social context that shapes his identity through the missteps of characters who misinterpret or underestimate him and through the relationship with a teacher and a school who do a better job. Lethem didn't invite people with Tourette's to become equal partners in his novel, yet he is emphatic about "the fallacy of the linear" diagnostic spectrum and about the inseparability of Lionel and his symptoms. By contrast, McCarthy thanks people who "generously shared their experience of post-trauma with me" on his acknowledgments page.[42] But he also links his narrator's trauma to his tyrannical terrorism.

The ethics of narrating neurological difference in fiction resist easy conclusions. As Phelan argues, "any character's action will typically have an ethical

dimension" and "the author's treatment of the narrator and of the authorial audience will indicate something of his or her ethical commitments toward the
telling."[43] But Phelan's "something" leaves a lot of room for ambiguity, for
what Garland-Thomson calls the "misfittings" between people and their
worlds—or in this case, between characters and the real-world people they
inevitably represent. These novels are not works of advocacy, as so many brain
memoirs are. Instead, they afford simulated experiences of neurological differences, experimenting with styles of narration to explore the possibilities for
meaning in those differences. Affordances are unpredictable: A tree affords
shelter, shade, play, and nutrients; a narrative experiment affords an enormous
range of possible responses, including those imagined by its author and many
more made possible by the diversity of readers. The biggest problem these
particular narrative experiments raise is their propensity to be received as
portraits of lived neurological difference. It would be a conceptual mistake with
serious political consequences to study novels to learn about what life entails
for an autistic, Tourettic, or traumatized person. The only way to do that is
through intimate involvement with people who identify as autistic, Tourettic, or
traumatized—and of course, those people will never represent the range of
experiences of others who identify similarly. What we can—and should—learn
from these novels is that the affordances and misfittings involved in the *representation* influence the circulation of ideas about neurological difference. We
won't understand the potential of neurodiversity politics or the implications of
neurodivergent identities unless we attend to the specific representational techniques that construct the cultural niches that make debates about the brain
possible and necessary.

5

Touching Brains in the Neuronovel

*The first time I held Dum's brain in my hands, I was surprised first by
its weight, and then by what I had suppressed—an awareness of the once-
living man, a stocky seventy-year-old who had died of heart disease.
When the man was alive, I thought, it was all there—internal pictures
and words, memories of the dead and the living.*
—Siri Hustvedt, *The Sorrows of an American*

THE WEIGHT OF DUM'S BRAIN MAY BE surprising, but it's simple to measure. An
average human brain weighs about three pounds. In *The Feeling of What
Happens: Body and Emotion in the Making of Consciousness* (1999), Antonio
Damasio observes, "After considering how consciousness may be produced
within the three pounds of flesh we call brain, we may revere life and respect
human beings more, rather than less."[1] In other words, studying the brain to
determine its role in "the making of consciousness" need not be a reductive
enterprise. The weight of a brain is probably the crudest measurement we have,
and even that can vary by as much as a pound from one human to the next (and
the weight of a cadaver's brain depends on how it's preserved). Even the
simplest questions about physical brains provoke questions about immaterial
selves.

In contemporary fiction, the appearance of a physical brain leads swiftly to
an explicit focus on questions that proliferate from the explanatory gap. Writers
don't use the term, but they explore and contextualize its implications in considerable detail. In this chapter, I'll examine the portrayal of those three pounds of

intricately designed flesh in five novels: Thomas Harris's *Hannibal* (1999), Ian McEwan's *Saturday* (2005), Siri Hustvedt's *The Sorrows of an American* (2009), John Wray's *Lowboy* (2010), and Maud Casey's *The Man Who Walked Away* (2014). These novels are representative of a common literary phenomenon: the dramatization of a fantasy whereby touching brains may reveal the stuff of which self is made. Like so many neuronovels, they are revisionist mysteries, wrapped in conventions of detective fiction, but revising those conventions in fundamental ways. Their protagonists' affiliations with science and medicine enable their authors to link the mysteries of plot to mysteries about brains. Harris's Clarice Starling hunts Hannibal, the brilliant psychopath, only to become his willing abductee (though at the novel's end, readers are primed for a sequel that will unravel the plot of its gothic melodrama); McEwan's Henry Perowne is a neurosurgeon hounded by a petty criminal whose Huntington's disease becomes a central plot device; Hustvedt's protagonist, Erik Davidsen, is a psychiatrist reluctantly embroiled in an anonymous extortionist's persecution of his sister, a mystery he can't solve without his eccentric friend Burton, a historian of memory science; Wray's Will Heller, aka Lowboy, is a schizophrenic teenager recently escaped from a psychiatric hospital and pursued through subway tunnels and city streets by a mystified Detective Lateef, with the help of the boy's mother, Violet, a failed student of neurochemistry;[2] Casey's Albert wanders Europe in fugue states, until he meets the Doctor, a practitioner of moral medicine determined to unravel the mystery of his lost memories. In each of these novels, the representation of physical brains provokes questions about the relationship between physiology and the self, which become central to narrative closure.

In each novel, plot resolution depends only partly on the solving of crimes. Harris's Hannibal feeds a drugged Starling the brain of her professional rival, with the intent to control her mind; McEwan's Perowne fights off a violent intruder out for revenge after the smug, wealthy protagonist insults his pride during an argument about a fender bender; Hustvedt's Erik uncovers the identities of his sister's extortionists; Wray's Detective Lateef discovers that Will's mother, Violet, is also schizophrenic, momentarily apprehending Will before the novel closes with its teenage protagonist falling onto subway tracks as a train approaches; Casey's Doctor uncovers traumatic memories from Albert's childhood through hypnosis (though he can't quite assemble them into a narrative explanation for his fugues). These resolutions are necessary but insufficient to the closure of the novels—which dramatize impossible quests for *interiority*. The process of solving crimes becomes a vehicle for characters to develop new understandings about relationships between brain, body, self, and world.

These novels portray physical brains as vehicles for a fantasy: that their characters might find elusive, intangible, or ethereal elements of self by dissecting brains, holding them, examining them, or just thinking about them. In these fictions, touching brains provokes a philosophical question their characters cannot answer: How does the interplay of physiology and the material world produce the felt states whose sum we call self? Plot resolution requires philosophical reflection to become concrete, guiding protagonists' actions and relationships. In short, they must find ways to escape or transcend the insularity of their inner lives. In the process, the novelists question—or revise—conventional understandings of interiority, suggesting that our shorthand term for the representation of what Damasio calls "the feeling of what happens" may obscure fundamental elements of the literary experiments it describes.

With their emphasis on physical brains, these novels recast the idea of interiority—the portrayal of inner states, or mental experience. Because interiority is so fundamental to the history of the novel, they represent a new phase of the genre's development and provoke some reconsideration of its history. The term "interiority" became pervasive in literary studies after interior monologues and stream of consciousness became the primary focus of the big modernist experiments. *Ulysses, Mrs. Dalloway,* and *The Sound and the Fury* disrupted literary conventions in order to find formal means of representing what mental experience feels like.[3] "Interiority" is so standard a term that we've forgotten it's a metaphor, one that conflates the fact that our brains reside inside our skulls with the idea that our mental experience must also live in a container. In its usage, the term both encompasses and obscures the inexorable interplay between body, mind, and environment central to the literary experiments it describes. We can touch physical brains. We know where they are. But where is the self, or the mind, or consciousness? Inside what? Our bodies? Our skulls? Not exactly. But sort of.

In neuronovels, interiority is recast with a range of narrative techniques for representing felt states produced through the dynamic interaction of an organism (or character) and environment. Interiority, they remind us, is not all about interiors. In his book *Embodied: Victorian Literature and the Senses,* William A. Cohen uses the term "material interiority" to describe the "literary depiction of ethereal inner qualities in a language of tangible objects" in nineteenth-century fiction. Cohen's concept expands the purview of interiority, emphasizing its dynamic and relational qualities. The impulse is similar to that of neuronovels, which represent the brain as one component in a dynamic and elusive system through which consciousness and selfhood emerge. As Cohen observes, various material objects—body parts, excrement, tombs, and architecture, for example—become entangled with "ethereal inner qualities" in novels by Charles Dickens, Charlotte Brontë, Anthony Trollope, and Thomas Hardy. Through metaphors of entombment, excrement, penetration, and pollution, Victorian novels reflect the wide-ranging objects of inquiry of their era's quickly evolving and increasingly public psychological sciences, whose purview was more diffuse than twenty-first-century brain research.[4] Phrenology focused on the skull and face; physiognomy on physical traits and demeanor; vivisection on nerves and muscles; evolutionist psychology on the relationship between behavior and genetic inheritance; and sexology on genital behavior.[5] Of course, twenty-first-century science examines skulls, faces, nerves, muscles, genes, and genitals—but neuroscience, with its acute focus on the brain and nervous system, currently attracts more cultural attention and social influence than any other branch of psychology or human physiology. As responses to neuroscience, neuronovels tend to focus primarily on the brain. In these neuronovels, brains are both metaphorical and literal. While the conscious or semiconscious thought of imagination or affect cannot be found in physical brains, there is also a sense that various forms of unconscious cognition take place in the activity of our nervous systems. In one sense, mental states happen outside place, immaterially, where we can't quite locate them. In another, they happen in our bodies, through the activities of our nervous systems, the circulation of hormones, and responses of muscles, skin, and hair.

When Marco Roth argues that neuronovels "capitulate" to neuroscience, he's partly right. The brain is central in these novels. According to Roth, the problem with neuronovels is that they mirror reductionist and determinist tendencies in neuroscience. Of course, neuroscience is a range of disciplines, and it would be a mistake to reduce all this science to a singular philosophical point of view or mode of practice. Similarly, it's impossible to generalize about all neuronovels. However, many of them exploit the centrality of the brain to suggest a paradox: When the brain is at the center, its contexts and its ambiguities become resoundingly visible, revealing the impossibility of reducing the self to mechanistic models of cellular interaction. In this sense, many of the novels Roth discusses engage in a more robust dialogue with the sciences than the one he caricatures.[6]

Neuronovels ask us to take biology seriously, to include cells, genes, and organs in our estimation of selfhood, but not necessarily to oversimplify biology's role. It's possible to argue (as Roth does) that where Virginia Woolf emphasizes the subjective experience of consciousness, McEwan reduces consciousness to brain activity or diseases.[7] But that would be to miss the irony implicit in his dramatization of his protagonist's fantasy of finding the selves of his patients when he cuts open their brains. Like Woolf's Clarissa Dalloway, McEwan's Henry Perowne is bourgeois, privileged, and myopic. But like Woolf, Perowne gives readers plenty of cues to see his failings, to sympathize with his epistemological limitations. In a different vein, Wray's *Lowboy* is a social and political novel, a critique on establishment medical practices for treating mental illness and an exploration of the ways that race and class shape identity. Siri Hustvedt adopts a more philosophical—almost theoretical—stance, dramatizing the impossible overdetermination of identity, whose contours are shaped by social relations, memory, physiology, sensory experience, emotion, and history. In each case, the writer "assimilates" science so as to "expand the writ of literature" to examine new inflections of the subject Roth argues they eschew: "the personal, the self." Like their modernist predecessors, neuronovels are experiments in narrative representation, experiments that challenge long-standing assumptions about subjectivity and interiority. They exploit twenty-first-century forms of material interiority to give readers an expanded view of what Antonio Damasio calls "the feeling of what happens."

Stuck in the Explanatory Gap

It's significant that Hustvedt's Erik Davidsen is wrong about Dum's brain. He's confounded by material interiority. "When the man was alive," he reports, "it was all there—internal pictures and words, memories of the dead and the living."[8] That "once living man" was never found *in* the brain Erik once held. To use Cohen's terms, his words and memories were "ethereal," his body "tangible." But his body didn't simply house his mind. The resolution of Erik's crisis—a midlife depression exacerbated by self-imposed isolation—requires a philosophical reorientation. Selfhood, he comes to learn, emerges from a dynamic interaction of brain, body, and world. Erik must learn that he, like

Dum, is more than the sum of his brain cells. In short, he must return to the messy world of social relationships by getting involved in the novel's two-pronged mystery plot, which involves questions about a trauma in his father's childhood and the blackmail of his sister by a former lover of her dead husband. The memory, regret, and desire that animate this plot feel ineffable, but they are dependent on the bodies and relationships of those involved. Hence Erik's reluctance.

Erik is stuck in the gap between the material and the immaterial, along with the protagonists of *Lowboy* and *Saturday*. In *Lowboy,* Will hides on a New York City subway platform, reflecting on the bewildering interplay of environmental stimuli, the current of his thoughts, and the physiology of his brain: "Lowboy listened to the sound of the wheels, to the squealing of the housings at the rail-heads and the bends, to the train's manifold and particulate elements functioning effortlessly in concert. Welcoming, familiar, almost sentimental sounds. His thoughts fell slackly into place. Even his cramped and claustrophobic brain felt a measure of affection for the tunnel. It was his skull that held him captive, after all, not the tunnel or the passengers on the train. I'm a prisoner of my own brainpan, he thought. Hostage of my limbic system. There's no way out for me but through my nose."[9] Throughout the novel, Will's conviction about the origin of his selfhood vacillates. Sometimes he's sure it's his brain; other times, the "particulate elements" of his world. But neither answer is sufficient. Wray makes it clear that to find Will, readers should look to the dense and elusive interplay of the brain to which he's captive, the tunnels he roams, and the body that differentiates him from all the others crowding those tunnels even when his psyche seems to merge with theirs. During surgery, McEwan's Henry Perowne does exactly that, probing brains more literally and thoroughly than the characters in the other two novels: "For all the recent advances," he reports during surgery, "it's still not known how this well-protected one kilogram or so of cells actually encodes information, how it holds experiences, memories, dreams and intentions. He doesn't doubt that in years to come, the coding mechanism will be known."[10]

As with Erik Davidsen and Will Heller, Perowne is wrong about his conviction that neuroscience is all we need to understand selfhood. His certainty is shaken through his encounter with Baxter—and is mitigated by his fascination with nonverbal meaning in music and his evolving attitudes about poetry as a means of engaging the ineffable. Like Clarissa Dalloway's, Perowne's insights are both genuine and flawed. Throughout the narrative, he clings to the idea that physiology can explain selfhood, but the narrative's central conflict is resolved through a poem and a surgery whose musical accompaniment is central to its success. While Perowne shares the fantasy of class privilege that defines Clarissa's subjective limitations, his are equally shaped by his conviction that the brain is the key to all mythologies. Woolf is more subtle than McEwan, refusing to represent Clarissa's experience as transformative. When her world-view is challenged, she is confused; when Perowne's is challenged, he budges. McEwan's portrait of the self, written in the age of "neural plasticity," may suggest a too-easy transformation even while McEwan questions his protagonist's overly rigid ideas about cause-and-effect relationships between physiology and experience.

Contradiction and inconsistency are inevitable when a novelist explores relations between physiology and self; in fact, they may be the point. In neuronovels, the gap between the material and the immaterial complicates the representation of mental experience. For example, Will's fantasy of extracting his brain—and therefore himself—through his nasal passages neatly summarizes a central problem of these texts. He's looking for his ineffable, suffering self in the contact between two forms of matter: his brain and the subway tunnels. This impossible quest echoes the epistemological impossibilities inherent in an emerging doctrine in theoretical neuroscience and cognitive philosophy: the idea that consciousness and self are products of the dynamic interactivity between brain, body, and world. In Damasio's words, "Consciousness, as we commonly think of it, from its basic levels to its most complex, is the unified mental pattern that brings together the object and the self."[11] Philosopher Alva Noë articulates a similar idea more assertively: "to understand consciousness in humans and animals, we must look not inward, into the recesses of our insides; rather, we need to look to the ways in which each of us, as a whole animal, carries on the processes of living in and with and in response to the world around us."[12] While the recent advances in brain research are astounding, we are far from understanding the vicissitudes involved when physical bodies in material worlds produce the ineffable experience of an organism. As responses to recent developments in theoretical, empirical, and clinical neuroscience, the ingenuity of the novels under discussion lies in their experimenting with narrative techniques that can submerge readers in the "explanatory gap" between the material and the immaterial, or the physical and the phenomenological.

Fictional Brain Theorists

Harris's Hannibal and Casey's the great doctor (based on nineteenth-century French neurologist Jean-Martin Charcot) are brain theorists. Hannibal subscribes to *The Journal of Brain Physiology*, designs his life around his memory palace, and attempts to rewrite his personal history through mind control. The great doctor gives lectures about the invisible lesions he believes to be the cause of so-called hysterical symptoms of women patients he puts on theatrical display to educate his peers in the European medical community. Both characters are masters of manipulation whose certainties about relations between brain and self are central to their authors' depiction of them as villains.

As a character, Hannibal is imprinted on cultural imagination, impossible to disassociate with the face of Anthony Hopkins. Harris wrote four Hannibal books, two of them adapted into films starring Hopkins. While *Silence of the Lambs* (1991) was the more critically successful of the two films, the brain-eating scene in *Hannibal* (2001) is legendary. Both books were international best sellers, but their details tend to be obscured by the notoriety of the films. As a novel, Hannibal is not well remembered for its pervasive representation of theories about the mind, memory, cognition, and affect. Lecter fancies himself an expert on human minds, both a theorist and a practitioner. As Harris writes, "The memory palace was a mnemonic system well known to ancient scholars and much information was preserved in them through the Dark Ages while Vandals burned the books. Like scholars before him, Dr. Lecter stores an enormous amount of information keyed to objects in his thousand rooms, but unlike the ancients, Dr. Lecter has a second purpose for his palace; sometimes he lives there."[13] The memory palace is a form of material interiority devised by ancient rhetoricians, locating ephemeral mind stuff in imagined physical space. Lecter lives in his memory palace during his years of imprisonment or during periods of stress. He installs shades "to relieve the terrible glare" and statuary so he may soothe his face "against the cool marble flank of Venus." He envisions Starling's mind in similar physical terms, but inhabited by very different materials: "hard and stubborn nodes, like knots in wood, and old resentments still flammable as resin"—materials that prove challenging in his quest to rewrite her personality.[14]

In his gothic crime fiction, Harris portrays fantasies of mixing the mental and the material with an insistent complexity. In the climactic scene, Harris portrays

Lecter as a surgical aesthete—and chef: "Standing over Krendler with an instrument resembling a tonsil spoon, Dr. Lecter removed a slice of Krendler's prefrontal lobe, then another, until he had four. Krendler's eyes looked up as though he were following what was going on. Dr. Lecter placed the slices in the bowl of ice water, the water acidulated with the juice of a lemon, in order to firm them." He feeds Starling until the two of them have shared the whole of Krendler's frontal lobe. The scene becomes camp in his gothic melodrama, but in addition to appeasing an appetite for aestheticized horror (in readers as much as Lecter), it serves another narrative function. In the aftermath of the meal, Starling begins to develop her own memory palace, one that "shares rooms with Dr. Lecter's." As Harris writes, "He has discovered her in there several times." Lecter's brain theory focuses on "early experience matrices, frameworks by which later perceptions were understood."[15] In order to remake her, like a sculpture, he must rebuild the matrices so that her perceptions become malleable.

The insistent sensationalism of Harris's fiction might be understood to cast a shadow over more literary fictions that portray fantasies of finding or making selves in physical brains. More literary novels like Casey's or McEwan's borrow some of this gothic drama and put it to alternate uses. In *The Man Who Walked Away,* Casey's character, the great doctor, is also a manipulator of women's minds, but whereas Harris seems to portray Lecter's monstrosity mostly for the thrill it might induce, Casey does it to give fictional form to historical figures whose subjectivities are lost to us despite their central role in a history of medical probing of suffering selves. Like Lecter, the great doctor has a theory, about invisible lesions and their role in causing the symptoms of hysteria (or "conversion disorder," as it's labeled in the current edition of the *DSM*).

As Charcot did, the great doctor gathers large groups of male physicians to witness his theatrical experiments on "the girl"—his current favorite among the hysterical patients residing in his teaching hospital. Among these physicians is the Doctor, who is treating Albert, the novel's protagonist, whose fugue states seem to share some symptoms with those of hysterics. As the great doctor explains, "Today, we will witness a treatment that is not blind to the invisible lesion. It sees it. It speaks to it."[16] The irony of the great doctor's theory, based on a physical lesion he has never seen, is increased by his showmanship and his particular brand of hypnosis—a practice that "sees" and "speaks to" invisible lesions. In practice, the treatment is incidental to the theatrics, which replace the invisible lesion with a physical brain:

And the Doctor realizes that the something on the platter is not lunch after all. It is a brain.

"... notice the attractive exterior ..."

The monkey, punished? Was this the brain of his beloved pet?

"... the white matter, the flattened portion of the crura ... the gray layers of the island of Reil ..."

The Doctor's mind skips like a stone over logic into the frigid depths of panic. It is much worse than he had thought. It is not the monkey's brain at all. He wiggles his knee into the back of the high forehead in front of him. "Where is the girl?" he whispers.

Shhh, the forehead says. *Shhh,* says the audience. *Zzzzzz.* The Doctor finds himself wishing Monsieur Eager were here. He would know, or he would claim to know, what has happened to the girl. What has the great doctor done with the rest of her? Chopped her into pieces?[17]

The Doctor's panic results from his emotional attachment to the girl, formed on a previous visit to the theater, an attachment that implicates him in her objectification even though he is a harsh critic of the great doctor's treatment of her. When he sees the brain, he wonders who had to die for the sake of medical theatrics. The great doctor's pet monkey? The girl? Had the great doctor "chopped her into pieces"—as Lecter did with Krendler? As a fiction writer, though, Casey deals in lyric, not teleological narratives about cannibals. Nonetheless, she draws readers' attention to the barbarity of the scene, reminding us that nineteenth-century medical investigations of human subjectivity strayed into Hannibal Lecter–like territory, dissecting bodies to find selves.

Casey's Doctor is confused, and the girl becomes his guide. When she appears on the stage, "it is only then that he realizes he has been on the verge of tears. It is not the girl's brain." Casey makes the Doctor subject to a scene in which the girl—standing in, presumably, for centuries of women subjected to outrageous medical treatments for symptoms that eluded their doctors' theories—steals the show. He watches as "the girl does not look at the brain on the platter on the table, though it is close enough that she could reach out from the chair where she sits and touch it." Casey narrates the Doctor's confusion in the third person, but using indirect speech so intimate that readers become witnesses with him. The scene turns almost slapstick, as the camera that was set up to take still portraits of the girl's hypnotic states crashes to the floor, shattered glass spilling onto the stage. The girl seizes the moment of chaos: "At first she appears to be reaching for the brain itself, and the Doctor thinks, She will eat it." In the

Doctor's imagination, for that moment, readers are back in Hannibal Lecter territory, where humans eat brains. But the Doctor is wrong: "it isn't the brain she wants. She picks up the straitjacket instead, slipping her arms expertly through the sleeves."[18] Casey replaces gothic melodrama with feminist triumph. The girl reclaims the straitjacket, the symbol of her imprisonment in the great doctor's theory of her mental experience, his hospital with its locked wards, and his stage with its brutal medical apparatuses, on which she is the object of the collective gaze of physicians who travel great distances across Europe (like Albert) to witness her subjection. This brain will not reveal her mind.

Material Interiority

Cohen coined the term "material interiority" in an essay on Charlotte Brontë's *The Professor* and elaborates on the concept in his book, *Embodied: Victorian Literature and the Senses.* He asserts that the emphasis on material interiority in Victorian fiction "collapses dualistic notions of mind and body." In Cohen's words, "By portraying in palpable terms the human body's enclosure of intangible subjectivity, [Brontë] exploits the paradox of an immaterial soul, heart, or mind inhabiting the flesh. Pervaded by metaphors of entombment and boundary violation, the novel's language exaggerates and estranges the conditions of embodiment. In using the term 'material interiority,' I mean to designate this literary depiction of ethereal inner qualities in a language of tangible objects, a practice that collapses dualistic conceptions of mind and body (or body and soul) by making subjective inwardness and bodily innards stand for each other."[19] Cohen's argument, that Victorian fiction "exaggerates and estranges the conditions of embodiment" is applicable to contemporary neuronovels, which also make "subjective inwardness and bodily innards stand for each other." Like the Victorian texts Cohen examines, neuronovels remind readers that "the body is the inescapable condition of possibility for human existence."[20] However, neuronovels are less interested in "collapsing" dualism than they are in estranging relations between body and self in order to emphasize the "possibility" in Cohen's sentence—or, put another way, to highlight the epistemological and experiential uncertainties that emerge from the explanatory gap.

In McEwan's *Saturday,* for example, Henry Perowne touches brains for a living. In place of Clarissa Dalloway's flights into other characters' psyches, Perowne (as his narrator calls him) penetrates other characters' skulls. The novel features numerous surgery scenes, during which Perowne expertly cuts open people's skulls and cuts into their brain matter in the hope of changing, or saving, their lives. McEwan depicts these surgeries in exquisite detail. When he does so, his narrator assumes a double position, emphasizing Perowne's surgical techniques and speculating on philosophical questions about the capacity of the brain matter to animate his patients. The novel's primary conflict is resolved through a five-page surgery scene that sutures its climax and ensures denoue-ment. Henry performs this surgery on a character named Baxter, a thug whose portrayal resembles Dickens more than Woolf: "Now, using the same dissector, he lifts the whole free flap away from the skull, a large piece of bone like a segment of coconut, and lays it in the bowl with the other bits. The clot is in full view, red of such darkness it is almost black, and of the consistency of set jam. Or, as Perowne sometimes thinks, like a placenta. But round the edges of the clot, blood is flowing freely now that the pressure of the bone flap has been relieved. It pours off the back of Baxter's head, over the surgical drapes and onto the floor."[21] Perowne's observations are thick with metaphors that estrange the patient's brain, even for a neurosurgeon intimate with the anatomy. The skull is a "coconut," the clot "set jam." His placenta analogy suggests an unrep-resented history for Baxter. Before he was a man in middle age, like Perowne, Baxter was a fetus, then an infant, a child, an adolescent, and a young man. Now his vulnerable body "pours" out of him. Perowne's job is to inflict bodily trauma in order to heal, violating his body's boundaries in order to restore them.

Henry's colleagues don't know it, but Henry caused Baxter's injury, by pushing him down a flight of stairs, after Baxter broke into his house, terrorized his family, and threatened to rape his daughter. Henry keeps another secret from his colleagues. In addition to the blood clot, Baxter suffers from fairly advanced Huntington's disease. His life, however compromised, depends upon the success of the surgery, depicted in clinical detail: " 'Elevate the head of the table. Give me as much as you can,' Henry calls to Jay. If the bleed is higher than the heart, the blood will flow less copiously. The table rises, and Henry and Rodney step back in quickly through the blood at their feet and, working together, use a sucker and an Adson elevator to remove the clot. . . . But they can't close up yet. Perowne takes a scalpel and makes a small incision in the dura, parts it a little and peers inside. The surface of Baxter's brain is indeed covered with a clot, much smaller than the first. He extends the incision and Rodney tucks back the dura with stay sutures."[22] The scene may be contemporary literature's most elaborate (and meticulously researched) display of material interiority. The brain anatomy with which Perowne is so familiar is "estranged" because of his charged and overdetermined relationship with Baxter, setting the stage for the surgeon to fantasize about the "ethereal" aspects of self he might find as he dissects his antagonist's brain. In the novel's acknowledgments, McEwan thanks a number of neurosurgeons, including Neil Kitchen: "It was a privilege to watch this gifted surgeon at work in the theatre over a period of two years." McEwan's research shows in these passages. Their length and detail feel like they're coming from a writer who can't resist demonstrating what he's learned. However, the language of the passage is as lyrical as it is clinical. Metaphors are not uncommon in medical literature, but the emphasis on emotionally charged sensory experience—"[blood] pours off the back of Baxter's head, over the surgical drapes and onto the floor"—is where the craft of the novelist transforms the clinical into the literary. Baxter's body is commingling with the antiseptic environment of the operating room. Readers are asked to indulge the fantasy that an exchange of Baxter's immaterial self is taking place when Perowne cuts him open and lets the contents of his body pour "freely" into the room. Even Perowne, thoroughly a materialist, imagines that he'll learn something about the mind by touching the brain.

As the scene proceeds, philosophical reflections intrude upon the clinical. Like Damasio, Perowne finds all the evidence he needs to revere life in the brain as a physical organ. But his materialism seems to soften as the scene progresses, and it becomes clear that Perowne is looking for more than a blood clot under Baxter's skull:

> For all the recent advances, it's still not known how this well-protected one kilogram or so of cells actually encodes information, how it holds experiences, memories, dreams and intentions. He doesn't doubt that in years to come, the coding mechanism will be known, though it might not be in his lifetime. . . . But even when it has, the wonder will remain, that mere wet stuff can make this bright inward cinema of thought, of sight and sound and touch bound into a vivid illusion of an instantaneous present, with a self, another brightly wrought illusion, hovering like a ghost at its centre. Could it ever be explained, how matter becomes conscious?[23]

Perowne sounds like an Enlightenment naturalist when it comes to predicting epistemological revolutions just beyond reach—a gesture common among neuroscience enthusiasts. You could call these predictions rhetorical sleights of hand, whereby what we might know in the future stands in for what we don't know now, but you might also call them fantasy. It's debatable whether we'll ever understand the complex relationship between matter (our brains, our bodies, the physical world around us) and the immaterial or ineffable experience of self or consciousness. In the meantime, novelists offer aesthetic experience in place of epistemological certainty.

Whereas science deals in hypothesis, literature deals in the creation of speculative worlds. Both enterprises demonstrate the value of counterfactual thinking—imagining what we cannot yet know. Touching brains to find minds is a fantastical enterprise. In literature, the irony of a quest is explicit. Neuronovelists dramatize epistemological questions that confound science and philosophy, but they make no claim to resolving them. In the process, it becomes clear that moments of material interiority mirror a generalizable formal principle: Aesthetic experience involves the inexplicable traffic between the material and the immaterial in ways that feel automatic and often go unnoticed. Words on a page, images on a screen, or sound vibrating from a speaker act upon the bodies of readers, spectators, and listeners and in the process trigger a spectrum of immaterial experiences—affective responses, acts of inspiration or imagination, emotions, desire, memory—whose physiological correlates, felt and unfelt, trigger still more immaterial experiences. And so on. In this sense, a form of "material interiority" is fundamental to the capacity for the aesthetic "transmission of affect," to borrow a phrase from feminist philosopher Teresa Brennan. In the final section of this essay, I will argue that while Hustvedt, McEwan, and Wray begin by probing the origins of ineffable experience, they conclude by focusing on means for transmitting or sharing it.

Baxter's Blood, Will's Membrane, and Burton's Sweat

In the conclusion to *Embodied,* Cohen revisits "fractured moments that provide glimpses of the body unmaking any abstract idea of the human" in Victorian literature. He argues that such moments highlight "the contiguous and reciprocal contact between body and world by focusing on sensory influx and corporeal outflow." Cohen's key insight is that moments like this "draw attention to the conditions of embodiment itself. When the body obtrudes on the self and cannot be regarded merely as its container, we are shocked into recognition of the fullness of bodily existence. Such a recognition registers the primacy of the material that is the human and, at the same time, prevents that material from becoming fixed and left behind by an idea of the ethereal, transcendent, or universal personhood."[24] Scenes of "sensory influx and corporeal outflow" are central in the neuronovels I've been discussing. Cohen emphasizes obtrusions of the body on the self. These neuronovels extend that idea: As their narratives proceed toward resolution, they emphasize moments when characters' bodies "obtrude" on *each other,* catalyzing moments of shared subjectivity—whereby characters feel like they bridge the gap between one "ethereal" consciousness and another, however momentary or fleeting the experience. Ultimately, plot resolutions depend on these moments of shared subjectivity, arising from moments of contact between bodily organs or fluids, sometimes literally and sometimes metaphorically. In the process of solving the crimes that drive their plots, a great deal of bodily obtrusion enables characters to overcome the isolation of "the private, first-person phenomenon" of consciousness, to borrow a phrase from Damasio.[25]

Casey's Albert and Harris's Hannibal are characters for whom the boundaries of consciousness are porous by definition. They instigate plots driven by the magnetic pull of their own porous identities. When Albert is alone, "He blurs into the sky and the sky into the wind and the others are smeared into each other and into him. He feels himself spilling into the creek. What is himself? There is nowhere to go to escape; he is already part of nowhere. Nowhere. The word fills him until he begins to shake." When he joins the community at the asylum, his capacity to blend with his environment finds an outlet—other people: "Since the arrival of the new patient, the universe has shifted slightly. The simple vase of the asylum is not so simple after all. The arrival of someone new, and suddenly everyone is sloshing over its edges."[26] Albert's porous identity defines him, as a person who feels connection, to the degree that his sense of self is boundaryless. His ambivalence stems from his inherent capacity to connect and his struggle to feel himself in the process of doing it. Hannibal is altogether more controlled and controlling in his will to subsume the identities of others, particularly Agent Starling. Through hypnosis, he renovates her brain and her psyche—what he calls her memory palace—until he's satisfied the boundaries between them have dissolved. "Using hypnotic drugs and hypnotic techniques much modified from cameral therapy," Harris writes, "he was finding in Clarice Starling's personality hard and stubborn nodes, like knots in wood." Hannibal enjoys the challenge, probing the "matrix" of Starling's mind until he finds a portal: "tableaux of pitiless brightness, years old but well tended and detailed, that sent limbic anger flashing through Starling's brain like lightning in a thunder-head. Potential flexibility. The cerebral cortex rules." The result is all the more satisfying because he conceives his project as overcoming the challenges of a difficult subject, to create a mind he can share: "Clarice Starling's memory palace is building as well. It shares some rooms with Dr. Lecter's own memory palace—he has discovered her in there several times—but her own palace grows on its own. It is full of new things."[27]

Casey's and Harris's novels are unusual in their portrayal of characters who think, feel, and act outside the model of Damasio's "first-person" prison of identity. It's more common that plots trace the trajectory of characters' struggles to overcome isolation, through whatever means they can find to connect. In *Lowboy,* for example, Will spends much of the novel on a quest to lose his virginity. His first attempt, in the makeshift subway tunnel home of a woman character named Heather Covington, fails. Nonetheless, Will's reflections on the experience demonstrate his desire for psychological release through bodily obtrusion:

> She closed her eyes and opened her legs wider. He looked away for the length of a breath, then leaned forward until he could feel the warmth of her bare skin against his face. The smell forced his mouth and eyes shut. He thought about the inside of his body: how cold and shutaway it was, like a doll forgotten in an empty house. He thought about the end of the world, about the people above the grates, about the tunnel, about MUSEUM OF NATURAL HISTORY. The sparkling tiles, the unforgiving benches. The dinosaurs set like urns into the wall. He pictured his own skeleton there, then Heather Covington's, then Violet's. What he needed to do was as clear as if it had been burned into him with electric wire. He needed to break the membrane that had held him all his life, to slip out into the putrefying world. He had to put himself into another body. He had to bite down on his tongue and push.
>
> Above the grate someone was laughing softly.
>
> "I can't do it," he gasped, gagging on his own breath. "It's gone to sleep, Miss Covington. Take a look."[28]

Toward the end of the novel, Will finally does lose his virginity, with a prostitute who calls herself Secretary. The scene enables him, finally, to feel like he's broken "the membrane that had held him all his life": "The room had gone silent and the light had gone dim and he opened his mouth and the whole world went silent. Somewhere voices were screaming in amazement and victory but the screaming was too far off for him to hear. There was no need to hear. She was moving above him. He could see out of the holes in her eyes and taste with her mouth and feel every single thing that she was feeling. He felt the skin around him breaking and the silence breaking with it. He seeped out of his body like the yolk out of an egg. The world was outside his body now, which meant he was alone. His body was on the outside of the world."[29] Like Erik and Perowne, Will is an unreliable narrator. His delusions may account for his belief that he can "feel every single thing that she was feeling." But the moment, followed by a beating, in which Will's body is obtruded in another, more painful and violent way, motivates him to return to the Union Square subway stop, the scene of the crime that led to his incarceration—a place where Lateef and Violet are likely to find him. Lateef apprehends him momentarily. He bites the detective's cheek, tasting his blood as he falls onto the tracks. Will is relentless in his quest for connection through bodily obtrusion.

Will's feeling of shared subjectivity is grand and generalized. When he dies, the delusional narrator tells us, "the world ended by fire." While his case is extreme, it's contiguous with moments in other neuronovels, including the empathy McEwan's Perowne feels for Baxter. Before giving his assent to close, Perowne directs a nurse to put on Barber's "Adagio for Strings"—to replace the Bach that played during surgery. Music is the only form of art that seems not to leave Perowne cold, and he chooses the soundtracks to his surgeries carefully. Barber becomes the vehicle for Perowne's empathy:

> When at last the head bandage is in place and secured, everyone in the theatre, the whole firm, converges on Baxter—this is the stage at which the patient's identity is restored, when a small area of violently revealed brain is returned to the possession of the entire person. This unwrapping of the patient marks a return to life, and if he hadn't seen it many hundred times before, Henry feels he could almost mistake it for tenderness. While Emily and Joan are carefully pulling away the surgical drapes from around Baxter's chest and legs, Rodney makes sure the tubes, leads and drains are not dislodged. Gita is removing the pads taped over the patient's eyes. Jay is detaching the inflatable warming blanket from around Baxter's legs. Henry stands at the edge of the table, cradling the head in his hands. The helpless body is revealed in a hospital gown and looks small on the table. The meditative, falling line of the orchestral strings seems to be addressed to Baxter alone.[30]

Upon completion of the surgery, Perowne reflects on "the dream of absorption" or "benevolent dissociation" that transports him when he cuts people open and repairs their damaged flesh. "He's been delivered into a pure present," he thinks. ". . . It's a little like sex, in that he feels himself in another medium. . . . It's a feeling of clarified emptiness, of deep, muted joy." This particular case is more charged than most. Baxter, the man whose blood poured all over him during surgery, is his partner in this "pure present." He's become intimate with the physiology of his persecutor, the man who nearly raped his daughter. When Perowne expresses the feeling that the music "seems to be addressed to Baxter alone," he adopts Baxter's perspective—or his fantasy of it, momentarily bridging the divide between himself and this man who is so different from him in all worldly particulars. If Will is unreliable because of his delusions, Perowne, "the professional reductionist," is unreliable because of his rigid materialism, whose persistence is indicated by the scene's final sentence: "There must, he concludes as he stands to leave the theatre, be something wrong with him."[31] After risking his career by insisting on operating on a man whose injuries he caused, Perowne is unable to maintain reflection on his own motives or feelings. While he may dismiss his actions, it's clear to readers that he's been seeking empathy for his persecutor, because he needs it to resolve the psychological and epistemological confusion that their conflict exposed.

Genital contact is the vehicle for Will's feeling of shared subjectivity; for Perowne, it's Baxter's blood and brain. For Hustvedt's Erik Davidsen, it's his friend Burton's sweat. Hustvedt's psychiatrist narrator and protagonist is a serious man. He's divorced; his father has died; he's dedicated to his practice and patients; he's got an unrequited crush on his tenant; he's a devoted brother and uncle; he's smart, curious, well-read, dour, and isolated. In middle age, when readers meet him, Erik is not a man who's likely to give a nickname to a cadaver. When he thinks about holding Dum's brain in his hands, readers become privy to a history that haunts him. Erik was once a younger man, a medical student willing and able to participate in a little gallows humor. As he thinks about the "internal pictures and words" of the "once-living man" represented by that three pounds of flesh, readers are prompted to think about Erik in these terms. His "memories of the dead and the living" are internal pictures and words, as Dum's once were. If Erik were right that a life like Dum's could be found in the brain alone, there would be no crisis to resolve—simply a crime to be prosecuted. But life, Hustvedt's novel suggests, happens in the breach between materiality and consciousness. The power of the brain requires a context: a body in a world of other bodies and multitudes of organisms and objects that play roles in the emergence of a human life from systems of proteins, amino acids, chemicals, cells, and organs. Through self-imposed isolation, Erik has been avoiding the contexts that might change his life.

That's where his sweaty friend Burton comes in. Burton is a minor character with a noxious case of material interiority—hyperhidrosis—and a central role in the novel's resolution:

> Burton was a fat, waddling, red-faced person who had little luck with girls. His chief trouble, however, wasn't his looks, but his moistness. Even in winter, Burton had a steamy appearance. Bubbles of perspiration protruded from his upper lip. His forehead gleamed, and his dark shirts were notable for the great damp circles under his arms. The poor fellow gave the impression that he was humid to the core, a peripatetic swamp of a man with a single vital accouterment—his handkerchief. Once in medical school I had suggested that there were some treatments for hyperhidrosis. Burton had informed me that he had tried everything known to humankind that didn't risk turning him into a vegetable, and his was a hopeless case. "My ur-reality is sweat," he told me. The first year of residency had marked the end of his career as a practicing physician. His melancholy, dripping face, his sticky palms and sodden handkerchief had alienated nearly every conscious patient.[32]

Burton is a messy counterpoint to a protagonist who doesn't realize how much he needs his help. Perhaps unsurprisingly, his sweat has everything to do with his brain *and* his mind. Hyperhidrosis is a medical mystery. It can be localized to the spots where we all sweat most: armpits, hands, feet, groin. People with "generalized" hyperhidrosis like Burton's sweat profusely all over their bodies. While the cause of hyperhidrosis is the subject of some debate, the nervous system plays a role. Of course, many people sweat more when they're anxious. People like Burton sweat *a lot* more when they're nervous. At the end of the novel, Burton's sweat abates somewhat after the death of his mother. He confesses his concern to Erik that the change—and therefore the sweat itself—might be "symptomatic." A psychoanalyst might see Burton's sweat as a symptom of his feelings about his mother, or a childhood trauma. Nonsense, a physician might say. Burton's problem is physical. Hustvedt is careful not to resolve the impasse. In the words of Erik, the psychiatrist: "I wouldn't overinterpret what appears to be a good thing."[33]

Burton's sweat represents the murkiness of relations between psychological and physical experience, a visible sign of inarticulate and largely unknowable corporeal experience—what Damasio has sometimes called the body's "wordless storytelling." One of Burton's roles is to pull some murk out of the novel's other characters, who speak so deftly that their bodies, unlike Burton's, don't get much chance to communicate. In contrast to Burton, Erik is about as dry as a person gets. He's also the narrator of a novel populated by characters whose "ur-reality" is *ideas*—which aren't any closer to resolving the emotional conflicts or family mysteries that hamper them. They are frustrated, unhappy creatures searching for elusive meanings about their pasts, their deceased relatives, their spouses, their crushes, and their work. Ideas insulate them. Burton sweats all over these ideas, dons a wig, solves the novel's central mystery, and delivers some moist comfort to his dry friends.

Burton belongs to a tradition of literary characters who secrete too much, from the pissing giants in Rabelais's *Gargantua and Pantagruel,* to the farting Ignatius J. Reilly in John Kennedy Toole's *A Confederacy of Dunces.* Their secretions are palpable transmitters of affect. Of course, the root of the word "secretion" is "secret," meaning "something set apart or concealed as private." You might say these characters are leaking for the rest of us, whose secretions are taboo. Even though the experiences are unquestionably universal, we're not supposed to sweat or fart or puke or piss or bleed or ejaculate in public. *Keep your secretions to yourself,* the taboo reminds us. That taboo is violated by the characters in *Lowboy, Saturday,* and *The Sorrows of an American*—and, in another sense, by their authors. Like Rabelais and Toole, they printed and published accounts of their characters' leaking bodies. Their novels are public declarations that the taboo against public obtrusions of bodily boundaries may inhibit something integral to life—the material interiority that animates human beings and undergirds social connection. The protagonists of all three novels are seeking emotional and psychological connection through bodily contact.

Hustvedt's earlier novel *What I Loved* gives a name to what they seek. In that novel, Hustvedt's character Violet proposes a theory of "mixing" in a book she's writing about anorexia: "They find a way to separate the needs and desires of other people from their own. After a while, they rebel by shutting down. They want to close up all their openings so nothing and nobody can get in. But mixing is the way of the world. The world passes through us—food, books, pictures, other people."[34] Anorexia, Hustvedt's Violet theorizes, is an attempt to prevent mixing. In that sense, *not mixing* is pathological. Plot resolution in *Lowboy, Saturday,* and *The Sorrows of an American* requires characters to reconceive their relationship to "all their openings." The world, including elements of other people's bodies, passes through us—mostly in undetectable ways. In Cohen's words, "permeable and pervious to the world through our senses, our bodies are . . . dynamic selves."[35] The characters I've been discussing experience their own failures to mix with other people as a confounding obstruction; it inhibits their "dynamic selves" and their relationships. The narratives in which they star are propelled by their desires to find ways to mix, through sex, surgery, physical violence, the endurance of another's sweat, or listening compassionately while other people narrate their problems.

In many ways, neuronovels focus on material interiority as way of addressing E. M. Forster's famous dictum from the final pages of *Howards End:* "Only connect." Touching another person's brain to find that person's self is a fantasy of connecting: finding empathy, sharing feelings, exchanging affect, blending each other's stories. Recently, science has developed new methods to explore facets of human connection and exchange. Studies on mirror neurons and empathy are widespread in neuroscience. Studies on neuroaesthetics and the ways literary language affects readers are increasingly common. Research on "emotional contagion" enjoys a high profile in social psychology.[36] *"Only connect,"* Forster wrote. *This is how we do it,* the studies suggest. *If only I could,* these characters might reply. Understanding the physiology and psychology of connection would not satisfy Forster, and it won't help the suffering protagonists of these novels. Will's psychiatric treatment doesn't help; in fact, his medication inhibits connection. Nor does Perowne's strict materialism, nor Erik's psychiatric training and practice. But each of them encounters characters who provoke them to mix. For Erik, it's Burton; for Will, it's Heather Covington and Secretary; for Perowne, it's Baxter. Their leaking counterparts help them fulfill Forster's dictum, or Violet's axiom. These characters are reminders that we're all leaking substances that reveal aspects of self we're hardly aware of. The leakage is essential for the mixing.

At the end of *Embodied,* Cohen quotes *The Picture of Dorian Gray:* "to convey one's temperament into another as though it were a subtle fluid or a strange perfume: there was a real joy in that." "This is a transitivity," Cohen concludes, "beyond the boundaries of the self, soul, or indeed body itself, a material form of existence whose porousness puts it both outside and at the center of what it means to be human."[37] Ultimately, neuronovels explore this porousness, whose mechanisms and meanings are elusive partly because they occupy the explanatory gap that confounds neuroscience and philosophy. Rather than offering theories or proposals about the relationship between physiology and self, they create narratives that propel characters from the examination of bodies into the feeling of shared experience. By devising aesthetic means of representing the gap, they encourage readers to think about their own porousness. In the process, they recast traditional literary notions of interiority. Their leaking bodies catalyze moments of shared feeling. Like the nineteenth-century novels Cohen discusses, these neuronovels suggest that bodies are not "mere containers" for subjectivity. The fictional bodies—and brains—they portray both contain and leak feelings, both literally and metaphorically. These neuronovels suggest that interiority is both literal and metaphorical. The feelings of subjectivity happen in and through physical bodies but are not fully contained by them. What we call "interiority" straddles the explanatory gap, blends material and immaterial experience.

As Hustvedt's Violet points out, books are one form of material that "passes through us." In her book *Feeling Beauty: The Neuroscience of Aesthetic Experience,* Gabrielle Starr proposes a theory of aesthetics that complements Cohen's argument about porousness—and that may explain how and why novelists of the twenty-first century are responding in such great numbers to the exciting discoveries and confounding questions of neuroscience. Drawing on a blend of empirical research and literary analysis, Starr concludes, "the arts mediate our knowledge of the world around us by directing our attention, shaping perceptions, and creating dissonance or harmony where none had been before." In other words, art makes new experience possible—because, in Starr's words, "mental images serve to integrate a variety of information." In both cognitive and physiological terms, "imagery is, de facto, not just multidimensional but multisensory."[38] Aesthetic experience marshals the brain's interconnectivity to induce experiences that yield new combinations of sensory, cognitive, and emotional experience. As an aesthetic technique, material interiority requires readers (and characters) to live with the ambiguity inherent in the idea that our bodies are "both outside and at the center of what it means to be human." To do that, novelists develop narrative strategies that encompass both the harmony and dissonance central to Starr's proposition about art's capacity to exploit the porousness Cohen describes. Erik can't reconstruct the man whose body Dum's brain once occupied, but when he feels its weight, it provokes him to imagine the man's experience. It becomes an aesthetic engagement, like reading a novel. In their responses to the neuroscientific revolution, novelists play a unique role, crafting narratives that may forestall simplistic or reductive understandings of the relationship between brain and self, using the materiality of written words to shape the perception of readers—enabling them to feel the porousness of the explanatory gap.

Interlude: Interview with Maud Casey

JASON TOUGAW: You've talked about the fact that you discovered "Albert's Tale" in the appendix to Ian Hacking's *Mad Travelers: Reflections on the Reality of Transient Mental Illnesses*. Albert Dadas became the inspiration for Albert, the protagonist of your novel *The Man Who Walked Away*. What drew you to his story? How would you compare the Dadas of the case history with the Albert of your novel?

MAUD CASEY: What drew me to the story initially was, indeed, that appendix translated by Hacking. Part of the appendix was the transcript of the sessions of hypnosis Dadas underwent as treatment, called "Albert's Tale (1872–May 1886)." This was Dadas's account of his travels or, rather, his effort to tell his story. He had a way of telling it that was as if he were telling someone else's adventure—baffled, poignant, with great empathy for this tragic fellow who happened to be him. I found it profoundly moving. There was such tenderness in the telling, as well as an appreciation of the mystery of it all. And also a sense of seeking. At the heart of it all was a question. Or questions. I began writing my novel by copying down all of the phrases Dadas repeated in the piecing together of his story. "It seems," "it appears," "I found myself," "I discovered myself," "I woke up." There was a lot of astonishment involved. I was astonished to learn that I had been apprenticed to a traveling salesman, he says in telling the story of wandering off the first time, at the age of twelve. And: The next day I was astonished to find myself on the train and to hear the announcement, "Tours." These phrases launched me into the book. I can't pretend to know much about the real Dadas. My guess is that he was as much of a mystery to himself as I am to myself. Which is to say, there's a lot I don't know! My fictional Albert started with the real guy's lyrical language and lifted off from there.

JASON: The asylum in your novel, where Albert lands for a time, is a remarkable place—designed by your character, the Doctor, on the principle of moral treatment. What is moral treatment? What qualities of this nineteenth-century concept did you use to shape your portrayal of the asylum?

MAUD: The asylum in the novel grew out of reading I did about moral treatment, particularly as defined by an English Quaker named William Tuke in the eighteenth century. Tuke founded a place called the York Retreat in opposition to the harsher treatment employed by other asylums at the time. His retreat was a beautiful country home with a high staff-to-patient ratio and an emphasis on rest and spiritual development. There was a lot of talk of "family." In the early nineteenth century, Tuke's grandson, Samuel Tuke, wrote about the retreat and used the term "moral treatment," so it was part of the psychiatric conversation in the nineteenth century as well, but even though the real Albert Dadas's real doctor treated him very well, this place is largely my invention. I think often when we think Victorian asylum, we think horrific conditions and the mistreatment of patients, and mostly we would be right. But I think fiction can function as a kind of wish fulfillment, and there may have been some of that as I was writing it. At the York Retreat, there was a discussion of stillness as an aspiration. That resonated for me—what relief stillness would be for someone in constant motion. Which is to say, all of us.

JASON: You've written about your experience struggling with symptoms of mental illness in your essay "A Better Place to Live"—specifically depression, mania, and delusion. In your twenties, you got a bipolar diagnosis. Varieties of mental illness appear in all your fiction, from *The Shape of Things to Come* to *The Man Who Walked Away.* But diagnosis is never simple in your fiction. It's difficult to write about mental illness without either romanticizing or stigmatizing. You manage never to do either. So here's my question: How does your own experience living with and being treated for mental illness inform your choices about how to represent it in fiction?

MAUD: Once again, I turn to the inimitable Ian Hacking to guide me. From his book *Rewriting the Soul: Multiple Personality and the Sciences of Memory,* in which he describes being wary of the word "disorder": "a standard all-purpose word used in the *DSM* . . . a good choice but cannot help being loaded with values. The word is code for a vision of the world that ought to be orderly." Related to this is my feeling (which increases as I get older): Why isn't everyone walking down the street screaming? The way Hacking approaches "disorder" is how I feel about the words "mental illness" and "diagnosis." Let me quickly add, these are useful, often invaluable, terms. I've benefited from receiving a diagnosis in all sorts of ways—meds, health insurance, the relief of having my pain named, of knowing I wasn't the only one who believed Madonna was speaking to her through the TV. But I'm not—good thing!—a psychiatrist or a scientist. My vocation requires me to make things up, and a big part of the project of fiction has to do with the complexity of approximating/inventing a particular consciousness on the page, with all its freewheeling texture and idio-syncrasies and strangeness. What E. M. Forster called so aptly the "secret life" of a character. The secret life requires getting underneath, behind, and other-wise unraveling, the things we think we know—what mental illness *is,* what diagnosis *means.* I'm much more interested in the mystery of self, the fluidity of self (selves!), and it always feels to me as though the shorthand of diagnoses obscures all of that fascinating mess. One of the questions I wrestle with is how to create the patterns required to make a character legible without reducing the character to those patterns. We're a culture that demands answers. A diagnosis is, for the good and for the bad, an answer. Fiction, like all the arts, requires a certain amount of mystery.

JASON: I want to ask a question about narration technique in your novel *The Man Who Walked Away.* Your two primary characters are Albert, who wanders around Europe in fugue states, and the Doctor, who becomes fascinated—or fixated—by Albert. You describe them as "dreaming together" in hypnosis sessions. You narrate those sessions in what I'd call a doubly indirect style. Your narrator recounts the mixed thoughts and feelings of the Doctor.

For example: "When Albert trembled and shook, when he fell on his way to bed because he was that dizzy, when he was overcome by that urge that he could not find the words for, his father would take him to bed, first swaddling Albert's wrist and ankles in cloth to prevent the rope from burning. He was always gentle. He would always ask, 'Is the rope too tight?' " When I read these scenes, I'm convinced that you are narrating the Doctor's reception of Albert's words. The words belong to both of them, come from the two of them "dreaming together," blending with each other. It's an astounding technique, both jarring and very moving. I'm convinced that this is one of the ways you manage to convey the particular experience of Albert's eccentric mind, rather than reducing him to a diagnosis. When the doctor is subsumed by Albert's consciousness, he knows that simple diagnosis won't do. I'm curious: Did you conceive this narration technique in a conscious way? Did you stumble upon it or plan it? Does my reading resonate for you, or do you see it differently?

MAUD: I so dig your reading of the narrative technique! I spent a lot of time thinking about the narration of *The Man Who Walked Away* and tinkering with it. Narration in general has been fascinating me lately—its essential questions of from what distance and from what angle can alter a narrative so enormously. In *The Man Who Walked Away,* it seemed important to have an omniscient narration, which steps back at the beginning and in those interstitial sections when people are seeing Albert from afar, and then could also zoom in and become very intimate with Albert and the Doctor. In the first section, I wanted to establish that pattern—a panoramic view and then intense interiority (Albert's) and then back out again. I'm a big believer in teaching the reader how to read a book, so setting that up right at the beginning felt essential. The passage you quote from comes in one of the hypnosis sections. I think it's pretty deep into the book. That the "dreaming together" is, at that point, mirrored in the form thrills me. It wasn't conscious, and I'm not sure I could have articulated it, but that it reads that way thrills me because my hope is that in the sections of hypnosis, there is exactly that, a blending of perspective with the Doctor and Albert. In other words, it's kind of a happy accident that grew out of an effort to modulate the omniscient narration's proximity to the characters. In sum, yay that it reads that way to you!

JASON: I love the idea of "teaching the reader how to read a book." So many of my favorite writers do this: Jane Austen, George Eliot, Henry James, Ralph Ellison, Kazuo Ishiguro, David Mitchell. In all of these cases, that teaching involves asking readers to adapt to narration and assume particular angles of consciousness. With Austen and James, that means always inhabiting multiple perspectives; with Ellison and Ishiguro, it means becoming comfortable with disorientation. In *The Man Who Walked Away,* you do both. But you offer another kind of reading lesson, too—one with high stakes—about how to understand both the history and current practice of psychiatric medicine.

I'm thinking of the scene in which the Doctor goes to see the great doctor perform hypnosis on the girl, whom he has diagnosed with hysteria. It all goes wrong when the photographer hired to document the girl's evolving states of consciousness stumbles, drops his camera, glass shattering on the stage. At that point, the girl steals the show—grabbing a straitjacket from the great doctor and insisting, "Buckle me in." It's a complicated moment, because she's seizing authority by demanding to be restrained. A straitjacket is, of course, a notorious symbol of psychiatric abuse, so her performance is ironic. Am I right in thinking you're asking readers to assume an ironic stance in relation to psychiatric medicine?

MAUD: I'm not sure it's an ironic stance so much as one that accounts for the needs and desires and flaws of the patients and the doctors, both. The effect may have some irony, though, as you're pointing out in that "Buckle me in" scene. It's funny. In an earlier draft, she said, "Zip me in," and then a friend read it and was like, the zipper wasn't invented yet. Thank you, close reader friend. Anyway, yeah, maybe some irony. My hope there, too, and throughout is to illuminate the desire of these patients to be cared for, held, buckled, whatever, to the extent that they learn the language of the medicine of the time. Ian Hacking talks about a "symptom pool," in which patients learn the symptoms of their particular era, their particular disease. I think this extends to treatment too. So, in that scene, the girl understands her role and the script as a means of finding relief of some kind. Also, as you point out, she's seizing his power and understands, whether consciously or not, the power (however relative) she has as the star of the amphitheater. She's terrified but she's also aware that she is expected to behave in a certain way, to perform. There's another moment in the book where she tells the Doctor to "get rid of the snake in your pants," which is kind of hilarious. It comes directly from the transcripts of Charcot's *The Tuesday Lessons*. I mean, obviously, it's not something he asked her to say. She's improvising, riffing, given the sexualized nature of the treatment of hysteria (all that ovarian adjustment and women draped in sheets being asked to writhe erotically and be photogenic).

JASON: These days, there's a lot of debate—some of it quite heated—about the terms and labels available for describing various neurological and mental conditions. Back in 1995, Kay Redfield Jamison voiced her strong preference for "manic depression," instead of the more clinical, and at that time politically safer, term "bipolar disorder." Twenty years later, the terminology wheel has spun again, and there's a groundswell of dissatisfaction with the word "disorder" in general. Some writers and activists have started to use the term "bipolar" as a noun, as in "the symptoms of bipolar are variable." Given your own eloquent (and elegant) descriptions of the inadequacies of diagnosis to describe the full personhood of any individual, or literary character, I'm wondering where you stand on these evolving debates about terms and labels. One of Jamison's points—for the record—is that "bipolar disorder" is misleading because it makes it seem as though mania and depression are two poles that never touch, when in fact, people with the diagnosis often experience them together. How much do these terms matter? Do you have preferences? Does the elegance of language matter, or does the goal of eliminating stigmatizing language trump aesthetics? Is it possible to find a term that will do justice to or offer an accurate description of the experience diagnoses are devised to describe?

MAUD: I'm going to start at the end and work back, or more likely meander. It's not possible to find a term that will ever completely describe the experience of what lies behind a diagnosis, because the varieties of experience—miraculously!—are infinite. So there's that. And then there are very practical matters, like categories for health insurance, and treatment, and other essential things that allow people to navigate the world and survive. Fortunately for me, and lucky for everyone seeking treatment, I'm a fiction writer not a psychiatrist, and my task as I see it is, to paraphrase something I once heard Seamus Heaney say: to make the intimate universal. I'd say the intimate and the inimitable. I'm avoiding the question, I know, and actually I seem to recall a reviewer of my novel *Genealogy*—in which there is a woman who has what one might deduce is manic depression or bipolar disorder, though it is never named—wonder why I didn't just name it. Not naming it was a deliberate choice, and like all the choices you make when writing a story, it had its risks and even its flaws; still, I didn't want the character to be burdened with the fraught weight of a diagnosis, which in fiction tends to have the effect of reducing rather than expanding. I'm always pro the latter. In *The Man Who Walked Away* my interest was, in part, to illustrate why a diagnosis is necessary but never sufficient. I'm of two, maybe three or four, minds in relation to fiddling with the terminology. Language is power. It means something and it can be wielded for good and for bad. It creates and orders the world as much as it describes it. So I get the dissatisfaction and the discontent. Dissatisfaction and discontent are a big part of why art gets made. I'm all for it! And yet I'm kind of with Jamison. "Manic depression" has always been my preference. Maybe because I like the Jimi Hendrix song, and maybe because there are times it seems as good a label as any other.

JASON: You recently gave a lecture at Weill Cornell Medical College's History of Psychiatry Seminar. In that lecture, you suggested that "creating a space for mystery in fiction requires a certain amount of *unmaking*." There are many mysteries in *The Man Who Walked Away*: Why does Albert walk? What does fugue feel like? Does it have an organic cause? What are the origins of consciousness? In terms of craft, what did *unmaking* mean for you when you wrote the novel—especially in terms of the history of psychiatry that the real-life Albert played a minor role in making?

MAUD: My favorite kind of fiction is all about the uns. Unmaking, undoing, unraveling, unknowing. Knowing less in order to see something anew. There are surface-level questions, which get answered, and then deeper questions, which don't ever really get answered but which allow the reader to think and feel on a more intuitive level. The tricky fine line, it seems to me, is to create seductive mystery as opposed to murky mystery. In terms of how you make that happen, it sometimes has to do with providing enough information but not too much. The question of why Albert walks—well, there's kind of an answer or, rather, there's a lot of information the Doctor gathers, so the reader can mull that stuff over. What does fugue feel like? There's where the deeper mystery kicks in. The music of a character is very different than the diagnosis of a person. The sound a character makes on the page should be strange and singular, so it all comes back to the language. Albert's song, his cellular grammar, is less of a question than an experience. That's my hope, at least.

6

Neurocomics and Neuroimaging

Overturning the age-old axiom that a picture is worth a thousand words,
perhaps these PET images require millions of words to be understood!
—Joseph Dumit, *Picturing Personhood*[1]

MATTEO FARINELLA AND HANA ROŠ'S *NEUROCOMIC* (2013) is a basic neuroscience lesson in the form of a comic, wrapped loosely in a fictional narrative. Farinella is an illustrator with a PhD in neuroscience, and Roš is a research associate in neuroscience and pharmacology at the University College, London. Together they have created a hybrid text of literary neuroscience—a graphic neurology fairy-tale primer. *Neurocomic*'s quest narrative couldn't be more explicit, linking a search for self directly with the protagonist's journey through the human brain. A generic man finds himself trapped in a book read by a generic woman who attracts him. Unlike most contemporary brain narratives, *Neurocomic* tells a representative story, not a particular one. Its protagonists are allegorical composites. Like Alice through her rabbit hole, a man falls through the book into what appears to be his own brain—or a composite one (fig. 2). He meets a series of guides—famous figures from the history of neurology, including Santiago Ramón y Cajal, Charles Sherrington, and Eric Kandel—who lead him through the bewildering and often terrifying "forest" of his own brain and finally into the "castle of our consciousness" (where he's reunited with the reading woman who initiated his ambivalent quest).[2]

But the generic man doesn't exactly find his *self* through the journey. Instead he discovers he's an object of representation, twice over. He's a character in a

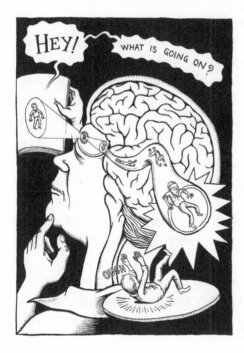

Fig. 2. From *Neurocomic* © Matteo Farinella and Hana Roš. Nobrow 2013.

book, made of pen strokes, panels, shapes, and words; and he's an animated being, made of bones, flesh, cells, electricity, chemicals, and proteins whose continuous interrelations would seem to create him—though, as in most literature inspired by neuroscience, it's not clear how his identity emerges from these interrelations. The making of self through the tools of artistic representation become a substitute for the more elusive making of self through physiology. In many ways, *Neurocomic* would appear to tell a simple—and even simplistic— story about a series of great men who made great discoveries in the history of brain research. But its frame-tale structure creates a more nuanced narrative, reminding readers that its facts are delivered through the tools of artistic representation.

When *Neurocomic*'s protagonist falls into the brain, readers see him tumbling into the explanatory gap. In addition to *Neurocomic,* a small number of graphic brain narratives published in recent years experiment with novel methods of visualizing the brain, most of which tell particular, even idiosyncratic stories about living with brains that complicate their authors' lives. In recent years, two renowned comic artists have published high-profile graphic brain narratives.

French comic artist David B.'s *Epileptic* (2006) tells the story of its author's family struggling to cope with his brother Jean-Christophe's epilepsy; American Ellen Forney's *Marbles: Mania, Depression, Michelangelo, and Me* (2012) tells the story of its author's evolving identity in response to a bipolar diagnosis. Whereas *Neurocomic* creates characters whose brains each become a vehicle for telling a story about the current state of neuroscientific knowledge, *Epileptic* and *Marbles* portray their characters' brains as part of an ensemble of images that define their search for what it means to suffer as a result of neurological conditions beyond their control. Like so many brain narratives, these books offer alternatives to "you are your brain" / "you are not your brain" debates. The interplay of image and text in these graphic narratives becomes an analogue to the inexorably unraveling binary between physiology and subjectivity.

Neurocomic's opening scenario and central conceit gives fictional form to a fantasy Dr. Michael E. Phelps, one of the key developers of the brain-scanning technology of positron emission tomography (PET), described in an interview with anthropologist Joseph Dumit:

> Your body looks like it is a physical, anatomical substance, but inside there are all kinds of cells that are metabolizing things, or moving around and doing things, signaling to each other. We'd like to be able to watch this action. That is the objective. You know the activity is there, and you'd like to build a camera that can watch it. Well, one way to do that is first to say, "Well, if I was really little, I could go in there, move around, and watch those things." But since you can't go in there, you can send a messenger. So you do that. . . . So you take a molecule that will go and participate in that portion. . . . This is really what PET does. It reveals to us something that we know is going on in your body, but that we can't get to.[3]

With *Neurocomic,* Farinella and Roš fulfill Phelps's impossible wish, creating a protagonist who shrinks, to become "really little," who can "go in there, move around, and watch" the "action" of his own brain. Farinella and Roš dramatize their protagonist's unwitting fulfillment of Phelps's explicit desire: to crawl around a living brain to see how it works.

The coincidence of these two narratives brings into focus a loose convergence among the sciences and the humanities as they circle the explanatory gap—and, in particular, the divergent tools they use to explore it. The two scenarios yoke two vastly different contemporary methods for visualizing the brain. Graphic narratives are a subcultural genre celebrated for their rebellious aesthetics and emphasis on narratives that challenge mainstream social and political assumptions. Brain-scanning technologies—including fMRI (functional magnetic resonance imaging), MRI (magnetic resonance imaging), PET (positron emission tomography), and SPECT (single photon emission computed tomography)—are highly specialized tools that have revolutionized brain research and gained considerable mainstream attention. The mainstreaming of brain-scanning technologies oversimplifies the images they produce, creating a widely held sense that they offer direct access to the brains they visualize. By contrast, graphic narratives put heavy emphasis on the aesthetic process involved in their making of images (and narratives) of brains. As cultural contributions to public perceptions of the brain's meaning, these two enterprises couldn't be more different in their methods or aims. While I don't intend to minimize these differences, I believe key similarities between these technologies of representing brains can be a means for clarifying the roles played by the sciences and the humanities in the cultural laboratory of contemporary neuromania.

A human cannot shrink to enter a brain, but a character in a comic can. In that sense, the representational tools of a comic enable what's not possible in life—as might happen in a dream. When they give visual form to Phelps's fantasy scenario, Farinella and Roš emphasize a host of disparities between comics and brain-scanning technologies—differences in aims, techniques, and cultural status. Their literary experiment involves play, irony, fantasy, and the breaking of boundaries. Scientific experiments involve observation, truth, and the boundaries of method. Graphic narratives blend fantasy and realism to tell particular stories about characters in a visual-verbal language. They are explicitly dream-like and speculative. Brain scans gather data by measuring the activity of gases and electricity and use complex algorithms to create images of neural activity. Graphic narratives aim to entertain, challenge, or inspire reflection. They can help people cope with or think about the meanings of brain-related experience. Brain scans aim to create statistical data about general brain function or visualize injuries, disease, or anomalies in individual brains. They can help save lives and improve health.

Nonetheless, Farinella and Roš's experiment also suggests some relations between literary and scientific experiment, which share the fundamental aims that motivate Phelps's fantasy: to know "something . . . we can't get to." The impetus for these very different enterprises is rooted in personal suffering, the mysteries of physiology, and the making of knowledge. Finally—and perhaps most obviously, though little discussed—they both require human practitioners. An fMRI image and a frame of a graphic narrative are both designed by people whose judgments shape their results and their meanings. As a form, neuro-comics remind readers that knowledge is made, not simply discovered. That's as true in the sciences as it is in the humanities, but too often scientific knowl-edge—and brain scans in particular—are circulated and received as transparent fact rather than the product of elaborately designed technology, methods, and interpretation.

As scholars in many disciplines have noted, brain scans appear—to the nonexpert—to speak for themselves; that is, to represent neural activity directly. Recently, Patricia Churchland has critiqued the "neurojunk" that proliferates when the claims of neuroscientific research are overstated or oversimplified.[4] Churchland's neurojunk can be understood as both an engine and product of neuromania. I propose that Churchland's neurojunk is the product of cultural forms of neuromania that obscure or erase the representational tools involved in the making of knowledge about the brain. The promises of that cultural neuromania will become more realistic and more productive if those of us involved can help each other develop language and rhetoric that emphasize the fundamental relations between the tools and the knowledge.

In the theoretical neurosciences, the brain is routinely described as a repre-sentational organ. "You are your synapses," writes Joseph LeDoux; the self is "a dynamic collection of integrated neural processes, centered on the represen-tation of the living body," writes Antonio Damasio.[5] LeDoux and Damasio disagree about quite a lot, but they agree that the brain works by representing the self—and the world—via patterns of cellular and intracellular interaction. Of course, neither of these leading neuroscientists can be sure about how the feeling of selfhood emerges from these patterns of representation. LeDoux believes the key to consciousness lies in the physiology of the cerebral cortex, and Damasio believes it lies in the evolutionarily older upper brain stem. They agree that either way it will involve the multiple interactions of many brain systems. While the debates continue and the research advances, the field of consciousness studies proceeds largely through two modes of investigating brain-self-world relations: the thought experiment and the brain scan. Both modes—perhaps we can call them genres—tend to obscure their representa-tional tools. Thought experiments about echolocating bats, color scientists locked in colorless rooms, or zombies are like fairy tales, too, but they are used to wage philosophical debates, and ultimately the positions they represent outshine the outlandish hypothetical stories they tell. Brain-scanning technologies represent brain activity through a complex process that involves the collection of data about the flow of chemicals, oxygen, or blood in the brain; the algorithmic representation of that data in visual forms; and the interpretation of the images by trained human experts.

I'm arguing that neurocomics visualize a particularly vivid version of an idea implicit in most brain memoirs and neuronovels: We need to find more effective means of communicating how knowledge about our brains is produced. We need rhetorical techniques that account for the epistemological gaps in research, the dynamic interplay of systems proposed by the theories (including physiological, environmental, and social ones), *and* the representational tools we use to develop those theories. We need rhetorical techniques with as much appeal as thought experiments and brain scans. If we develop these, we may redirect neuromania away from the production of neurojunk and toward ways of thinking about the epistemological and social implications of the idea that our biologies are, in the words of Rose and Abi-Rached, in "constant transaction" with our milieus.[6]

The Tools of Comics

Literary criticism of graphic narratives has exploded with the genre's growing popularity and circulation in the last decade. Its most influential critics emphasize the possibilities for representing fluid identity and experience made possible by the distinctive features of the genre, starting with the interplay of text and image, but also including the creation of visual voice, frames that contain meaning, disrupted frames that loosen it, and the gutters between pages that guide and pace the reading experience. Rocco Versaci argues that the interplay of text and image "reminds us at every turn (or panel) that what we are experiencing is a representation."[7] In their introduction to an influential 2006 issue of *Modern Fiction Studies,* Hillary Chute and Marianne DeKoven argue that graphic narrative "calls a reader's attention visually and spatially to the act, process, and duration of interpretation" because "it refuses a problematic transparency, through an explicit awareness of its own surfaces."[8] The hybrid form of graphic narrative enables modes of representation that bypass linear narrative. As Chute and DeKoven note, "the form's fundamental syntactical operation is the representation of time as space on the page." Following on this idea, they make several additional claims about the genre: (1) its hybridity is "a challenge to the structure of binary classification"; (2) it's "a mass cultural art," drawing on high and low art indexes; (3) it's multigeneric, composed, often ingeniously, from widely different genres and subgenres, and (4) its visual and verbal elements "do not merely synthesize" but can tug at or tussle with each other to create meaning of referents that can't be tamed by logical or linear structures.[9] For all of these reasons, graphic narratives tend to offer alternative or nonmainstream takes on the subjects they represent. Caroline Hong has observed that graphic narratives tend to "tell personal stories that are also profoundly collective." Hong argues that graphic narratives are ideally suited to representing Asian American identities, because "the form's unique interplay of words and images" enables narratives that account for the integral roles of culture, history, and particular (and varied) experience—through what comics theorist Scott McCloud calls the form's "silent dance between the seen and the unseen."[10] Collectively, these critics applaud the genre's capacity to represent multiple intersections of identity continuously in the process of becoming. Neurocomics, like so many graphic narratives, focus on the complexities of the self—both what's seen and unseen.

Forney offers a vivid example of her chosen form's capacity to transform ideas through images, with her depiction of a page from the *DSM* as a dream-like carousel, a pictorial metaphor designed to encompass her ambivalence about her bipolar diagnosis (fig. 3). Forney uses the carousel to parody the *DSM*'s linear list of bipolar symptoms. On her carousel, depression curls up under a pony; "mixed states" tears the pony in two, clinging to its upper torso and balancing precariously on its back; mania stands on the pony with a single foot, her head bumping against the merry-go-round's ceiling.[11] The carousel implies perpetual motion, representing time as space on the page; it revises the linearity of the *DSM*'s diagnostic criteria into a chaos of phenomenological mobility; it replaces the tome's serious, stigmatizing structure with a playful montage. In his critique of the *DSM,* Ian Hacking contends that "trying to get it right, in revision after revision, perpetuates the long-standing idea that, in our present state of knowledge, the recognized varieties of mental illness should neatly sort themselves out into tidy blocks, in the way that plants and animals do."[12] Ellen Forney resists the *DSM*'s "tidy blocks." Even her title emphasizes

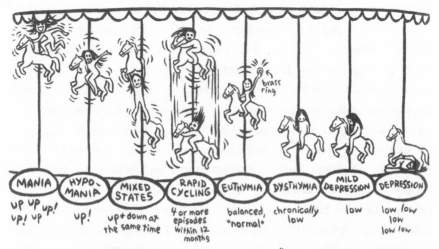

NOTE: "BIPOLAR DISORDER" + "MANIC DEPRESSION" ARE THE SAME THING.

Fig. 3. From *Marbles: Mania, Depression, Michelangelo, and Me: A Graphic Memoir* by Ellen Forney, copyright © 2012 by Ellen Forney. Used by permission of Gotham Books, an imprint of Penguin Publishing Group, a division of Penguin Random House LLC.

symptoms—mania and depression—rather than describing her *DSM* diagnosis: "*Bipolar I Disorder.*" She tells her story of coming to terms with the diagnosis in a chaos of graphic forms that seem designed to replace what Hacking calls "our present state of knowledge" with portraits of the phenomenology of mania and depression that are both playful and terrifying—a mixed emotional effect made possible by the illogic of her form's representational resources. The medium of the graphic narrative enables Forney to recontextualize the *DSM,* reclassifying it from that scary book that determines her identity as a mentally ill person into a malleable text whose context she can revise and adapt to find what she needs in it.

Forney is explicit about her urgent need for knowledge about the brain as well as her awareness that this knowledge can only be hypothetical and contingent. Like most authors of graphic narratives, she is as interested in how knowledge is made as she is in its contents. Her tools share a great deal with Freud's "dream work"—the four elements of dreaming that shape the relationship between a dream's content and its personal meanings. In *The Interpretation of Dreams* (1899), Freud names these elements condensation, displacement, representation, and secondary revision. When we dream, images, thoughts, and feelings "are whirled about, broken up, and pushed up against one another." Summarizing Freud in his introduction to a 1999 edition of the text, Ritchie Robertson observes, "The dream . . . excels at turning thoughts into pictures." Similarly, contemporary dream theorist Ernest Hartmann argues that dreams create "pictured metaphors" of waking concerns.[13] As in dreams, the pictorial emphasis of graphic narrative allows for condensation, projection, and a focus on the materiality of representation. Of course, Freud is a polarizing figure, but contemporary neuroscience is in the process of shedding its behaviorist history. During the twentieth century, psychoanalysis and behaviorist psychology became incompatible disciplines—competing for the job of explaining human behavior. Graphic narratives and neuroscience are not in competition; rather, they have the opportunity to complement each other, to fill in each other's gaps. The contiguities between the tools of graphic narrative and Freud's dreaming mind enable representation of aspects of identity that are difficult to see or feel, much less measure.

A person dreaming has no need for the logical cognition of waking life. Freud asks, "[W]hat has become of the bonds of logic which had previously given the structure its form? What kinds of representation does the dream give to 'when,' 'because,' 'just as,' 'although,' 'either-or,' and all the other relational terms without which we can understand neither sentence nor speech?" Freud exaggerates when he answers that "the dream has no means . . . of representing these logical relations." Ritchie Robertson explains that, through condensation, "dream-elements are fused." People, images, or ideas are condensed in a single image or thought; displacement involves "transferring the emotional intensity from the centre of the dream-thought to its marginal components"; a dream's "representational resources" enable its illogical or bizarre qualities; and secondary revision "censors the exuberance of the dream, reassures the dreamer by introducing thoughts like 'It's only a dream,' and fills in gaps in the dream's structure to make it more logical and coherent."[14] It would make little sense to reduce the tools of comics to these four elements, but varieties of them are integral to the work of graphic memoirists, whose representational tools, like those of dreams, blend the ordinary and the fantastic; condense apparently incongruous images, ideas, and feelings; frame emotional intensity in stylized forms; engage in forms of "secondary revision" that remind readers that a dream is an act of representation; and drag their fantastical elements back into ordinary settings governed by logic and realism.

Fig. 4. English translation: "They perform gaseous encephalograms on him. They shoot gas into his brain to inflate it so they can take photos in which they hope to find traces of a lesion or tumor. When my parents tell me about it, I visualize my brother in the clutches of mad scientists." From *L'Ascension du Haut Mal* by David B., © 1996, David B. and L'Association.

Both *Neurocomic* and *Epileptic* gesture toward a relationship between neuroimaging and the visualization of brains in comics. They don't duplicate or represent brain scans. Instead, they recast them in a visual language belonging to a long tradition of comic-book representations that resemble dreams, or nightmares, more than reality—for example, exposed brains or brains with agency who become characters (usually villains). In *Epileptic* (which Hillary Chute calls "the most famous of graphic illness narratives"[15]), Jean-Christophe undergoes gaseous encephalography, now an outdated and little used technology that replaces cerebrospinal fluid with gases in order to produce radiographic images (fig. 4). In his account, David B. is explicit here about the mediation of the image he presents for readers. His parents recount the scene of doctors who "shoot gas" into Jean-Christophe's brain "to inflate it so they can take photos in which they hope to find traces of a lesion or tumor." His knowledge about his brother's experience—and his brain—is filtered through the hope of the doctors and his parents. The doctors' knowledge is based on a complex process of representation using gas to produce images.

As Chute argues, *Epileptic* "is a deeply stylized text" that "signals itself as an imaginative reconstruction of the past on every page."[16] In this case, the reconstruction is a terrifying fantasy about encephalography. The adult David B., artist and author, portrays his childhood fantasy using stylistic features that appear throughout the memoir: the steampunk technology, the tiny doctors probing Jean-Christophe's outsized skull, the blank expression on his face, the snakelike tubes that recall the serpent of his epilepsy. If the doctors find a lesion or tumor, surgery might be able to help Jean-Christophe. But they don't. The brain scan becomes one more attempt in a long series of them to find a solution to explain or eliminate Jean-Christophe's seizures. David B. is careful to cue readers to notice the mediation of the image he presents, mediation that reflects the epistemological failures of his family's quest to save his brother. The hope created by each possible cure or treatment—most of them based on false certainties—is destroying the family. As a writer and comics artist, he works in a medium that proliferates uncertainty. Even his identity is in question. David B. is a pseudonym. As a character in his memoir the adult David B. and the child Pierre-François, his given name, are sometimes fused and sometimes distinct. If the memoir has a thesis, it's that he and his family need to find ways to live with this uncertainty.

By comparison, the stakes of *Neurocomic* are more academic, less personal and visceral, but equally focused on foregrounding its representational resources—and those of the neuroscience it portrays. When Farinella and Roš explain the synapse—one of neuroscience's most basic concepts—they do it almost as a parody of conventional textbook illustrations (fig. 5). Even the language Farinella and Roš use to explain the image closely resembles the language of textbooks: "Synaptic transmission has two great advantages: The first is that the same signal can have different meanings depending on the combination of molecules and receptors present in the synapse."[17] Synapses make meanings—multiple and mutable ones. Their representational resources are designed to create flexibility, to make meaning in fluid and unpredictable ways. This is a routine observation in basic neuroscience, but not one whose implications receive much attention. Whereas a conventional textbook elides the condensation of meaning in both the process of synaptic transmission and its own representation of that process, *Neurocomic* emphasizes both: A synapse is a gap, or cleft, between two cells; its meaning is composed of parts, like the triangle and square that make a house when you combine them; the generation of meaning is like the generation of life, drawn to resemble sperm cells; the process is embodied and mobile, an idea hinted at by the jointlike depiction of the pre- and post-synaptic neurons; its meanings become functional in the context of a brain's electrical oscillations, or brainwaves, hinted at by the wavy

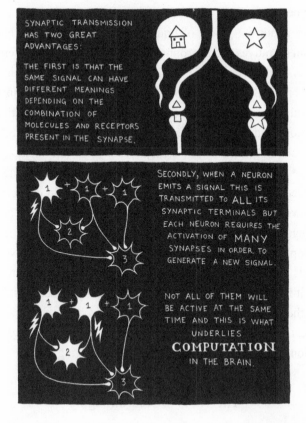

Fig. 5. From *Neurocomic* © Matteo Farinella and Hana Roš. Nobrow 2013.

tales of those spermlike thought bubbles. The graphic representation of the synapse proliferates its meanings. Farinella and Roš represent axons and dendrites like bones, the neurotransmitters as simple shapes (stars, squares, triangles), and the resulting signals in spermlike thought bubbles. The representational resources of the comic—like Freud's dreams—almost demand the condensation of multiple meanings in a single image. A nerve cell is a bone, a neural signal a sperm cell. But such proliferation of meaning isn't unique to comics or unheard of in neuroscience. The most conventional of textbooks describe a synapse as a gap or cleft, metaphorical language that involves similar condensation of meaning.

By emphasizing the representational tools of the comic as genre, *Neurocomic* suggests that synaptic gaps—or clefts—are like the gutter in a comic book or the distance between neural correlates and qualia. Gaps like these are central to controversies about the power of brain imaging to explain the human mind. Graphic brain narratives and neuroimaging could not be more different in terms of their goals or the technologies and strategies involved in their representations of the brain. But they are both technologies for creating images of the brain, and both types of image make claims on understanding relations between brain physiology and selfhood. The pervasive circulation of PET, SPECT, MRI, and fMRI technologies has been a major catalyst in the making of cultural neuromania.[18] By comparison, graphic brain narratives are a niche form, their cultural influence not nearly so strong or visible. The brain imagery in graphic narratives owes as much to science fiction films and comics as it does to neuroimaging. Its unique representational tools enable it to meld its sources in ways that emphasize the cultural mixing of very different media. Neuroimaging technology is more complex, more precise, and more targeted in terms of its goals—but it involves a set of representational tools nonetheless. It's possible to interpret the more playful representational forms of graphic brain narratives as a provocation, demanding more attention to the myriad questions about representation that are seldom asked about neuroimaging.

The Tools of Neuroimaging

Brain-imaging techniques are driving forces in widespread cultural neuromania. In popular culture, they tend to be described as direct images of brains at work, rather than images of brains created through a complex process of measurement, statistical analysis, and computer-aided representations. As neurobiologist Susan M. Fitzpatrick explains, "the brain images displayed in scientific publications and in the popular media are not representations of changes in brain neuronal activity, or areas of 'activation,' or the brain 'lighting up' or 'switching on.' Brain scans acquired with fMRI do not even graphically depict the magnitude of the BOLD [blood oxygen level dependent] signal. Rather, the images are computer-generated, color-coded 'maps' of statistically significant comparisons among data sets."[19] Concrete examples of the oversimplifications Fitzpatrick laments are plentiful, and they come in a variety of forms. Many of these are well-intended translations of medical jargon designed to provide readers with accessible shorthand, though it's difficult to dismiss the dramatic effects created by the shorthand. For example, in her biography of famous neurology patient H. M., Suzanne Corkin makes a dramatic shorthand claim: "Using MRI scans, we could look through Henry's scalp and skull to see his brain."[20] Corkin is aiming to create a feeling of intimacy with her subject. Looking through his scalp to see his brain, as a character in a comic book might be able to, adds a physical dimension to that intimacy. In general, the apparent motives of such translations are more neutral, as with Cornell University's website advertising its MRI facilities: "Neuroscientist Valerie Reyna compares functional MRI—an imaging technique that allows researchers to see the brain in action—to the microscopes and telescopes that allow scientists to peer into cells and the cosmos to explore the mysteries of life. For the first time on Cornell's Ithaca campus, she and fellow researchers can observe how the brain fires when we think and react and compare how such activity differs among age groups and populations. Such work promises to bring into focus what was once out of sight—the hidden factors that drive human behavior."[21] Again, the writer eschews a detailed description of the technology's representational resources, describing instead a fantastical version that, again, resembles a comic book scenario: researchers "see the brain in action," revealing "hidden factors that drive human behavior." Those hidden factors—what we don't know about ourselves—appear fairly routinely in writing that makes promises about the powers of brain-imaging technologies. In his book *Affective Neuroscience,* Jaak Panksepp offers a more accurate description that nonetheless is likely to be read in the tradition of rhetorical oversimplification: "During the past decade, remarkable progress has been made in our ability to visualize what is going on inside the living human brain."[22] The word "visualize"—as opposed to "see"— presupposes an acknowledgment of the complex representational resources entailed in brain imaging, akin to the speculative practices of literary narratives that envision or reenvision possible realities. But it's a subtle presupposition, one readers accustomed to broader and more dramatic claims are likely to miss without more explicit rhetorical cues and detailed explanations of those resources.

While scholars from multiple disciplines have made a clear-cut case that brain imaging does not provide direct access to brains, popular publications, neuro-self-help programs, and even published scientific papers promise— continuously and emphatically—that they do just that. As Dumit argues, this elision of technological complexity is bound up with assumptions about human behavior and identity: "Brain-imaging technologies like PET offer researchers the potential to ask a question about almost any aspect of human nature, human behavior, or human kinds and design an experiment to look for the answer in the brain. Each piece of experimental design, data generation, and data analysis, however, necessarily builds in assumptions about human nature, about how the brain works, and how person and brain are related. No researcher denies this. In fact, they constantly discuss assumptions as obstacles to be overcome as trade-offs between specificity and generalization."[23] That trade-off between specificity and generalization is both rhetorical and methodological. Too much specialization means a smaller audience, but it also leads to more circumscribed conclusions. The potential Dumit describes is exciting, and it makes perfect sense that researchers and practitioners are interested in making the most of it. As he observes, they are well aware of the complexities involved. If the general public is not aware, it's because so much of the rhetoric about brain imaging involves misleading translations of specific research designs for the sake of emphasizing the dramatic potential of the technology.

Academic examinations of the representational tools of brain-scanning technologies are plentiful. These studies reveal and explicate the varieties of mediation involved in making meaning, but they aren't widely read. As Bunge and Kahn observe, fMRI and PET belong to a "class" of neuroimaging techniques that "consists of methods for indirectly measuring neuronal activity, which operate under the principle that neural activity is supported by increased local blood flow and metabolic activity."[24] A brain scan's relation to an actual brain or a composite one involves a great deal of expert construction and interpretation, a fact whose complexities have been well documented by scholars in a variety of disciplines. For example, Alač and Hutchins observe an expert reader of fMRI scans teaching a novice, detailing "how scientists use such semiotic resources as gesture, language, and material structure" in order to argue that such images are by no means transparent but require active constructions in order to become legible. Dumit's *Picturing Personhood* is an ethnographic study of experimental PET research and cultural responses to images produced in the process; Fitzpatrick's "Functional Brain Imaging: Neuro-Turn or Wrong Turn?" offers a detailed explanation of the methodologies involved in producing PET and BOLD fMRI scans, with an emphasis on "what neuroimaging can and cannot reveal about the mind." Hayles's "Brain Imaging and the Epistemology of Vision: Daniel Suarez's *Daemon* and *Freedom*" analyzes the influence of fMRI scans on the work of novelist Daniel Suarez as a case study in the popular circulation of ideas in response to the ubiquity of neuroimaging. Johnson's "'How Do You Know Unless You Look?': Brain Imaging, Biopower, and Practical Neuroscience" examines the representation of SPECT (single photon emission computed tomography) scans "presented as visual evidence that is highly legible even to an untrained audience" in the neuro-self-help books by Daniel Amen. McCabe and Castel's "Seeing Is Believing: The Effect of Brain Images on Judgments of Scientific Reasoning" reports on empirical research documenting the "persuasive power" of brain images among nonexpert readers of fabricated news articles on various topics in cognitive psychology.[25]

The complex technologies and methodologies that translate data into images are not news to scientists, but as these scholars observe, the popular circulation of these images tends to occlude their representational complexities. As Johnson observes, "The complex averaging procedures and statistical work that go into producing such images are lost in the neat, simple-looking images presented for the readers' consumption and interpretation."[26] In other words, the image of a brain scan is a fabrication of a complex process that requires enormous expertise both to create and to interpret, but the vivid and colorful results seem to present transparent meaning to nonexperts—a fact exacerbated by a tendency in science journalism, popular neurological texts, and even textbooks to bypass the technical details involved in their production. The meaning of brain scans suggests serious implications, both medically and philosophically. As Dumit observes, "These brain images make claims on us because they portray *kinds* of brains. As people with obviously one or another kind of brain, we are placed among the categories that the set of images offers. To which category do I belong? What brain type do I have? Or more nervously: Am I normal? Addressing such claims requires an ability to critically analyze how these brain images come to be taken as facts about the world."[27] Brain scans portray serious knowledge whose representational complexities are often occluded. In the process, kinds of brains become stand-ins for actual brains and the people who live with them.

Medical anthropologist Rayna Rapp is interested in reuniting brain scans with the people whose brains are scanned—and those who scan them. She offers a concrete, evenhanded account of the stakes of fMRI research and its mediation in her article "A Child Surrounds This Brain: The Future of Neurological Difference According to Scientists, Parents and Diagnosed Young Adults"—an account of her ethnographic work with L-CAN (the Laboratory for Child and

Adult Neuroscience) in New York City. L-CAN is well known for its research on ADHD, but it also conducts studies on autism, Tourette's, and dyslexia. Observing relationships among the lab's staff, parents, and children who are research subjects, Rapp observes that the images produced by fMRI acquire enormous social power. "If the somatic truth of a child's school problems is lodged in specific brain regions and dysfunctional connections," she writes, "the materiality of the condition can be dislodged from putative parental shortcomings, enabling a partner or teacher to accept childhood differences with potentially less frustration and more compassion. The future of brain studies may thus seem comforting to some parents." As Rapp argues, neuroimaging offers physiological evidence that may counter social stigma. However, as she notes, the researchers with whom she works consistently acknowledge the mediation of the technologies involved, which precludes any direct cause-effect relationships between physiology and behavior. L-CAN's research focuses on a "dispersed view of how children's brains actually function." Yet, as the lab's director tells Rapp, "The one consistent thing about ADHD is that it's inconsistent." As Rapp notes, "no matter how I framed the question, not one member of the scanning staff ever pointed to significant direct brain-to-behaviour differences beyond those of age."[28] This doesn't indicate a flaw in the research, which is in its early stages and designed by practitioners whose disciplinary sophistication makes them comfortable with a scientific process that involves hypothetical knowledge whose applications may be imagined not predicted. Yet the disparity between apparent social stakes and scientific meanings of the images produced is one of many examples of the misconceptions created by the cultural circulation of brain scans.

Researchers like those at L-CAN are after statistics, rather than insight about individual brains. For that reason, the lab "has taken the lead in establishing an international consortium where brain images and the databases that accompany them can be uploaded and analyzed across at least four continents. There may not, for example, be enough left-handed children of both sexes between 6 and 10 with an autism diagnosis who can be recruited to a specific study in lower Manhattan—but when compared to databases derived from similar subjects enrolled in Europe, Latin America, and Japan, findings may well become statistically robust." Rapp argues that "social collaborations aim to harmonise research strategies," but that the process involves smoothing out the differences across the lumpiness of laboratory life in its diverse national contexts." The "lumpiness" Rapp describes takes many forms: methodological differences, variations in subject populations (sometimes documented, sometimes not), the mood or ambience of laboratories, or social and cultural factors that shape both research practices and subject responses to a given study's methods. Rapp argues that the promise of brain research represents an "existential gap." By her account, neuroscientists, clinicians, research subjects, patients, and their families have come to conceive neurodiversity "as a polysemic metaphor for the acceptance of human difference lodged in the physiological brain."[29] Metaphor proliferates when the complex mediation of brain-scanning technologies circulates in forms that simulate direct correlations between the images they produce and human experience or behavior. Brain scans become metaphors for actual brain matter and for the subjective experiences they appear to describe—or even produce. Of course, graphic narratives excel at representing polysemic metaphors. Their job, in the age of the brain scan, is to represent the child, or person, who surrounds the brain, lumpiness and all.

N. Katherine Hayles articulates something like a critical consensus when it comes to the lack of attention to the representational tools of brain-scanning technologies in popular—and many specialized—accounts of their results: "The point is that interpretations of brain scans require careful consideration of the experimental design, knowledge of previous research linking behavior and regional brain activity, accuracy of the statistical analysis, and so forth. While the images themselves may appear seductively transparent, non-experts and even research professionals who have not read the original article should be very cautious about deciding what the images actually show."[30] Transparency is seductive, as Hayles argues, but it's also illusory. Like literary texts, brain scans require context and interpretation in order to be useful.

Of course the same is true of graphic narratives. When they call attention to their representation tools—ink strokes, interplay of words and images, frames, gutters—they do it to encourage attentive interpretation. The authors of graphic novels render psychological experience in physical forms whose narratives are sutured with words. The juxtaposition of words and images reminds readers that representation is never transparent. Words and images translate or distort experience. When the narrative in question focuses on neurological experience, this emphasis on the representational resources of the artists becomes a vehicle for the elusiveness of the explanatory gap between physiology and subjectivity. That same explanatory gap is at play in neuroimaging, but too often it is bypassed when the meaning of brain scans appear—or are presented or received as—transparent. It's my contention that learning to read graphic brain narratives can be helpful in demystifying the representational qualities of neuroimaging, and that understanding the techniques and methods through which brain scans are created and interpreted can deepen a reader's understanding of graphic brain narratives.

A Person Surrounds This Brain

As a thought experiment, examine an early image from *Neurocomic,* a rendering of the human nervous system (fig. 6). Imagine the central figure isolated in negative space—minus the bird, sun, flower, and thorns, or the sensory words that accompany them. You would see a human organism, with a schematic version of its brain and nervous system made visible (presumably through medical imaging technologies). At best, the figure would appear clinical; at worst, monstrous. In either case, it would feel uncanny. The text at the top of the page is narration, offered by one of the protagonist's first guides, Santiago Ramón y Cajal, the 1906 Nobel Laureate famous for his detailed drawings of neurons emphasizing their treelike structure, and proponent of the once controversial idea that brain matter is composed of distinct (rather than fused) cells we now call neurons. Ramón y Cajal explains to the tiny protagonist, "It all begins and ends with neurons: From your sensory receptors to the nerves that control your muscles. Everything you feel, remember or dream is written in those cells."[31]

Like all thought experiments, the exercise I just asked you to consider replaces real-world complexity with a hypothetical scenario. The image on the page represents a human being in the fullness of experience—thinking, feeling, sensing. This human is represented as an organism, stripping away the barriers of flesh, bone, and hair to reveal the organs that enable life. Other elements in the image create a montage—a very different kind of representation—that seems to contradict Ramón y Cajal's exposition. As Scott McCloud explains in *Understanding Comics,* a montage creates an image "where words are treated as integral parts of the picture."[32] Farinella and Roš create tension between text and image through what McCloud calls the "interdependent" combination, "where words and pictures go hand in hand to convey an idea that neither could convey alone."[33] The image adds motion, context, and feeling to the text. Text and image create tension: The words "all" and "everything"—standing in here

IT ALL BEGINS AND ENDS WITH NEURONS : FROM YOUR
SENSORY RECEPTORS TO THE NERVES THAT CONTROL YOUR
MUSCLES. EVERYTHING YOU FEEL, REMEMBER OR DREAM
IS WRITTEN IN THESE CELLS.

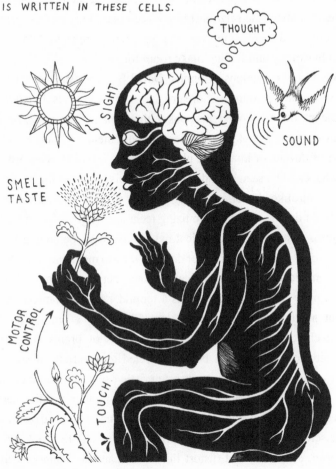

Fig. 6. From *Neurocomic* © Matteo Farinella and Hana Roš. Nobrow 2013.

for the fullness of experience—are misleading. A thorny thistle provides the
content of touch and gives it meaning that's only possible through interconnections with other senses, with feelings, with memories: *Don't touch this plant.*
The same is true for the sight of the sun, the sound of a bird, or the smell of a
flower. The montage of words and objects surrounding the figure gives visual
form to the experience correlated with those neurons. The resulting meaning is
akin to Damasio's argument that the objects of perception are integral to the

making of consciousness, or feeling. Of course, tensions between text and image are central to all graphic narratives. I argue that authors of neurocomics adapt these tensions for a particular purpose, making them stand-ins for unresolved debates about the relationship between neurology and experience. The contradictions and competing ideas that proliferate from the explanatory gap between physiology and feeling make room for stories.

With his visual depictions of brains, David B. emphasizes overlap between the representational resources of dreams and comics. Comics, like dreams, give form to the impossible. I open this book with an image from *Epileptic* that visualizes David's fantasy that a neuroscientist could meld his brain with his brother's—one of dozens of images of physical brains David B. uses, ironically, to portray what can't be seen or understood about his brother's illness. In a related image, two birdlike doctors climbing ladders to peer into Jean-Christophe's exposed brain demonstrates his ironizing technique (fig. 7). The doctors' semi-human forms cast them as fantastical hybrid creatures, belonging more to the representational world of comics (or dreams) than to medicine. The ladders give physical form to the epistemological distance between them and a cure for Jean-Christophe. The exposed brain is a reminder that in comics, you can see just about anything. In life, seeing Jean-Christophe's brain would require invasive techniques. David B. alternates images of brains with images of Jean-Christophe's skull as it's being subjected to a variety of such invasive techniques—generally figured as retro-futuristic canisters and tubes (figs. 8, 9, and 10). In a typical example, Jean-Christophe's mother steadies herself atop her son's skull, while his doctors look on from a distance, poised on the head and tail of the serpent that represents his epilepsy throughout the book. Images like this collapse, condense, and distort time and space, a common technique in comics. The invasive technology belongs to a brutal history of medical experiments and to a future imagined by Jean-Christophe's doctors, one that involves the successful applications of their theoretical cures. The patient's skull, and therefore his brain, is outsized, larger than most of the other human bodies in the frame. Of course, this represents the size (or severity) of the problem, but it also represents that same epistemological distance between theoretical cures and successful applications.

In other frames, David B. represents his own brain. "Unbeknownst to me," he writes, "this flood of absurdities takes root in my brain. Images are born."[34] He depicts himself in exaggerated anatomical terms, entwined with the serpent of his brother's epilepsy. He exposes his brain using the same visual language he uses to depict his brother's, and crude lightning bolts represent what's "unbeknownst." His brother's seizures are visible to the family but knowable to Jean-Christophe only through the symptoms that precede their onset and the effects that linger as he recovers consciousness. In frames like this one, David B. develops the idea that his vocation—as storyteller—involves an analogous form of unconscious cognition. He is gripped and shaped by his brother's seizures, which become the subject of his narratives. In another set of panels, David B. represents his frustrated agency in relation to his brother's suffering— but in fantastical terms that undermine it. "I'd been dreaming," he writes, "of saving my . . . brother."[35] His portrayal of the dreams casts him in the role of the mad scientists who experiment on his brother. He wields their steampunk technologies: their tubes, drawn as extensions of his own arms, become his route into his brother's brain—but also his experience.

Like David B., Ellen Forney represents the mind in physical terms in *Marbles,* her memoir about learning to live with mania and depression. In her title, Forney repurposes a common pictorial metaphor, one that's only used when said marbles are *lost,* when something seems to go wrong with a person's mind. The image on the upper panel sets a complex affective tone, a flying crown and confetti substituting for marbles, apparently radiating from her forehead, up through the crown of her skull, and into the air (fig. 11). The text in the montage—"POP!"—is like the "POW!" of children's comics. It indicates the completion of unseen physical action. It's a common convention in comics to depict figures about to punch each other, while the text or context lets us know they've followed through. The confetti, crown, and general cartoonishness imply something like a party, but Forney's self-portrait reads more like a hangover. The text frames the image on three sides, but is pushed toward the margins of the page, like footnotes or captions. "It occurred to me," Forney writes," that a sense of electrical current was part of my own experience of being manic." Forney describes "the sensation that my mind was spinning & overheating," a feeling that "would sometimes build to a sensation like an electrical short—a burst of light, a melting, or dissipating."[36] In this case, text and image complement each other; the affective ambiguity of the image is framed by explanatory text that fleshes out Forney's representation of her phenomenology, her sense that mania gives physical form to her immaterial mind. But the lower panel complicates her portrayal. Forney's skeptical friend creates a new context for

Fig. 7. English translation: "The doctor who's treating him is stymied by my brother's epilepsy. He prescribes a new experimental therapy." From *L'Ascension du Haut Mal* by David B., © 2000, David B. and L'Association.

Fig. 8. English translation: "In her mind, this sends us all back to square one. She has a vision of her son in the hospital, with his head shaved. It's as if she's being pulled backward. She reminds herself that Master N. is no longer there." From *L'Ascension du Haut Mal* by David B., © 1997, David B. and L'Association.

Fig. 9. English translation: "Unbeknownst to me, this flood of absurdities takes root in my brain. Images are born." From *L'Ascension du Haut Mal* by David B., © 1998, David B. and L'Association.

Fig. 10. English translation: "It's odd how my mother and I have the same dreams. I'd been dreaming of saving my grandfather and my brother." From *L'Ascension du Haut Mal* by David B., © 1999, David B. and L'Association.

Fig. 11. From *Marbles: Mania, Depression, Michelangelo, and Me: A Graphic Memoir* by Ellen Forney, copyright © 2012 by Ellen Forney. Used by permission of Gotham Books, an imprint of Penguin Publishing Group, a division of Penguin Random House LLC.

her celebration of her electrified mind. The relation between the panels condenses affective and temporal experience. Forney is the bursting, dancing woman who delights in magical thinking and the woman whose worried friend reminds her of the more skeptical strains of her identity. Courtney Donovan, a critical geographer whose research focuses on health and disease, argues that "Forney offers insight through her body into the process of diagnosing and managing her illness," a process that foregrounds "her changing mood and its interplay with her body."[37] Language enables Forney to be explicit about diagnosis and the management of symptoms, while she uses her visual voice—drawing her body, her feelings, and circumstances with visual cues that indicate changing moods whose subtleties or semiconscious qualities elude language.

As a graphic memoirist, Forney can visualize all these qualities of affective experience through images that encompass the neural underpinnings and cultural construction of her feelings. The image of Forney's popping head dominates the panel, as if to represent the persistence and all-encompassing power of mania. But the horizontal panel at the bottom seems to represent mania's aftermath. Forney acquires a body—a guarded one—and a friend, who asks her, ironically, "If you put a light bulb in your mouth, would it light up?" Forney's character answers, "No, it's a little more subtle than that." But she hasn't depicted it as particularly subtle. She's asked us to imagine feelings so physical that they suggest—almost—that her body is so electric it might fuel a light bulb. With mania comes belief and confidence. With depression comes humility and doubt. The two states are analogous to the push-pull between neuromania, with its epistemological optimism, and neuro-skepticism, with its countervailing reminders of epistemological limits.

Even while they revel in their dreamlike capacity to revise and reinvent, graphic narratives also tend to emphasize the pedagogical power of the visual. While these particular graphic narratives are explicit about their pedagogical aims, which range from countering stigmas associated with mental illness to tracing the history of neurology, they do not offer easy educations. The quality they share is mixing words and images—as well as characteristics of genre—to forestall the resolution of the explanatory gap. In the words of Farinella and Roš, "Finding a biological explanation for the mind is really the hardest challenge of neuroscience" (fig. 12).[38] Of course, a work of literature isn't going to resolve neuroscience's most difficult challenges. Toward the ends of the neurocomics I've been discussing, they offer an alternative to resolution: increasing

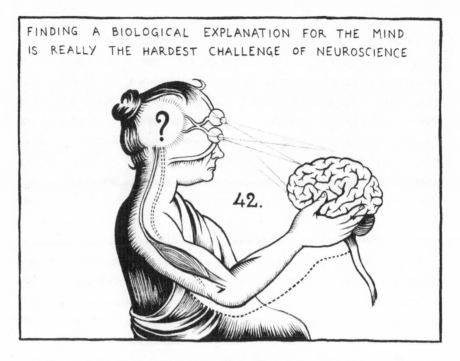

Fig. 12. From *Neurocomic* © Matteo Farinella and Hana Roš. Nobrow 2013.

attention to their identities as writers and artists. In *Epileptic,* for example, David B. describes his writing as a series of "electrical discharges" in his brain, "like explosions" or "tiny epileptic seizures" (fig. 13). He portrays a fantasy of severing his own head with macabre irony, likening himself visually to Hamlet holding Yorick's skull (fig. 14). He imagines he could bleed feelings: "It would all come out at last! The anxiety, the fear, the justice, the rage." But he revises the fantasy—and reattaches his head—within a few frames (fig. 15). "It's just another way of telling stories. . . . I've read many stories that have helped me. I want to touch people with my books in return."[39] The fantasy is a personal response to the explanatory gap. Like so many theoretical accounts, it imagines that physiology and feeling are identical, and like these accounts, it undoes itself. But in this case, the undoing directs readers' attention to the tools of representation. In place of his morbid fantasy, David B. offers a revision on the fantasy of finding the immaterial in the material—that his art might *touch* other people, that the materials of his books will touch readers via their immaterial responses to it.

Fig. 13. English translation, middle row, left panel: "It'd be wonderful to let myself go."
Middle panel: "I could pretend to be an epileptic. I could imitate a seizure. I know
how." Right panel: "Anyway, I am an epileptic. These electrical discharges in my brain,
like explosions, that's what they are! They're tiny epileptic seizures!" From *L'Ascension
du Haut Mal* by David B., © 2003, David B. and L'Association.

Fig. 14. English translation, left panel: "I want to spill all the blood in my body." Middle panel: "It would all come out at last! The anxiety, the fear, the justice, the rage." Right panel: "Then I could sleep to my heart's content." From *L'Ascension du Haut Mal* by David B., © 2003, David B. and L'Association.

Fig. 15. English translation, left panel: "It's just another way of telling stories. You can't help yourself. Middle panel: "It's a way of conjuring unhappiness. It's magic." Right panel: "I've read many stories that have helped me. I want to touch people with my books in return." From *L'Ascension du Haut Mal* by David B., © 2003, David B. and L'Association.

Early in *Marbles,* Forney portrays herself in the position of a reader much like the ones David B. imagines. At her therapist's suggestion, she reads Kay Redfield Jamison's memoir *An Unquiet Mind,* probably the most influential memoir about manic depression (fig. 16). As she reads, her brain buzzes with

Fig. 16. From *Marbles: Mania, Depression, Michelangelo, and Me: A Graphic Memoir* by Ellen Forney, copyright © 2012 by Ellen Forney. Used by permission of Gotham Books, an imprint of Penguin Publishing Group, a division of Penguin Random House LLC.

manic electricity, but she tells us, "I dismissed her story as not pertaining to me at all."[40] Toward the end of her own book, though, she returns to a quest initiated by her reading. Skeptical, she returns to Jamison—in particular a running theme in *An Unquiet Mind,* the relationship between mania and creativity (fig. 17). Forney, not quite convinced, turns Jamison's supposition into a question: "Are bipolar disorder and creativity actually linked?"[41] She maps her reading onto a cartoon brain, inscribing cognitive activities onto its flat surface.

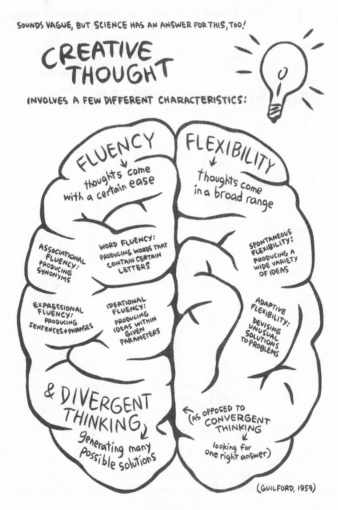

Fig. 17. From *Marbles: Mania, Depression, Michelangelo, and Me: A Graphic Memoir* by Ellen Forney, copyright © 2012 by Ellen Forney. Used by permission of Gotham Books, an imprint of Penguin Publishing Group, a division of Penguin Random House LLC.

Despite the irony, Forney becomes less dismissive of Jamison's optimism about creativity and manic depression. The cognitive components of the creative brain she diagrammed—fluency, flexibility, association, divergent thinking, and spontaneity—might just as easily describe her chosen genre, which enables her to represent the flux and range of her identity.

Questions about the relationship between her physical brain and her buzzing mind lead her to a portrait of her bipolar self on facing pages—emphasizing relations between experience and physiology (fig. 18). On these pages, Forney represents herself as the person surrounding the cartoonlike, schematic brain she's been probing for signs that her mental illness is in fact a source of creative genius, as Jamison claims it may have been for Michelangelo, Van Gogh, and O'Keeffe. Both pages remove frames from around human figures, taking them outside time and space, and put the text into frames and speech bubbles, a strategy Forney uses to indicate stable, or rational, thinking. The frameless, floating figures indicate both a collapsing and a condensing of time and space, performing a representation of Forney across time and in various spaces. Four floating figures dominate the left page: Forney, with a tear on her face, writing in a journal to document her moods, at a desk whose surface looks like water; her therapist, Karen, holding a box of tissues; a friend who's a recurring figure of support throughout the novel; and a composite head that is a tool for diagramming Forney's brain in its current state. As a whole, the spread emphasizes a combination of cognitive behavioral strategies, drug treatments, therapies, work, and social relationships—a holistic representation of Forney's commitment to tame her mania and depression, without any expectation or desire to eliminate them. The composite brain figure at the bottom of the panel is a visual schematic of the contents of Forney's journal, which is blank apart from the words "Keep track." She uses circles, arrows, and boxes to demonstrate relationships between moods and behaviors, and connects them with lines to the figure's bean-shaped brain, but—significantly—not to brain regions represented with any particularity. She lists "symptoms, side effects, & triggers": "not sleeping well," "memory problems," and "upcoming art show." Insomnia is a symptom, memory problems a side effect of lithium, and an upcoming art show is a possible trigger for mania. Possible solutions include making a sleep chart, taking an antianxiety drug, talking to Karen, and remaining alert to "revving," a precursor to mania.

The page on the right feels more dynamic, its wavier lines implying motion and life—emphasizing living as coping. "Managing my disorder," she writes in

Fig. 18. From *Marbles: Mania, Depression, Michelangelo, and Me: A Graphic Memoir* by Ellen Forney, copyright © 2012 by Ellen Forney. Used by permission of Gotham Books, an imprint of Penguin Publishing Group, a division of Penguin Random House LLC.

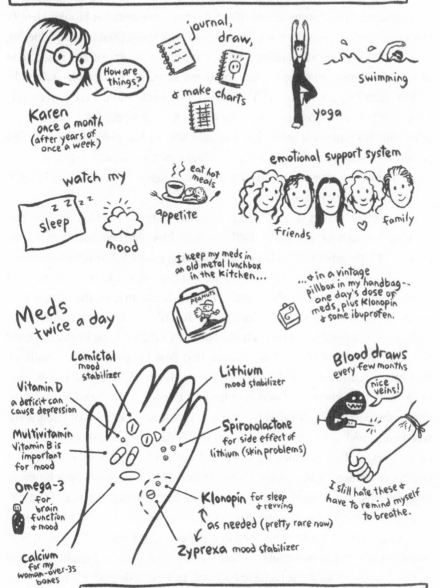

a frame at the top of the page, "means a multifaceted treatment plan." And in the frame at the bottom: "Bipolar disorder is for keeps—I'll be doing these, or a variation of these, for my whole life."[42] Forney represents her bipolar identity in a variety of contexts. Karen is there, along with more friends, a bewildering host of pills, a demonic creature with a syringe who draws her blood, and images that represent sleep, work, food, and exercise. Her bipolar self talks with a therapist, socializes with friends, takes medication, experiences side effects, offers her veins up so her blood may be examined, does yoga, reads, cries, and documents it all in her journal—and in her published work. The person who surrounds Forney's creative brain uses visual and verbal irony to make room for her variety of responses to her diagnosis: resignation, delight, resistance, fear, confusion, clarity.

Like Forney, David B. emphasizes the materiality of reading, writing, and drawing throughout *Epileptic*. Both authors link detailed accounts of the process of representation—what Freud might have called their representational resources—in relation to the making of identity. Also like Forney, he uses facing pages to represent the complexity of his identity, or the person who surrounds his own brain (and his brother's). In a ribbonlike frame spanning the tops of both pages, he inscribes an invitation: "Come visit the inside of David B.'s head at the end of the 70s"—words that flow backward from a bullhorn held by a circuslike figure (fig. 19). This time, the inside of David B.'s head is not a brain, but a chaotic collection of fragments from stories he wrote and drew during the period. Stories that represent a decade's work, a lot of geographic wandering, and a rapidly evolving sense of identity collapse onto a single page—images from comics he's created and read, images of his brother's doctors condensed with images of the "madmen" who populate both brothers' imaginations, and images of Jean-Christophe both healthy and sick. David B. represents himself as writer and artist, in two bubbles, one on each page. He sits at a desk, with the tools of his medium: paper, pens, bright light. The speech bubble in the first image reads: "There's a feverish, confused quality to these stories." In the second: "A pathetic bulwark, and yet it does shield me."[43] As it is for Forney, creating comics is a means of reconciling complex and apparently contradictory aspects of identity—and the flexible fluency of the form is key to ensuring that the reconciliation does not require tidy integration, that it can encompass the lumpiness of experience.

David B.'s and Forney's strategies both involve creating images that empha-size the intimate proximity and distant epistemology of the brain's relationship to the self and mind. In numerous images, David B. depicts Jean-Christophe's brain as an object probed by doctors, healers, and philosophers—and, more occasionally, his own brain, which comes to feel more porous and vulnerable with its proximity to his brother's suffering and the treatments designed to alle-viate it.

Forney represents her brain differently—mostly via the sensations to which she attributes it. When she does include a drawing of a physical brain, it's a diagram explaining a neuropsychological theory of creativity. More often, she alludes to her brain through drawings of her head and face, surrounded by imagery that externalizes her mental experience. Dots, lines, and words— "POP!"—create a montage that suggests physical feelings. When Forney describes her mind "spinning and overheating" like an "electrical short," she mixes the physical and the mental, describing affective experience as embodied feeling—a kind of visual translation of recent theories of affect. In the words of neuroscientist Jaak Panksepp, "All objective bodily measures [of "interior experiences"], from facial expressions to autonomic changes, are only vague approximations of the underlying neural dynamics—like ghostly tracks in the bubble chamber detectors of particle physics."[44] In the words of cultural critic Ann Cvetkovich, "I tend to use affect in a generic sense, . . . as a category that encompasses affect, emotion, and feeling, and that includes impulses, desires, and feelings that get historically constructed in a range of ways. I also like to use *feeling* as a generic term that does some of the same work: naming the undifferentiated 'stuff' of feeling; spanning the distinctions between emotion and affect central to some theories; acknowledging the somatic or sensory nature of feelings as experiences that aren't just cognitive concepts or construc-tions."[45] It's not surprising that the neuroscientist emphasizes the "underlying neural dynamics" of affect, and the cultural critic emphasizes its historical construction. What they share—with each other and with the authors of neuro-comics—is an emphasis on the elusive or ineffable quality of feelings, their subtle but immense range of expression, and the confusion those feelings tend to create. In other words, they portray affect as a form of what McCloud calls one of graphic narrative's specialties, the interplay of "the seen and the unseen," or the felt and the unfelt.

Fig. 19. English translation, banner: "Come visit the inside of David B.'s head at the end of the 70s." From *L'Ascension du Haut Mal* by David B., © 2003, David B. and L'Association.

Neurocomic is a more explicitly pedagogical text than *Epileptic* or *Marbles,* using the form of a graphic narrative to offer an accessible introduction to brain physiology and the history of neurology. But it's also a hybrid of fiction and nonfiction—and its fictional frame is by no means incidental. Farinella and Roš might have created a straightforward illustrated history of neurology, but instead they wrap it in a fictional fantasy about a shrinking man who wanders in metaphorical forest, his own brain. Near the beginning of the story, a hypothetical human, brain exposed, examines the book page on which the protagonist is trapped (fig. 20). That hypothetical human is figured as the protagonist

Fig. 20. From *Neurocomic* © Matteo Farinella and Hana Roš. Nobrow 2013.

himself, in the role of reader, but also as the reader of this text. By analogy, the protagonist and reader are condensed into this hypothetical human. Near the end of the story, the woman courted by the protagonist explains: "Our existence relies on the brain of the reader which is able to see motion and hear sounds . . . on a flat sheet of paper."[46] This text begins on a panel featuring an unidentified character, holding a copy of *Understanding Comics.* It's an expandingly meta moment that captures *Neurocomic*'s central preoccupation with the brain as a representational organ that enables both the making and interpretation of more representation. Readers are asked to imagine their own brains imagining these characters' brains—and to generalize the lesson to all readers, all brains. The result is a kind of recasting of the message attributed to Ramón y Cajal near the book's beginning. The "It" in "It all begins and ends with neurons" becomes the reader, trapped in an epistemological loop. This hypothetical reader can only learn about its brain by using that brain, and it can't quite know if its flesh and blood are real or products of its own ability to "see motion and hear sounds on a flat sheet of paper." In other words, human brains mediate reality, and consciousness of that reality is subjective by definition. Meaning, as a result, is always contingent—and in the case of graphic narrative—that contingency flows from the continuous interplay of text and image. Like these characters, a neural pattern is a representation of the world—one composed of neurotrans-mitters and electricity, whose meanings are further shaped by variables like location, the rhythms of brain waves, and the support of glial cells that surround neurons (and whose variety of functions—support, insulation, regulation—are ever expanding in the neuroscientific literature. Any psychology textbook will tell you that a perception is a construction—or a functional distortion—of the objects it represents.

In that sense, graphic narratives are corollaries to academic critiques of the oversimplification of brain-scanning technologies. As Fitzpatrick writes, "brain-imaging scans are highly technical and difficult to interpret without expert knowledge of the subjects participating in the studies, the tasks performed, the techniques used to acquire the data, and the complicated statis-tical tools used to analyze the data and create the images."[47] It's worth reiter-ating that brain-scanning technologies and graphic narratives are far from equivalent. Meta-representational techniques are integral to the representa-tional tools of graphic narratives, part of the reading experience. The dissection and digital reconsolidation of brains, the measurement of their electrical patterns, or the imaging of their blood flow are powerful tools for gaining knowledge of their functions. The expert knowledge necessary to make and interpret the images created through brain-scanning technologies involves a great deal of meta-representation, but their cultural circulation mostly obscures this fact. Clinicians, subjects, laboratories, machines, and algorithms disappear behind appealing images.

Despite obvious and vast differences, these technologies share one significant quality with neurocomics. They are representations of brains, built not found. Simply put: The images produced by brain scans will continue to circulate as "neurojunk" unless the people doing the circulating—including journalists, marketers, clinicians, researchers, and artists—find the rhetorical means to situate them in the representational frameworks that make them meaningful. The sentiment in the epigraph to this chapter, from Dumit's *Picturing Personhood,* extends from the PET images he examines to brain-scanning technologies in general: "Overturning the age-old axiom that a picture is worth a thousand words, perhaps these PET images require millions of words to be understood." Of course, it's not the quantity of words that matters, but their quality. Graphic narratives foreground the materials they use to make pictures of personhood. Experts in neuroscience are attuned to the complexity of the materials they use to make images of brains—and to the fact that these images don't so much represent personhood as an incomplete and highly mediated set of pictures of physiology. Nonetheless, they often translate the complexities of the technology into rhetoric that makes the images in question appear to be transparent images of brains. Panksepp's description of these images as visualizations is an example of a more accurate description, but it doesn't go far enough to combat the widely articulated idea that brain scanning provides direct access to brains.

By definition, expert knowledge belongs to specialists, but the stakes of neuroimaging belong to anybody with a brain—and that's as good a reason as I can imagine to work hard to develop a set of explanatory and rhetorical techniques that can describe the meaning of brain scans to a larger public. But neurocomics, like so many literary responses to neuroscience, demonstrate an imbalanced relationship among the arts and sciences. The writers of brain memoirs and neuronovels—including the graphic varieties of both—are highly conscious of the personal, social, and philosophical stakes of representing and circulating expert knowledge. Individual experts in the neurosciences share this awareness, but collectively, as a set of disciplines, the sciences aren't designed to respond to concepts or tools emerging from the arts and humanities. Literary writers and critics make a vocation of working with the intricacies of representations of all varieties of human experience and knowledge. Graphic narratives demonstrate one of literature's salient contributions to contemporary understandings of the brain: their emphasis on meta-representation. To imagine collective, multidisciplinary collaboration among scientists and humanists interested in the meaning of brain images—or the relationship between brain and self more generally—remains an exercise in speculative fiction. Nonetheless, graphic brain narratives offer an implicit but concrete suggestion to those involved in the circulation of brain-scan images. Simply to include the word "representation" (or its equivalent) in descriptions of these images would help to clarify their meanings—in no small part because the word would require some follow-up explanation, in accessible prose, of what's entailed in the representation of a brain—and, ideally, the person (or people) surrounding that brain.

Epilogue: Reading Organisms in the Age of Neuroscience

IN THIS BOOK, I'VE TOLD A PRETTY optimistic story about relations between literature and neuroscience. I'm optimistic because I believe neuroscience does the world a lot of good (despite my queasiness about the dissection of sea slugs or inserting gene mutations in mice). I believe literature does its own kinds of good (despite my wariness of the literary as a narrow category used to prop up elitist attitudes or inequitable social structures). Throughout the writing, it's been clear to me that it would be possible to tell this story another way, emphasizing the limitations of neuroscience, literature, or both. I chose not to do that, because my aim is to demonstrate what's valuable about advances in neuroscience and literary responses to them—and, more basically, what's valuable about science and literature, as disciplines that help us make new knowledge and new ways of knowing. Nonetheless, I also believe an uncritical or myopic neuromania obscures the value of neuroscience *and* literature, whose methods and technologies for representation work through the overlapping modes of hypothesis and fantasy. To recognize the value, we need to be attuned to the specificities of speculative knowledge in both disciplines.

You can touch a brain or a book, but you can't touch a literary world. A book is a material object that stimulates subjective, personal, and immaterial reading experiences. The material elements of a literary world are distributed. They're represented among the pages of books or on screens, the black marks of letters, words, and paragraphs. They're represented in bodies of readers, who might notice their hearts racing, their eyes moistening, or their bellies, lungs, and heads laughing. They're located in the brain activity both of writers and of readers. They're represented in conversations among readers, spoken or written. Black marks on a page stimulate qualia—the perceptual building blocks of consciousness—floods of them: sensory qualia, affective ones, intellectual ones. When we read a novel, memoir, or poem, the immaterial world emerging from those qualia seeps into the physical ones we inhabit (say a beach, bus, or classroom). When we say we lose ourselves in a book, we mean it hijacks our awareness of those physical worlds. Reading becomes something like what Damasio calls "private, first-person" experience,[1] but not quite. It may be highly personal, and private in the sense that nobody can share another reader's experience, but reading is a first-person experience that invites the perspective of the writer to blend with it. It's social *and* private, first- *and* third-person. A literary representation uses words to stimulate a reader's brain (and body) to experience a remix of the physical world. Representation makes new experience, new feelings, new ideas possible. A literary world built around the brains of its protagonists invites readers to consider physiological dimensions of reading, to imagine themselves as organisms, to consider neurological identity, and to remember that the brain itself is a representational organ. Like writers, brains represent worlds.

Neurological identity is made possible by the brain of an organism representing itself. The concept requires leaps of faith or imagination, to bypass the explanatory gap between brain activity and lived experience. The leap is necessary because we live with brains—brains that confound and surprise, go awry, become damaged. Brains are urgent objects of investigation because they are so fundamental to human experience, from the curiosities that arise from consciousness to the crises that arise from damage or disease. The advances of neuroscience and the popularity of all things neuro (marketing, film, economics, identity) reflect the urgency. When critics worry about the cultural circulation of *neurojunk, neuromania,* or *brainhood,* they object to ideas about the brain that ignore ambiguities inherent in representation. Brains create ambiguities when they represent both the world and the self: Expectation shapes perception; the triggers of the present prime memory, which is already primed by the triggers of the past; consciousness creates the illusion of unrestrained free will. To compound the matter, we can only investigate or communicate about the brain by representing it. The tools of a journalist, novelist, brain-scanning technician, or computational modeler mediate what we can know about the brain. The contributions of literary responses to neuroscience lie in their reminder that understanding brains requires attention to questions about representation.

In recent years, new representational tools in the sciences have catalyzed new questions about how the brain represents literary worlds—how it represents representation: What are the neural correlates of aesthetic experience? What cognitive experiences do certain texts or genres afford? How might the physiology involved in social interaction overlap with the physiology involved in aesthetic engagement? What does it mean to read as an organism? For obvious reasons, this research is inherently multidisciplinary, requiring careful negotiation of the representational tools—methodologies, rhetorics, styles of writing and thinking—of disciplines as disparate as neuroscience, literary studies, anthropology, economics, and history. These questions of the neurohumanities exceed the epistemological reach of any particular disciplinary lens—and, of course, multidisciplinary lenses too. They require speculation. The neurohumanities blend thought styles: the fantasy of the literary and the hypothesis of the scientific; the historical and the physiological; the conceptual critique of social theory with the aspirational imagination of scientific theory.

The brain's representation of aesthetic engagement requires multiple frames. A literary writer like Siri Hustvedt can speculate, in *The Shaking Woman,* about reading's power to recast her "internal narrator" through engagement with the narrator who emerges from those black marks on the page:

> The closest we can get to this entrance into another person's psyche is through reading. Reading is the mental arena where different thought styles, tough and tender, and the ideas generated by them become more apparent. We have access to a stranger's internal narrator. Reading, after all, is a way of living inside another person's words. His or her voice becomes my narrator for the duration. Of course, I retain my own critical faculties, pausing to say to myself, *Yes, he's right about that* or *No, he's forgotten this point entirely* or *That's a clichéd character,* but the more compelling the voice on the page is, the more I lose my own. I am seduced and give myself up to the other person's words.[2]

Hustvedt blends philosophical reflection and literary speculation. Her evidence is personal experience. She needs no statistical data, feels no onus to make her claims definitive. Of course, reading doesn't give us access to "another person's psyche." Hustvedt argues it's as close as we get, not that it gets us there. She describes the capacity of a writer's voice to become her narrator, to mix with the stream of her consciousness, to give her access to unfamiliar "thought styles" that may lead to new ideas, new ways of understanding the world—and, ultimately, living with it.

In a very different register, neuroscientist Stanislas Dehaene argues that "the human brain never evolved for reading. . . . The only evolution was cultural— reading itself progressively evolved toward a form adapted to our brain circuits." By his account, preexisting brain systems devoted to representing shapes, sounds, and speech enable—and constrict—black marks on pages to make meaning and, by my account, to create imaginary worlds. Reading is a human invention, or tool, built through universal principles that make use of those brain circuits, a "morpho-phonological principle" that represents "word roots and phonological structures" as well as "a small inventory of shapes shared throughout the world." Nonetheless, Dehaene acknowledges that "an exponential number of cultural forms can arise from the multiple combinations of restricted selection of fundamental traits."[3] In other words, the malleability of the brain's representational systems enables the continuous evolution of new forms of representation.

The literary wing of the neurohumanities is busy with researchers and theo- rists investigating what it might mean to "live inside another's words" and the variations of reading possible within the physiological constraints Dehaene describes. Some of this research has gotten a lot of press—for example, Natalie Phillips's fMRI research on reading Jane Austen, featured on NPR, *The Huffington Post,* and *Salon* well before it was published in journals. Phillips conducted her research on a fellowship at Stanford, which touted it with the headline "This Is Your Brain on Jane Austen." Phillips's research is a multidis- ciplinary collaboration—whose process mirrors its premises with a productive irony Austen might appreciate. Phillips is interested in the limits of attention, studying Austen's fiction to make arguments about how it challenges readers to adopt multiple perspectives that challenge those limits. Samantha Holmsworth, a neuroimaging expert on the project, describes the challenges: "We were all interested, but working at the edge of our capacity to understand even 10 percent of what each other were saying"—an estimate revised to 30 percent in an academic article that finally fleshed out the results that had received so much preliminary hype.[4] Phillips presents her research with the enthusiasm of a hypothesis that requires further study. In short, close reading (attending to questions about form) and pleasure reading (getting lost in a book) involve related but different forms of representation. The "neural signatures"—read: representations—involved multiple brain systems, and Phillips envisions future research using a "functional connectivity" approach to measure "synchronous patterns that emerge in parallel across the brain and investigates how these connections change as we engage with a stimulus over time."[5] Close reading seems to initiate more widespread activity than pleasure reading, including the somatosensory cortex and motor cortex—areas involved in space and movement. This is nascent research, and its hypotheses are tentative. Phillips's framework is a lot like the worlds Jane Austen builds for her characters, worlds in which all knowledge is hypothetical, meaning-contingent, and analysis-tentative.

The headlines emphasize what neuroscience might tell us about literary experience. In this book, I've turned the tables, asking what literary writers can tell us about neuroscience and the brain. What are literature's contributions to conversations and debates generated by neuroscience and neuromania? Of course, every literary text is different, but collectively—as a literary movement that builds on a history of novels and memoirs that experiment with form to represent the physiology of self—brain memoirs and neuronovels suggest a set of meaningful propositions:

- Literary experiments turn Malabou's question—"What should we do with our brain?"—into narrative, a form that instigates attention to the meanings, especially the unruly or ambiguous ones, afforded through representation. One thing we should do with our brains is understand them as representational organs. In addition, we should value the representation of particular, subjective experiences that may resonate with but don't require the arguments and conclusions of academic inquiry.
- As the neurosciences, the social sciences, and philosophy have begun to engage in cross-disciplinary dialogue, one result has been a multiplication of variables in the making of mind: The mind is embodied, situated, relational, and dynamic. The mind is plastic, within limits, its various functions distributed. The minds and brains of individuals differ, both subtly and dramatically. There is no singular or normative mind. These appraisals—which have fast become commitments—create a misalignment between their truth claims, the traditional methodologies, and available evidence. The variables are too many—and too different—to be

addressed with a single set of disciplinary tools. They are too hypothetical to be exhausted or resolved. Multidisciplinary research about the functions and meanings of the brain must take stock of the forms of knowledge gained or obscured by particular methods and pay serious attention to how the refraction of multiple methodologies might enable new research questions or the refinement of methodologies. To be effective, though, they require curious audiences attuned to the value of tentative knowledge and nascent methods.

- Difference is a motivating element in literature—and, as such, literary experiments responding to neuroscience have a great deal in common with disability studies. Rosemarie Garland-Thomson coined "misfitting" to describe disjunctions between particular bodies and environments that render differences from norms disabling to particular people.[6]

- Neurocognitive difference is often difficult to notice (as when a person is depressed or has trouble reading) and just as often dramatically disruptive (as when a person experiences a seizure or an uncontrollable urge to echolalia).

- Literary representations of "all manner of neurologies" help make what's hard to see visible and invite engagement with difference. They emphasize the difficulties and disjunctions as well as the benefits and opportunities for personal and cultural transformation involved.

- Beginning in the 1990s, theoretical neuroscience began to sound like post-structuralist theory. The key difference is that neuroscience located the malleability of self in material bodies, before or outside language. With productive irony, literary writers responded by using language to explore the inarticulate malleability and dynamism of the self. Contemporary literary experiments that foreground mind or consciousness are heirs to modernist ones, using language as a kind of mimesis for the limits of language and turning to peculiarities of embodiment for sources of identity that elude conscious articulation. To describe mental experience as interiority—to speak of an "inner self" or "internal narrator"—is to use a metaphor that bypasses the explanatory gap, locating consciousness in the container of the body. The metaphor associates the self with a body. Fair enough. But it also suggests the body is a container for immaterial experience and obscures the dynamic interplay involved among physiology, affect, feeling, thought, and identity. We need language and rhetoric that encompass the interplay of material and immaterial experience entailed in consciousness.

- Mind reading—or mentalizing—may be fundamental to both social relations and to literary experience. But mind reading is misreading. While this may be surprising in some disciplines, it's fundamental in literary studies. Misreading is no disaster though. The legacy of semiotics is relevant here: Signifiers are unstable. It's the way things are. The study of empathy, mirror neurons, aesthetics, or the cognition of reading will all benefit from a fundamental embrace of the instability of the mental models we make of other minds, both fictional and real ones—all of them acts of representation.

NOTES

Introduction

1. Levine, "Materialism and Qualia."
2. David B., *Epileptic,* 168.
3. Malabou, *What Should We Do with Our Brain?*
4. Damasio, *Self Comes to Mind,* 130.
5. Houser, *Ecosickness in Contemporary U.S. Fiction.*
6. Chalmers, *The Character of Consciousness,* 5.
7. Satel and Lilienfeld, *Brainwashed.*
8. Jamison, *An Unquiet Mind,* 5–6.
9. Houser, *Ecosickness in Contemporary U.S. Fiction.*
10. Pitts-Taylor, *The Brain's Body,* 5, 15, 13.
11. Panksepp, *Affective Neuroscience,* 9; Solms and Turnbull, *The Brain and the Inner World;* Damasio, *The Feeling of What Happens;* Edelman and Tononi, *A Universe of Consciousness.*
12. LeDoux, *Synaptic Self,* 324.
13. Ibid., 2–3.
14. Seung, *Connectome,* xiv, xiii, xv.
15. Crick, *The Astonishing Hypothesis,* 3.
16. Swaab, *We Are Our Brains,* 3.
17. Ibid., xxiv.
18. Noë, *Out of Our Heads,* 7.
19. In the social sciences, critiques of neuroscience focus on its tendency to reductivism and determinism, the distortions that occur when its data and methods are disseminated, and an overzealous rush to overstate the power of its emerging technologies. The following are among the strongest of these critiques: Davi Johnson, "'How Do You Know Unless You Look?'"; Jordan-Young, *Brain Storm;* Martin, "Mind-Body Problems"; Pitts-Taylor, "Social Brains, Embodiment, and Neuro-Interactionism"; and, from within the sciences, Roy, "Asking Different Questions."

20. Rose and Abi-Rached, *Neuro,* 2–3.
21. Churchland, *Touching a Nerve.*
22. Gazzaniga, *Who's in Charge?* 3.
23. Ibid., 4, 7.
24. Damasio, *The Feeling of What Happens,* 20.
25. Damasio, *Self Comes to Mind,* 45, 206.
26. LeDoux, *Anxious,* 227.
27. Damasio has developed his evolving theories of consciousness, emotion, embodiment, and self in several books. *The Feeling of What Happens* (1999) and *Self Comes to Mind* (2010) are most relevant for his theory of consciousness. For a summary of his theories, see "Minding the Body" (2006), a collaboration with Hannah Damasio.
28. Churchland, *Touching a Nerve,* 11.
29. Ibid., 10, 13.
30. Ibid., 256–57.
31. Ibid., 13.
32. Ibid., 263.
33. Noë, *Out of Our Heads,* 49.
34. Ibid., 49.
35. Ibid., 185.
36. Damasio, *The Feeling of What Happens,* 20.
37. Malabou, *What Should We Do with Our Brain?* 63.
38. Ibid., 56, 63, 69.
39. Swaab, *We Are Our Brains,* xxiv.
40. Ramachandran, *The Tell-Tale Brain,* xiii.
41. Hustvedt, *The Blazing World,* 159.
42. Ibid., 125.
43. Heider and Simmel, "An Experimental Study of Apparent Behavior."
44. Powers, *The Echo Maker,* 3–4.
45. Ibid., 18–19.
46. Ibid., 36–37.
47. *New York Times,* "Can 'Neuro Lit Crit' Save the Humanities?"
48. Snow, *The Two Cultures and the Scientific Revolution,* 4.
49. *New York Times,* "Can 'Neuro Lit Crit' Save the Humanities?"
50. Rose and Abi-Rached, *Neuro,* 9.
51. Legrenzi and Umiltà, *Neuromania,* 102; Satel and Lilienfeld, *Brainwashed,* xx; Martin, "Mind-Body Problems," 569.
52. Roth, "Rise of the Neuronovel"; Ortega and Vidal, "Brains in Literature / Literature in the Brain," 330.
53. Ortega and Vidal, "Brains in Literature / Literature in the Brain," 328.
54. Richardson, "Once upon a Mind," 361; Patricia Cohen, "Next Big Thing in English."
55. Zunshine, *Introduction to Cognitive Cultural Studies,* 6; Raymond Williams, *The Long Revolution,* 36.
56. In Sedgwick's "Paranoid Reading and Reparative Reading, Or, You're So Paranoid You Probably Think This Essay Is about You" (from her 2002 book *Touching Feeling*), she credits Paul Ricoeur with coining the term "hermeneutics of suspicion." For a more

recent discussion, emphasizing the destructive power of the hermeneutics of suspicion as a norm so strong it marginalizes or even precludes scholarship like Turner's and Spolsky's, see Ruddick, "When Nothing Is Cool."

57. Turner, *The Literary Mind,* 4.
58. Spolsky, *Gaps in Nature,* 2.
59. Eakin, *Living Autobiographically,* 14–15.
60. Hogan, *Cognitive Science, Literature, and the Arts,* 2.
61. Hogan, *The Mind and Its Stories,* 86.
62. For a discussion of the history, social implications, and methodological limitations of mirror-neuron research, see Pitts-Taylor's *The Brain's Body,* chap. 3, "I Feel Your Pain."
63. Keen, *Empathy and the Novel,* 14.
64. Vermeule, *Why Do We Care about Literary Characters?* 245, 11.
65. Paul Armstrong, *How Literature Plays with the Brain,* 10.
66. Starr, *Feeling Beauty,* xiv.
67. Ibid., 29, 50, 14.
68. Groes, *Memory in the Twenty-First Century,* 4, 3.
69. Ibid., 82.
70. Snow, *The Two Cultures,* 170.
71. Ortega and Vidal, "Brains in Literature / Literature in the Brain," 27.
72. Charles Harris, "The Story of the Self," 243.
73. Ibid.
74. Gaedtke, "Cognitive Investigations," 143.
75. Savarese and Zunshine, "The Critic as Neurocosmopolite," 20.
76. Ibid.

Chapter 1. Before Neuromania

1. Powers, *Galatea 2.2,* 23.
2. Sacks, *An Anthropologist on Mars,* viii.
3. Sacks, *The Man Who Mistook His Wife for a Hat,* 97.
4. Ibid., 93.
5. Sacks, *An Anthropologist on Mars,* 78.
6. Ibid.
7. Ibid., 83.
8. Ibid., 85.
9. Ibid., 92, 94, 99.
10. Ibid., 98–99.
11. Brown, "Profile."
12. Kandel, "Eric Kandel: Oliver Sacks shows disease brings out courage, beauty," 822.
13. Shakespeare, Review of *An Anthropologist on Mars.*
14. Cassuto, "Oliver Sacks," 329, 332.
15. Couser, *The Cases of Oliver Sacks,* 4, 8, 9; Walker, *Neurocosmopolitanism;* Savarese and Zunshine, "The Critic as Neurocosmopolite."
16. Marshall, "In the Region of Lost Minds."

17. Couser, *The Cases of Oliver Sacks,* 5.
18. Sacks, *The Man Who Mistook His Wife for a Hat,* 25.
19. Ibid., 24–25.
20. Ibid., 38.
21. Couser, *The Cases of Oliver Sacks,* 6.
22. Ibid., 7.
23. Sacks, *On the Move,* 137.
24. Jamison, *An Unquiet Mind,* 172.
25. Grandin, *Thinking in Pictures,* 82.
26. Ibid., 3.
27. Ibid., 217.
28. Jamison, *An Unquiet Mind,* 79–80.
29. Ibid., 6–7.
30. Clark, *Supersizing the Mind.*
31. Grandin, *Thinking in Pictures,* 84–85.
32. Jamison, *An Unquiet Mind,* 118.
33. Ibid., 174, 143.
34. Ibid., 141.
35. Gary Johnson, "Consciousness as Content," 180.
36. Ortega and Vidal, "Brains in Literature / Literature in the Brain," 337.
37. Powers, *Galatea 2.2,* 15.
38. Ibid., 129.
39. Ibid., 171.
40. Lodge, *Thinks . . .,* 1.
41. Ibid., 51–52.
42. Ibid., 53.
43. Gaedtke, "Cognitive Investigations," 195.
44. Lodge, *Thinks . . .,* 317.
45. Scarry, *Dreaming by the Book,* 9, 4.
46. Ibid., 37–38.
47. Ibid., 38.
48. Starr, *Feeling Beauty,* 18.
49. Ibid., 24.
50. Lodge, *Thinks . . .,* 45. See Damasio, *Descartes' Error;* Picard, *Affective Computing;* and Panksepp, *Affective Neuroscience.*
51. Ortega and Vidal, "Brains in Literature / Literature in the Brain," 337.
52. Grandin, *Thinking in Pictures,* 217.

Interlude: Neurodiversity in the Age of the Brain Atlas

1. Human Brain Project, "The Human Brain Project"; National Institutes of Health (NIH), "Brain Research through Advancing Innovative Neurotechnologies (BRAIN)."
2. For a detailed description of brain atlas technologies, see Toga et al., "Towards Multimodal Atlases of the Human Brain."
3. Honigsbaum, "Human Brain Project."

4. Ibid.
5. Markram, Rinaldi, and Markram, "The Intense World Syndrome—an Alternative Hypothesis for Autism," 2.
6. Silberman, *NeuroTribes,* 470.
7. Walker, "Neurodiversity."
8. National Institutes of Health (NIH), "What Is the Brain Initiative?"
9. Requarth, "Bringing a Virtual Brain to Life."
10. "Open Message to the European Commission concerning the Human Brain Project."
11. "Mapping the Mind—Smart Thinking for Brain Health?"; Marcus, "The Trouble With Brain Science"; Bartlett, "Can the Human Brain Project Be Saved? Should It Be?"; Feder, "The Brain Is Big Science."
12. Marcus, "The Trouble With Brain Science."
13. Schaber, *neurowonderful;* Schaber, "Ask an Autistic."
14. Frances and Longden, "Psychiatry and Hearing Voices: A Dialogue With Eleanor Longden."
15. Luhrmann, "Redefining Mental Illness."
16. Baggs, "In My Language"; Human, *Erin Human;* Walker, *Neurocosmopolitanism;* Faulds, *Un-Boxed Brain;* Ryskamp, *NeuroQueer;* Fleischmann, "Speechless Intro."
17. Marcus, "The Trouble With Brain Science."
18. Ortega, "The Cerebral Subject and the Challenge of Neurodiversity," 440–41.

Chapter 2. Brain Memoirs

1. Smith and Watson, *Reading Autobiography,* 27.
2. Eakin, *Living Autobiographically,* 2–3.
3. Dully and Fleming, *My Lobotomy,* x, 256.
4. In that sense, her perspective resounds with William James's lectures "On Mysticism," from *The Varieties of Religious Experience,* where he insists that subjective accounts of mystical experience needed to be taken seriously on their own terms, and with the work of proponents of drug-induced psychedelic experience like Aldous Huxley, Timothy Leary, and (more recently) Daniel Pinchbeck.
5. Taylor, *My Stroke of Insight,* 38.
6. Ibid., 38, 139.
7. Hustvedt, *The Shaking Woman,* 7.
8. Ibid.
9. Ibid., 4, 6, 30.
10. Ibid., 116.
11. Damasio, *Self Comes to Mind,* 8–9.
12. Smith and Watson, *Reading Autobiography,* 1.
13. Ibid., 9–10.
14. Eliot, *Middlemarch.*
15. Noë, *Out of Our Heads,* 47.
16. Shulman, *To Love What Is,* 33.
17. Ibid., 135.
18. Ibid.
19. Ibid., 139–40.

20. Damasio, *Self Comes to Mind,* 9; Taylor, *My Stroke of Insight,* 137.
21. Taylor, *My Stroke of Insight,* 141.
22. Ibid., 39–43.
23. Taylor, "My Stroke of Insight."
24. James, "The Stream of Consciousness," 30–31.
25. Ibid., 40.
26. Eakin, *Living Autobiographically,* 70; Damasio, *The Feeling of What Happens,* 174.
27. Eakin, *Living Autobiographically,* 71.
28. Ibid., 70–71.
29. Ibid., 84–85.
30. Shulman, *To Love What Is,* 115, 116.
31. Hustvedt, *The Shaking Woman,* 6.
32. Taylor, *My Stroke of Insight,* 143.
33. Ibid., 144.
34. Smith and Watson, *Reading Autobiography,* 86; see also Nancy K. Miller, *But Enough about Me.*
35. Shulman, *To Love What Is,* 116.
36. Ibid., 165.
37. Hustvedt, *The Shaking Woman,* 88.
38. Ibid.

Chapter 3. Three Autistic Autobiographers

1. Murray, *Representing Autism,* 5, 23, 31, 32.
2. Ibid., 32.
3. Draaisma, "Stereotypes of Autism," 769.
4. Robison, *Look Me in the Eye,* ix.
5. Heilker and Yergeau, "Autism and Rhetoric," 487.
6. Hacking, "Autistic Autobiography," 1472.
7. Heilker and Yergeau, "Autism and Rhetoric," 486.
8. Silberman, *NeuroTribes,* 14.
9. Murray, *Representing Autism,* 33.
10. Mukhopadhyay, *How Can I Talk If My Lips Don't Move?* 4.
11. Murray, *Representing Autism,* 149.
12. Robison, *Look Me in the Eye,* 3.
13. Ibid., 255, 99–100.
14. Higashida, *The Reason I Jump,* 10.
15. Heilker and Yergeau, "Autism and Rhetoric," 489.
16. Ibid.
17. Dehaene, *Consciousness and the Brain,* 43.
18. Murray, *Autism,* 4, 7, 5–9.
19. Ibid., 11.
20. Higashida, *The Reason I Jump,* 99.
21. Ibid., 18.
22. Mukhopadhyay, *How Can I Talk If My Lips Don't Move?* 187.

23. Ibid.
24. Ibid., 115–16.
25. Ibid., 117.
26. Damasio, *Self Comes to Mind,* 148.
27. Dehaene, *Consciousness and the Brain,* 177.
28. Robison, *Switched On,* 132–33.
29. Ibid., 34, 23.
30. Dehaene, *Consciousness and the Brain,* 151–52.
31. Robison, *Switched On,* 68–69.
32. Ibid., 145.
33. Ibid.
34. Murray, *Autism,* 89, 94.
35. Straus, "Autism as Culture," 467–69.
36. Robison, "I Resign My Roles at Autism Speaks."
37. Higashida, *The Reason I Jump,* 175.

Interlude: If You've Met One Autistic Reviewer . . .

1. Flood, "Curious Incident of the Dog in the Night-Time Pulled from Children's Reading List."
2. Laura Miller, " 'The Curious Incident of the Dog in the Night-Time' by Mark Haddon"; Kakutani, "Maths and Physics?"; McInerney, "The Remains of the Dog"; Ashapoorv, "The Curious Incident of the Dog in the Night-Time by Mark Haddon—Review."
3. The quotation is generally attributed to Stephen Shore, an Adelphi University professor specializing in autistic education—though it circulates in a variety of forms and is often circulated or quoted with no attribution.
4. Schofield, "A Journey to Shock and Enlighten."
5. Olear, "When Popular Novels Perpetuate Negative Stereotypes."
6. Vermeule, *Why Do We Care about Literary Characters?* 64.
7. Ray, "Normalcy, Knowledge, and Nature in Mark Haddon's *The Curious Incident of the Dog in the Night-Time*"; Wooden, "Narrative Medicine in the Literature Classroom."
8. Hacking, "Autism Fiction," 645.
9. Draaisma, "Who Owns Asperger's?" 46, 48.
10. Bartmess, "Review."
11. Haddon, "asperger's & autism."
12. Bartmess, "Review."
13. Ibid.
14. Semino, "Pragmatic Failure, Mind Style and Characterisation in Fiction about Autism," 141.
15. Ibid., 142.
16. Silberman, *NeuroTribes,* 469.
17. The slogan is a founding principle of the Autistic Self Advocacy Network (ASAN). For a discussion of ASAN's history, development, and role in the neurodiversity movement, see Silberman, *NeuroTribes,* 450–64.
18. Bartmess, "Review."

19. Draaisma, "Eye on Fiction," 769.
20. Shore, *Beyond the Wall,* 158, 159.

Chapter 4. Narrating Neurological Difference

1. Savarese and Zunshine, "The Critic as Neurocosmopolite."
2. Zunshine, *Why We Read Fiction,* 124.
3. Cave, *Thinking with Literature,* 47, 48.
4. Ibid.
5. Lewontin and Levins, *Biology Under the Influence,* 32–33.
6. Kendal, Tehrani, and Odling-Smee, "Human Niche Construction in Interdisciplinary Focus."
7. Thomas Armstrong, *Neurodiversity in the Classroom,* 13–21.
8. Garland-Thomson, "Misfits," 592.
9. Cave, *Thinking with Literature,* 53, 50, 56.
10. Wood, *How Fiction Works,* 5.
11. Tom McCarthy, *Remainder,* 3.
12. Ibid., 264.
13. Lethem, *Motherless Brooklyn,* 192.
14. Haddon, *The Curious Incident of the Dog in the Night-Time,* 3.
15. Hacking, "Lost in the Forest."
16. Phelan, *Living to Tell about It,* 51.
17. Ibid., 20–21.
18. Haddon, *The Curious Incident of the Dog in the Night-Time,* 19.
19. Lethem, *Motherless Brooklyn,* 178.
20. Ibid., 1–2.
21. Ibid., 1.
22. Ibid., 1–2.
23. Quoted in Logan, "Private Defective."
24. Schleifer, "The Poetics of Tourette's Syndrome," 138–39.
25. Tom McCarthy, *Remainder,* 240.
26. Garland-Thomson, "Misfits," 592.
27. Cave, *Thinking with Literature,* 47.
28. Herman, "Re-Minding Modernism," 243–72, 255–56.
29. Lethem, *Motherless Brooklyn,* 131.
30. Ibid., 57.
31. Ibid., 4.
32. Haddon, *The Curious Incident of the Dog in the Night-Time,* 25.
33. Ibid., 73.
34. Loftis, *Imagining Autism,* 25, 26.
35. Ibid., 127.
36. Ibid.
37. Tom McCarthy, *Remainder,* 20.
38. Ibid., 15.

39. Ibid., 64, 67.
40. Nicolaidis, "What Can Physicians Learn from the Neurodiversity Movement?" 503–10.
41. Haddon, "asperger's & autism"; Logan, "Private Defective."
42. Tom McCarthy, *Remainder.*
43. Phelan, *Living to Tell about It,* 20–21.

Chapter 5. Touching Brains in the Neuronovel

1. Damasio, *The Feeling of What Happens,* 28.
2. *Lowboy* is narrated in alternating chapters by Will and Lateef. In an interesting formal parallel, Patrick and Henry Cockburn's collaborative memoir, *Henry's Demons: Living with Schizophrenia, A Father and Son's Story,* is narrated in alternating chapters by Patrick Cockburn and his schizophrenic son, Henry. In both texts, the alternating chapters have the effect of juxtaposing the first-person experience of schizophrenia with the perspective of an observer, preventing the dismissal or stigmatization of schizophrenic subjectivity.
3. *Oxford English Dictionary* documents the use of the term "interiority" to mean "inner life" to a text published in 1701, though it doesn't list uses of the term to describe a literary technique until the 1960s. Google Books Ngram Viewer, which searches digitized texts dating to 1500, reveals marginal use of the term throughout the nineteenth and twentieth centuries, with a rapid rise in use during the 1960s to the present.
4. William Cohen, *Embodied,* 22.
5. On phrenology, see Shuttleworth; on physiognomy, see Hartley; on vivisection, see Straley; on evolutionary psychology, see Block; on Darwin's literary influence, see Beer; on sexology, see Tougaw, *Strange Cases,* and Bland and Doan.
6. Roth, "The Rise of the Neuronovel."
7. Influential reviews of *Saturday,* notably in *Slate* magazine and *The New York Times,* characterize the novel as an explicit reworking of Woolf's *Mrs. Dalloway* for a neuroscientific era. In a recent public discussion with psychologist Paul Bloom, McEwan denied any awareness of the connection while he was writing the novel, but he conceded the possibility of an unconscious influence.
8. Hustvedt, *The Sorrows of an American,* 5.
9. Wray, *Lowboy,* 5.
10. McEwan, *Saturday,* 262.
11. Damasio, *The Feeling of What Happens,* 11.
12. Noë, *Out of Our Heads,* 7.
13. Thomas Harris, *Hannibal,* 270, 432, 513, 483, 484.
14. For a classic history of the memory palace and other mnemonic systems of ancient Greece and Rome, see Yates, *The Art of Memory.*
15. Thomas Harris, *Hannibal,* 503.
16. Casey, *The Man Who Walked Away,* 175.
17. Ibid., 174.
18. Ibid., 175, 176.
19. William Cohen, *Embodied,* 476.

20. Ibid., 131.
21. McEwan, *Saturday,* 260.
22. Ibid.
23. Ibid., 262.
24. William Cohen, *Embodied,* 131.
25. Damasio, *The Feeling of What Happens,* 12.
26. Casey, *The Man Who Walked Away,* 55, 83.
27. Thomas Harris, *Hannibal,* 510, 543.
28. Wray, *Lowboy,* 68.
29. Ibid., 221.
30. McEwan, *Saturday,* 264.
31. Ibid., 266, 264, 281, 266.
32. Hustvedt, *The Sorrows of an American,* 67.
33. Ibid., 233.
34. Hustvedt, *What I Loved,* 88.
35. William Cohen, *Embodied,* 132.
36. For a sociological study of mirror-neuron research, see Pitts-Taylor, "I Feel Your Pain: Embodied Knowledges and Situated Neurons." For an excellent discussion of neuroaesthetics, See Starr, *Feeling Beauty: The Neuroscience of Aesthetic Experience.* For a brief survey of influential research on emotional contagion, see Hatfield, Cacioppo, and Rapson, *Emotional Contagion.*
37. William Cohen, *Embodied,* 136.
38. Starr, *Feeling Beauty,* 78.

Chapter 6. Neurocomics and Neuroimaging

1. Dumit, *Picturing Personhood,* 24.
2. Farinella and Roš, *Neurocomic,* 113.
3. Dumit, *Picturing Personhood,* 2–3.
4. Churchland, *Touching a Nerve,* 18–20.
5. LeDoux, *Synaptic Self,* 324; Damasio, *Self Comes to Mind,* 8.
6. Rose and Abi-Rached, *Neuro,* 2–3.
7. Versaci, *This Book Contains Graphic Language,* 6.
8. Chute and DeKoven, "Introduction," 767.
9. Ibid., 769.
10. Hong, "Disorienting the Vietnam War."
11. Forney, *Marbles,* 59.
12. Hacking, "Lost in the Forest," 5.
13. Freud, *The Interpretation of Dreams,* 237; Robertson in Freud, *The Interpretation of Dreams,* xiv; Hartmann, *Dreams and Nightmares,* 2.
14. Freud, *The Interpretation of Dreams,* 237; Robertson in Freud, *The Interpretation of Dreams,* xiv.
15. Chute, "Our Cancer Year, . . ." 423.
16. Ibid.

17. Farinella and Roš, *Neurocomic,* 39.

18. Bunge and Kahn, in their "Cognition: An Overview of Neuroimaging Techniques," offer a thorough introduction to the most widely used methods of neuroimaging, including another class I don't discuss here, EEG (electroencephalography) and MEG (magneto-encephalography), which work by measuring electrical activity emanating from the brain.

19. Fitzpatrick, "Functional Brain Imaging," 186.

20. Corkin, *Permanent Present Tense,* 80.

21. Booker, "A Window into the Brain."

22. Panksepp, *Affective Neuroscience,* 90.

23. Dumit, *Picturing Personhood,* 16.

24. Bunge and Kahn, "Cognition," 1063.

25. Alač and Hutchins, "I See What You Are Saying," 629; Dumit, *Picturing Personhood;* Fitzpatrick, "Functional Brain Imaging," 180; Hayles, "Brain Imaging and the Epistemology of Vision"; Davi Johnson, "'How Do You Know Unless You Look?'" 151; McCabe and Castel, "Seeing Is Believing," 343.

26. Davi Johnson, "'How Do You Know Unless You Look?'"

27. Dumit, *Picturing Personhood,* 5.

28. Rapp, "A Child Surrounds This Brain," 12, 9, 13.

29. Ibid., 15, 25.

30. Hayles, "Brain Imaging and the Epistemology of Vision," 322.

31. Farinella and Roš, *Neurocomic,* 20.

32. McCloud, *Understanding Comics,* 154.

33. Ibid., 155.

34. David B., *Epileptic,* 117.

35. Ibid., 202.

36. Forney, *Marbles,* 171.

37. Donovan, "Representations of Health, Embodiment, and Experience in Graphic Memoir," 2, 6.

38. Farinella and Roš, *Neurocomic,* 116.

39. David B., *Epileptic,* 289–90.

40. Forney, *Marbles,* 28.

41. Ibid., 201.

42. Ibid., 229.

43. David B., *Epileptic,* 278–79.

44. Panksepp, *Affective Neuroscience,* 9.

45. Cvetkovich, *Depression,* 4.

46. Farinella and Roš, *Neurocomic,* 132.

47. Fitzpatrick, "Functional Brain Imaging," 194.

Epilogue

1. Damasio, *The Feeling of What Happens,* 12.

2. Hustvedt, *The Shaking Woman,* 148.

3. Dehaene, *Reading in the Brain,* 303–4.
4. Goldman, "This Is Your Brain on Jane Austen, and Stanford Researchers Are Taking Notes"; Phillips, "Literary Neuroscience and the History of Mind," 57.
5. Phillips, "Literary Neuroscience and the History of Mind," 61–62, 69.
6. Garland-Thomson, "Misfits."

BIBLIOGRAPHY

Alač, Morana, and Edwin Hutchins. "I See What You Are Saying: Action as Cognition in fMRI Brain Mapping Practice." *Journal of Cognition and Culture* 4, no. 3, 629–61.

Amen, Daniel. *Change Your Brain, Change Your Life: The Breakthrough Program for Conquering Anxiety, Depression, Obsessiveness, Lack of Focus, Anger, and Memory Problems.* Rev. and exp. ed. New York: Harmony, 2015.

Amen, Daniel, and Tana Amen. *The Brain Warrior's Way: Ignite Your Energy and Focus, Attack Illness and Aging, Transform Pain into Purpose.* New York: Berkeley, 2016.

Anderson, M. T. *Feed.* Cambridge, MA: Candlewick, 2012.

Annese, Jacopo, Natalie M. Schenker-Ahmed, Hauke Bartsch, Paul Maechler, Colleen Sheh, Natasha Thomas, Junya Kayano, Alexander Ghatan, Noah Bresler, Matthew P. Frosch, Ruth Klaming, and Suzanne Corkin. "Postmortem Examination of Patient H.M.'s Brain Based on Histological Sectioning and Digital 3D Reconstruction." *Nature Communications,* April 25, 2016. http://www.nature.com/ncomms/2014/140128/ncomms4122/full/ncomms 4122.html.

Ansermet, François, and Pierre Magistretti. *Biology of Freedom: Neural Plasticity, Experience, and the Unconscious.* Translated by Susan Fairfield. New York: Other, 2007.

Ariely, Dan, and Gregory S. Berns. "Neuromarketing: The Hope and Hype of Neuroimaging in Business." *Nature Reviews Neuroscience* 11, no. 4 (April 2010): 284–92.

Armstrong, Paul B. *How Literature Plays with the Brain: The Neuroscience of Reading and Art.* Baltimore, MD: Johns Hopkins University Press, 2013.

Armstrong, Thomas. *Neurodiversity in the Classroom: Strength-Based Strategies to Help Students with Special Needs Succeed in School and Life.* Alexandria, VA: Association for Supervision and Curriculum Development, 2012.

Ashapoorv. "The Curious Incident of the Dog in the Night-Time by Mark Haddon—Review." August 6, 2015. http://www.theguardian.com/childrens-books-site/2015/aug/06/ the-curious-incident-of-the-dog-in-the-nighttime-mark-haddon-review.

Asperger, Hans. "'Autistic Psychopathy' in Childhood." Translated by Uta Frith. In *Autism and Asperger Syndrome,* edited by Uta Frith. Cambridge: Cambridge University Press, 1991.

Austin, Michael. *Useful Fictions: Evolution, Anxiety, and the Origins of Literature.* Lincoln: University of Nebraska Press, 2011.

Backderf, Derf. *My Friend Dahmer.* New York: Abrams, 2012.

Baggs, Amanda. "In My Language." YouTube video, posted January 2007. https://www .youtube.com/watch?v=JnylM1hI2jc.

Barash, David P., and Nanelle R. Barash. *Madame Bovary's Ovaries: A Darwinian Look at Literature.* New York: Delta, 2007.

Bardsley, Alyson. "Interspecies Limbic Love: Jane Smiley's *Horse Heaven.*" *MFS Modern Fiction Studies* 61, no. 2 (2015): 251–70.

Bartlett, Tom. "Can the Human Brain Project Be Saved? Should It Be?" *Chronicle of Higher Education,* June 21, 2016. http://chronicle.com/article/Can-the-Human-Brain-Project-Be/ 190031/.

Bartmess, Elizabeth. "Review: *The Curious Incident of the Dog in the Night-Time* by Mark Haddon." *Disability in Kidlit,* April 4, 2015. http://disabilityinkidlit.com/2015/04/04/ review-the-curious-incident-of-the-dog-in-the-night-time-by-mark-haddon/.

Bauby, Jean-Dominique. *The Diving Bell and the Butterfly.* Translated by Jeremy Leggatt. New York: Vintage, 1998.

Bayley, John. *Elegy for Iris.* New York: Picador, 1999.

Beatty, Paul. *The Sellout.* New York: Farrar, Straus and Giroux, 2015.

Becker, Robin. *Brains: A Zombie Memoir.* New York: Harper Collins, 2010.

Beer, Gillian. *Darwin's Plots: Evolutionary Narrative in Darwin, George Eliot, and Nineteenth-Century Fiction.* New York: Cambridge University Press, 2009.

Berns, Gregory S., Kristina Blaine, Michael J. Prietula, and Brandon E. Pye. "Short- and Long-Term Effects of a Novel on Connectivity in the Brain." *Brain Connectivity* 3, no. 6 (2013): 590–600.

Bernstein, Charles, ed. *Close Listening: Poetry and the Performed Word.* 1st ed. New York: Oxford University Press, 1998.

Bland, Lucy, and Laura Doan. *Sexology in Culture: Labelling Bodies and Desires.* Chicago: University of Chicago Press, 1999.

Block, Ed, Jr. "James Sully, Evolutionist Psychology, and Late Victorian Gothic Fiction." *Victorian Studies* 25, no. 4 (Summer 1982): 443–68.

Bonker, Elizabeth M., and Virginia G. Breen. *I Am in Here: The Journey of a Child with Autism Who Cannot Speak but Finds Her Voice.* Ada, MI: Revell, 2011.

Booker, Karene. "A Window into the Brain." *Human Ecology* 41, no. 2 (Fall 2013): 5–7. http://mri.cornell.edu/files/2013/12/MRI_feature-1xc686k.pdf.

Brain, Robert. *The Pulse of Modernism: Physiological Aesthetics in Fin-de-Siècle Europe.* Seattle: University of Washington Press, 2015.

Broks, Paul. *Into the Silent Land: Travels in Neuropsychology.* New York: Atlantic Monthly Press, 2004.

Brown, Andrew. "Profile: Oliver Sacks." *The Guardian,* March 5, 2005. http://www .theguardian.com/books/2005/mar/05/booksonhealth.whauden.

——. "Seeing Double," *The Guardian,* March 4, 2005. http://www.theguardian.com/ books/2005/mar/05/booksonhealth.whauden.

Bunge, S. A., and I. Kahn. "Cognition: An Overview of Neuroimaging Techniques." In *Encyclopedia of Neuroscience,* edited by Larry R. Squire, 1063–67. Cambridge, MA: Academic Press, 2009.

Buñuel, Luis. *My Last Sigh: The Autobiography of Luis Buñuel.* New York: Vintage, 2013.

Burn, Stephen J. "Neuroscience and Modern Fiction." *MFS Modern Fiction Studies* 61, no. 2 (2015): 209–25.

Butler, Octavia. *Fledgling.* New York: Seven Stories, 2005.

Carroll, Joseph. *Literary Darwinism: Evolution, Human Nature, and Literature.* New York: Routledge, 2004.

———. *Reading Human Nature: Literary Darwinism in Theory and Practice.* Albany: SUNY Press, 2011.

Carruthers, Mary, and Jan M. Ziolkowski, eds. *The Medieval Craft of Memory: An Anthology of Texts and Pictures.* Philadelphia: University of Pennsylvania Press, 2003.

Casey, Maud. "A Better Place to Live." In *Unholy Ghost: Writers on Depression,* edited by Nell Casey. New York: William Morrow, 2001.

———. *Genealogy.* New York: Harper Perennial, 2006.

———. *The Man Who Walked Away: A Novel.* New York: Bloomsbury USA, 2014.

———. *The Shape of Things to Come.* New York: Harper Perennial, 2002.

Casper, Stephen T. "History and Neuroscience: An Integrative Legacy." *Isis* 105, no. 1 (2014): 123–32.

Cassuto, Leonard. "Oliver Sacks: The P. T. Barnum of the Postmodern World?" *American Quarterly* 52, no. 2 (2000): 326–33.

Cave, Terence. *Thinking with Literature: Towards a Cognitive Literary Criticism.* Oxford: Oxford University Press, 2016.

Chalmers, David J. *The Character of Consciousness.* New York: Oxford University Press, 2010.

Chapman, Wes. "The Cognitive Literary Theory of Richard Powers's *Galatea 2.2.*" *MFS Modern Fiction Studies* 61, no. 2 (2015): 226–50.

Churchland, Patricia S. *Touching a Nerve: Our Brains, Our Selves.* New York: W. W. Norton, 2014.

Chute, Hillary. "*Our Cancer Year,* and: *Janet and Me: An Illustrated Story of Love and Loss,* and: *Cancer Vixen: A True Story,* and: *Mom's Cancer,* and: *Blue Pills: A Positive Love Story,* and: *Epileptic,* and: *Black Hole* (review)." *Literature and Medicine* 26, no. 2 (2008): 413–29.

Chute, Hillary, and Marianne DeKoven. "Introduction: Graphic Narrative." *MFS Modern Fiction Studies* 52, no. 4 (2006): 767–82.

Clark, Andy. *Supersizing the Mind: Embodiment, Action, and Cognitive Extension.* Oxford; New York: Oxford University Press, 2010.

Clegg, Bill. *Portrait of an Addict as a Young Man.* New York: Little Brown, 2010.

Cockburn, Patrick, and Henry Cockburn. *Henry's Demons: Living with Schizophrenia, A Father and Son's Story.* New York: Scribner, 2011.

Cohen, Patricia. "Next Big Thing in English: Knowing They Know That You Know." *New York Times,* April 1, 2010. http://www.nytimes.com/2010/04/01/books/01lit.html.

Cohen, William A. *Embodied: Victorian Literature and the Senses.* Minneapolis: University of Minnesota Press, 2008.

——. "Material Interiority in Charlotte Brontë's *The Professor.*" *Nineteenth-Century Literature* 57, no. 4 (2003): 443–76.

Cole, Teju. *Open City.* New York: Random House, 2011.

Cook, Gareth. "Brain Games Are Bogus." *New Yorker,* April 5, 2013. http://www.newyorker.com/tech/elements/brain-games-are-bogus.

Corkin, Suzanne. *Permanent Present Tense: The Unforgettable Life of the Amnesic Patient, H. M.* New York: Basic, 2013.

Couser, G. Thomas. *The Cases of Oliver Sacks: The Ethics of Neuroanthropology.* Bloomington: Poynter Center, Indiana University, 2001.

Crick, Francis. *The Astonishing Hypothesis: The Scientific Search for the Soul.* New York: Scribner, 1995.

Cunningham, Darryl. *Psychiatric Tales: Eleven Graphic Stories about Mental Illness.* New York: Bloomsbury, 2011.

Cvetkovich, Ann. *Depression: A Public Feeling.* Durham: Duke University Press, 2012.

Damasio, Antonio. *Descartes' Error: Emotion, Reason, and the Human Brain.* London: Penguin, 2005.

——. *The Feeling of What Happens: Body and Emotion in the Making of Consciousness.* New York: Houghton Mifflin Harcourt, 1999.

——. *Looking for Spinoza: Joy, Sorrow, and the Feeling Brain.* Orlando, FL: Harvest, 2003.

——. *Self Comes to Mind: Constructing the Conscious Brain* (2010). New York: Vintage, 2012.

Damasio, Antonio, and Hannah Damasio. "Minding the Body." *Daedalus* 135, no. 3 (Summer 2006): 15–22.

Dames, Nicholas. *The Physiology of the Novel: Reading, Neural Science, and the Form of Victorian Fiction.* 1st ed. Oxford: Oxford University Press, 2007.

David B. *Epileptic.* New York: Pantheon, 2006.

——. *L'Ascension du Haut Mal.* Paris: L'Association, 2011.

Davide-Rivera, Jeannie. *Twirling Naked in the Streets and No One Noticed: Growing Up with Undiagnosed Autism.* N. P.: David and Goliath, 2013.

Dehaene, Stanislas. *Consciousness and the Brain: Deciphering How the Brain Codes Our Thoughts.* New York: Viking, 2014.

——. *Reading in the Brain: The New Science of How We Read.* New York: Penguin, 2010.

Doctorow, E. L. *Andrew's Brain.* New York: Random House, 2014.

Donovan, Courtney. "Representations of Health, Embodiment, and Experience in Graphic Memoir." *Configurations* 22, no. 2 (2014): 237–53.

Draaisma, Douwe. "Eye on Fiction: Generic Images of Autism." *The Psychologist,* April 24, 2016. https://thepsychologist.bps.org.uk/volume-27/edition-10/eye-fiction-generic-images-autism.

——. "Stereotypes of Autism." *Philosophical Transactions of the Royal Society B: Biological Sciences* 364, no. 1522 (May 27, 2009): 1475–80.

——. "Who Owns Asperger's Syndrome?" *Sartoniana* 21 (2008): 23–48.

Dully, Howard, and Charles Fleming. *My Lobotomy.* New York: Broadway, 2008.

Dumit, Joseph. *Picturing Personhood: Brain Scans and Biomedical Identity.* Princeton: Princeton University Press, 2004.

Eagleman, David. *The Brain: The Story of You.* New York: Pantheon, 2015.

Eakin, Paul John. *How Our Lives Become Stories: How Photography Complicates the Picture.* Ithaca, NY: Cornell University Press, 1999.

———. *Living Autobiographically: How We Create Identity in Narrative.* Ithaca, NY: Cornell University Press, 2008.

Edelman, Gerald M. *Wider Than the Sky: The Phenomenal Gift of Consciousness.* New Haven: Yale University Press, 2005.

Edelman, Gerald, and Giulio Tononi. *A Universe of Consciousness: How Matter Becomes Imagination.* New York: Basic, 2001.

Elliott, Stephen. *The Adderall Diaries.* New York: Graywolf, 2009.

Fallon, James. *The Psychopath Inside: A Neuroscientist's Personal Journey into the Dark Side of the Brain.* New York: Penguin, 2013.

Farinella, Matteo, and Hana Roš. *Neurocomic* (2013). London: Nobrow, 2014.

Fauconnier, Gilles, and Mark Turner. *The Way We Think: Conceptual Blending and the Mind's Hidden Complexities.* New York: Basic, 2003.

Faulds, Cas. *Un-Boxed Brain.* http://un-boxedbrain.com.au/.

Feder, Toni. "The Brain Is Big Science." *Physics Today* 66, no. 12 (2013): 20–22.

Fitzpatrick, S. M. "Functional Brain Imaging: Neuro-Turn or Wrong Turn?" In *The Neuroscientific Turn: Transdisciplinarity in the Age of the Brain.* Ann Arbor: University of Michigan Press, 2012.

Flaherty, Alice Weaver. *The Midnight Disease: The Drive to Write, Writer's Block, and the Creative Brain.* New York: Houghton Mifflin, 2004.

Fleischmann, Carly. "Speechless Intro." Video series, 2016–17. https://www.youtube.com/channel/UCeKKQlMB1NeOLN31_CSJFRQ.

Fleischmann, Carly, and Arthur Fleischmann. *Carly's Voice: Breaking through Autism.* New York: Touchstone, 2012.

Flood, Alison. "Curious Incident of the Dog in the Night-Time Pulled from Children's Reading List." *The Guardian,* August 12, 2015. http://www.theguardian.com/books/2015/aug/12/curious-incident-of-the-dog-in-the-night-time-pulled-from-childrens-reading-list.

Forney, Ellen. *Marbles: Mania, Depression, Michelangelo, and Me: A Graphic Memoir.* New York: Avery, 2012.

Frances, Allen, and Eleanor Longden. "Psychiatry and Hearing Voices: A Dialogue With Eleanor Longden." *Huffington Post,* June 21, 2016. http://www.huffingtonpost.com/allen-frances/psychiatry-and-hearing-vo_b_4003317.html.

Franzen, Jonathan. "My Father's Brain." *New Yorker,* September 10, 2001, 80–91.

Freud, Sigmund. *The Interpretation of Dreams* (1899). Translated by Joyce Crick. Oxford: Oxford University Press, 1999.

Gaedtke, Andrew. "Cognitive Investigations: The Problems of Qualia and Style in the Contemporary Neuronovel." *Novel* 45, no. 2 (2012): 184–201.

———. "Neuromodernism: Diagnosis and Disability in Will Self's *Umbrella.*" *MFS Modern Fiction Studies* 61, no. 2 (2015): 271–94.

Galchen, Rivka. *Atmospheric Disturbances.* New York: Farrar, Straus and Giroux, 2008.

Garland-Thomson, Rosemarie. "Misfits: A Feminist Materialist Disability Concept." *Hypatia* 26, no. 3 (August 1, 2011): 591–609.

Gazzaniga, Michael S. *Human: The Science Behind What Makes Us Unique.* New York: Harper Perennial, 2009.

——. *Who's in Charge?: Free Will and the Science of the Brain.* New York: Ecco, 2011.

Genova, Lisa. *Still Alice.* New York: Gallery, 2009.

Goldman, Corinne. "This Is Your Brain on Jane Austen, and Stanford Researchers Are Taking Notes." *Stanford Report,* September 7, 2012. http://news.stanford.edu/news/2012/september/austen-reading-fmri-090712.html.

Goldstein, Rebecca. *The Mind-Body Problem.* New York: Penguin, 1993.

Grandin, Temple. *Thinking in Pictures: My Life with Autism* (1995). Exp. ed. New York: Vintage, 2010.

Grandin, Temple, and Richard Panek. *The Autistic Brain: Helping Different Kinds of Minds Succeed.* Boston: Mariner, 2014.

Grandin, Temple, and Margaret M. Scariano. *Emergence: Labeled Autistic* (1986). Reissued ed. New York: Warner, 1996.

Greenberg, Lynne. *The Body Broken: A Memoir.* New York: Random House, 2009.

Groes, Sebastian. "Information Overload in Literature." *Textual Practice* (January 20, 2016): 1–28. http://www.tandfonline.com/doi/full/10.1080/0950236X.2015.1126630.

——, ed. *Memory in the Twenty-First Century: New Critical Perspectives from the Arts, Humanities, and Sciences.* New York: Palgrave Macmillan, 2016.

Hacking, Ian. "Autism Fiction: A Mirror of an Internet Decade?" *University of Toronto Quarterly* 79, no. 2 (2010): 632–55.

——. "Autistic Autobiography." *Philosophical Transactions of the Royal Society B: Biological Sciences* 364, no. 1522 (May 27, 2009): 1467–73.

——. "Lost in the Forest." *London Review of Books,* August 8, 2013. http://www.lrb.co.uk/v35/n15/ian-hacking/lost-in-the-forest.

——. *Mad Travelers: Reflections on the Reality of Transient Mental Illnesses.* Cambridge: Harvard University Press, 2002.

——. *Rewriting the Soul: Multiple Personality and the Sciences of Memory.* Princeton: Princeton University Press, 1995.

Haddon, Mark. "asperger's & autism," July 16, 2009. http://www.markhaddon.com/aspergers-and-autism.

——. *The Curious Incident of the Dog in the Night-Time* (2003). New York: Vintage, 2004.

Harris, Charles B. "The Story of the Self: *The Echo Maker* and Neurological Realism." In *Intersections: Essays on Richard Powers,* edited by Stephen J. Burn and Peter Dempsey, 230–59. Champaign, IL: Dalkey Archive Press, 2008.

Harris, Thomas. *Hannibal: A Novel.* 1st ed. New York: Delacorte, 1999.

Hartley, Lucy. *Physiognomy and the Meaning of Expression in Nineteenth-Century Culture.* Cambridge: Cambridge University Press, 2001.

Hartmann, Ernest. *Dreams and Nightmares: The Origin and Meaning of Dreams.* New York: Basic, 2000.

Hatfield, Elaine, John T. Cacioppo, and Richard L. Rapson. *Emotional Contagion: Studies in Emotion and Social Interaction.* Cambridge: Cambridge University Press, 1993.

Hayles, N. Katherine. "Brain Imaging and the Epistemology of Vision: Daniel Suarez's *Daemon* and *Freedom.*" *MFS Modern Fiction Studies* 61, no. 2 (2015): 320–34.

——. *How We Think: Digital Media and Contemporary Technogenesis.* Chicago: University of Chicago Press, 2012.

Hearing Voices Network. "Welcome." http://www.hearing-voices.org/.

Heider, Fritz, and Marianne Simmel. "An Experimental Study of Apparent Behavior." *American Journal of Psychology* 57, no. 2 (1944): 243–59.

Heilker, Paul, and Melanie R. Yergeau. "Autism and Rhetoric." *College English* 73, no. 5 (2011). https://experts.umich.edu/en/publications/autism-and-rhetoric.

Herman, David. "Re-Minding Modernism." In *The Emergence of Mind: Representations of Consciousness in Narrative Discourse in English,* edited by David Herman, 243–72. Lincoln: University of Nebraska Press, 2011.

Higashida, Naoki. *The Reason I Jump: The Inner Voice of a Thirteen-Year-Old Boy with Autism* (2007). Translated by KA Yoshida and David Mitchell. New York: Random House, 2013.

Hofstadter, Douglas. *I Am a Strange Loop.* New York: Basic, 2008.

Hogan, Patrick Colm. *Cognitive Science, Literature, and the Arts: A Guide for Humanists.* New York: Routledge, 2003.

———. *The Mind and Its Stories: Narrative Universals and Human Emotion.* New York: Cambridge University Press, 2003.

Hong, Caroline. "Disorienting the Vietnam War: GB Tran's *Vietnamerica* as Transnational and Transhistorical Graphic Memoir." *Asian American Literature: Discourses and Pedagogies* 5 (2014): 11–22.

Honigsbaum, Mark. "Human Brain Project: Henry Markram Plans to Spend €1bn Building a Perfect Model of the Human Brain." *The Guardian,* October 15, 2013. https://www.theguardian.com/science/2013/oct/15/human-brain-project-henry-markram.

Houser, Heather. *Ecosickness in Contemporary U.S. Fiction: Environment and Affect.* New York: Columbia University Press, 2014.

Human, Erin. *Erin Human: Writing, Cartooning, and Neurodiversity Designs.* https://erinhuman.com/.

Human Brain Project. "The Human Brain Project." https://www.humanbrainproject.eu/.

Hustvedt, Siri. *The Blazing World: A Novel.* New York: Simon and Schuster, 2014.

———. *Living, Thinking, Looking: Essays.* New York: Picador, 2012.

———. *The Shaking Woman or A History of My Nerves.* New York: Picador, 2010.

———. *The Sorrows of an American: A Novel.* New York: Picador, 2009.

———. *What I Loved: A Novel.* New York: Picador, 2004.

Huxley, Aldous. *The Doors of Perception.* New York: Harper Perennial, 2009.

Intervoice. "Intervoice.org," June 21, 2016. http://www.intervoiceonline.org/.

Isherwood, Christopher. *A Single Man: A Novel.* New York: Farrar, Straus and Giroux, 2013.

Ishiguro, Kazuo. *The Buried Giant.* New York: Vintage, 2015.

———. *The Unconsoled.* New York: Vintage, 1996.

James, William. *Psychology: The Briefer Course.* Mineola, NY: Dover Publications, 2001.

———. "The Stream of Consciousness." In *Psychology: The Briefer Course.* Mineola, NY: Dover, 2001.

———. *The Varieties of Religious Experience.* In *William James: Writings 1902–1910.* New York: Library of America, 1988.

Jamison, Kay Redfield. *An Unquiet Mind: A Memoir of Moods and Madness.* 1st ed. New York: Vintage, 1996.

Johnson, Davi. "'How Do You Know Unless You Look?': Brain Imaging, Biopower, and Practical Neuroscience." *Journal of Medical Humanities* 29, no. 3 (2008): 147–61.

Johnson, Gary. "Consciousness as Content: Neuronarratives and the Redemption of Fiction." *Mosaic* 41, no. 1 (2008): 169.

Johnson, Steven. *Mind Wide Open: Your Brain and the Neuroscience of Everyday Life*. New York: Scribner, 2005.

Jordan-Young, Rebecca M. *Brain Storm: The Flaws in the Science of Sex Research*. Cambridge: Harvard University Press, 2010.

Jung, C. G., and Sonu Shamdasani. *Dreams*. Translated by R. F. C. Hull. With a new foreword by Sonu Shamdasani. Princeton: Princeton University Press, 2010.

Kakutani, Michiko. "Math and Physics? A Cinch. People? Incomprehensible." *New York Times*, June 13, 2003. http://www.nytimes.com/2003/06/13/books/books-of-the-times-math-and-physics-a-cinch-people-incomprehensible.html.

Kalanithi, Paul. *When Breath Becomes Air*. New York: Random House, 2016.

Kandel, Eric. "Eric Kandel: Oliver Sacks shows disease brings out courage, beauty." *CBS This Morning*, February 20, 2015. http://www.cbsnews.com/news/neuroscientist-eric-kandel-on-neurologist-oliver-sacks-storytelling-neurology-contributions/.

———. *In Search of Memory: The Emergence of a New Science of Mind*. 1st ed. New York: W. W. Norton, 2006.

Kanner, Leo. "Autistic Disturbances of Affective Contact." *Nervous Child* 2 (1943): 217–50.

Kapp, Steven K., Kristen Gillespie-Lynch, Lauren E. Sherman, and Ted Hutman. "Deficit, Difference, or Both? Autism and Neurodiversity." *Developmental Psychology* 49, no. 1 (2013): 59–71.

Keen, Suzanne. *Empathy and the Novel*. 1st ed. New York: Oxford University Press, 2007.

Keenan, Julian. *The Face in the Mirror: The Origins of Consciousness*. New York: Harper Collins, 2003.

Kendal, Jeremy, Jamshid J. Tehrani, and John Odling-Smee. "Human Niche Construction in Interdisciplinary Focus." *Philosophical Transactions of the Royal Society B: Biological Sciences* 366, no. 1566 (March 27, 2011): 785–92.

Knapp, Caroline. *Drinking: A Love Story*. New York: Dial, 1997.

Knausgaard, Karl Ove. "The Terrible Beauty of Brain Surgery." *New York Times Magazine*. December 30, 2015. https://www.nytimes.com/2016/01/03/magazine/karl-ove-knausgaard-on-the-terrible-beauty-of-brain-surgery.html.

Konnikova, Maria. *Mastermind: How to Think Like Sherlock Holmes*. New York: Penguin, 2013.

Krasner, James. "Doubtful Arms and Phantom Limbs: Literary Portrayals of Embodied Grief." *PMLA* 119, no. 2 (2004): 218–32.

Krauss, Nicole. *Man Walks into a Room*. New York: Doubleday, 2002.

Lakoff, George, and Mark Turner. *More than Cool Reason: A Field Guide to Poetic Metaphor*. 1st ed. Chicago: University of Chicago Press, 1989.

Leary, Timothy. *The Psychedelic Experience: A Manual Based on the Tibetan Book of the Dead*. New York: Citadel Press, 1992.

LeDoux, Joseph. *Anxious: Using the Brain to Understand and Treat Fear and Anxiety*. 1st ed. New York: Viking, 2015.

———. *Synaptic Self: How Our Brains Become Who We Are*. New York: Penguin, 2003.

Legrenzi, Paolo, and Carlo Umiltà. *Neuromania: On the Limits of Brain Science*. 1st ed. New York: Oxford University Press, 2011.

Lethem, Jonathan. *Motherless Brooklyn* (1999). Vintage, 2000.

Levine, Joseph. "Materialism and Qualia: The Explanatory Gap." *Pacific Philosophical Quarterly* 64 (October 1983): 354–61.

Lewontin, Richard, and Richard Levins. *Biology Under the Influence: Dialectical Essays on Ecology, Agriculture, and Health.* New York: Monthly Review Press, 2007.

Lodge, David. *Consciousness and the Novel: Connected Essays.* 1st ed. Cambridge: Harvard University Press, 2002.

——. *Thinks . . .* New York: Penguin, 2001.

Loftis, Sonya Freeman. *Imagining Autism: Fiction and Stereotypes on the Spectrum.* Bloomington: Indiana University Press, 2015.

Logan, Brian. "Private Defective." *The Guardian,* April 17, 2016. http://www.theguardian .com/books/2000/jan/24/crime.artsfeatures.

Luhrmann, T. M. "Redefining Mental Illness." *New York Times,* January 17, 2015. http://www .nytimes.com/2015/01/18/opinion/sunday/t-m-luhrmann-redefining-mental-illness.html.

Malabou, Catherine. *What Should We Do with Our Brain?* Translated by Sebastian Rand. New York: Fordham University Press, 2008.

"Mapping the Mind—Smart Thinking for Brain Health?" *The Lancet* 381, no. 9874 (April 2013): 1247.

Marcus, Gary. "Obama's Brain." *New Yorker,* February 18, 2013. http://www.newyorker .com/news/news-desk/obamas-brain.

——. "The Trouble With Brain Science." *New York Times,* July 11, 2014. http://www .nytimes.com/2014/07/12/opinion/the-trouble-with-brain-science.html.

Markram, Henry, Tania Rinaldi, and Kamila Markram. "The Intense World Syndrome—an Alternative Hypothesis for Autism." *Frontiers in Neuroscience* 1, no. 1 (October 15, 2007): 77–96.

Marsh, Henry. *Do No Harm: Stories of Life, Death, and Brain Surgery.* New York: Thomas Dunne, 2015.

Marshall, John C. "In the Region of Lost Minds." *New York Times,* March 2, 1986. https:// www.nytimes.com/books/98/12/06/specials/sacks-mistook.html.

Martin, Emily. "Mind-Body Problems." *American Ethnologist* 27, no. 3 (August 2000): 569–90.

McBride, Eimear. *A Girl Is a Half-Formed Thing.* Minneapolis: Coffee House, 2014.

McCabe, David P., and Alan D. Castel. "Seeing Is Believing: The Effect of Brain Images on Judgments of Scientific Reasoning." *Cognition,* May 24, 2016, 343–52.

McCarthy, Jenny. *Louder than Words: A Mother's Journey in Healing Autism* (2007). New York: Plume, 2008.

McCarthy, Tom. *Remainder* (2005). Richmond, UK: Alma, 2007.

McCloud, Scott. *Understanding Comics: The Invisible Art.* New York: William Morrow Paperbacks, 1994.

McEwan, Ian. *Enduring Love: A Novel.* New York: Anchor, 1998.

——. *Saturday: A Novel.* New York: Doubleday, 2005.

McInerney, Jay. "The Remains of the Dog." *New York Times,* June 15, 2003. http://www .nytimes.com/2003/06/15/books/the-remains-of-the-dog.html.

Merleau-Ponty, Maurice. *The Phenomenology of Perception.* Translated by Donald Landes. Princeton: Princeton University Press, 2013.

Miller, Laura. "'The Curious Incident of the Dog in the Night-Time' by Mark Haddon." *Salon,* April 24, 2016. http://www.salon.com/2003/06/12/haddon/.

Miller, Nancy K. *But Enough about Me: Why We Read Other People's Lives.* New York: Columbia University Press, 2002.

Mitchell, David. *Slade House.* New York: Random House, 2015.

Mukhopadhyay, Tito Rajarshi. *The Gold of the Sunbeams* (2005). New York: Arcade, 2011.

——. *How Can I Talk If My Lips Don't Move?: Inside My Autistic Mind.* New York: Arcade, 2008.

——. *The Mind Tree: A Miraculous Child Breaks the Silence of Autism* (2000). New York: Arcade, 2003.

Mukhopadhyay, Tito Rajarshi, and Lorna Wing. *Beyond the Silence: My Life, the World and Autism.* London: National Autistic Society, 2000.

Murakami, Haruki. *1Q84.* New York: Knopf, 2011.

Murray, Stuart. *Autism.* New York: Routledge, 2011.

——. *Representing Autism: Culture, Narrative, Fascination.* Liverpool: Liverpool University Press, 2008.

Nagel, Thomas. "What Is It Like to Be a Bat?" *Philosophical Review* 83, no. 4 (1974): 435–50.

Nalbantian, Suzanne. *Memory in Literature: From Rousseau to Neuroscience.* New York: Palgrave Macmillan, 2004.

Nalbantian, Suzanne, Paul M. Matthews, and James L. McClelland, eds. *The Memory Process: Neuroscientific and Humanistic Perspectives.* Cambridge: MIT Press, 2010.

National Institutes of Health (NIH). The Brain Initiative®. "What Is the Brain Initiative?" http://www.braininitiative.nih.gov/.

New York Times, "Can 'Neuro Lit Crit' Save the Humanities?" *Room for Debate* (blog), April 5, 2010. http://roomfordebate.blogs.nytimes.com/2010/04/05/can-neuro-lit-crit-save -the-humanities/.

Nicolaidis, Christina. "What Can Physicians Learn from the Neurodiversity Movement?" *AMA Journal of Ethics: Illuminating the Art of Medicine* 14, no. 6 (2012): 503–10.

Noë, Alva. *Out of Our Heads: Why You Are Not Your Brain, and Other Lessons from the Biology of Consciousness.* 1st ed. New York: Hill and Wang, 2009.

——. *Strange Tools: Art and Human Nature.* New York: Hill and Wang, 2015.

——. *Varieties of Presence.* Cambridge: Harvard University Press, 2012.

Norman, Don. *The Design of Everyday Things.* Rev. and exp. ed. New York: Basic, 2013.

Olear, Greg. "When Popular Novels Perpetuate Negative Stereotypes: Mark Haddon, Asperger's and Irresponsible Fiction." *Huffington Post,* April 24, 2011. http://www .huffingtonpost.com/greg-olear/curious-incident-dog-night-time_b_1099692.html.

"Open Message to the European Commission Concerning the Human Brain Project." *Neurofuture,* July 7, 2014. http://www.neurofuture.eu/.

Ortega, Francisco. "The Cerebral Subject and the Challenge of Neurodiversity." *BioSocieties* 4, no. 4 (December 2009): 425–45.

Ortega, Francisco, and Fernando Vidal. "Brains in Literature / Literature in the Brain." *Poetics Today* 34, no. 3 (September 21, 2013): 327–60.

——. *Neurocultures: Glimpses into an Expanding Universe.* 1st ed. New York: Peter Lang, 2011.

Page, Tim. *Parallel Play: Growing Up with Undiagnosed Asperger's.* New York: Doubleday, 2009.

Panksepp, Jaak. *Affective Neuroscience: The Foundations of Human and Animal Emotions.* New York: Oxford University Press, 1998.

——. *The Archaeology of Mind: Neuroevolutionary Origins of Human Emotions.* 1st ed. New York: W. W. Norton, 2012.

Park, Clara Claiborne. *The Siege: A Family's Journey into the World of an Autistic Child* (1967). New York: Back Bay, 1982.

Phelan, James. *Living to Tell about It: A Rhetoric and Ethics of Character Narration.* Ithaca, NY: Cornell University Press, 2004.

Phillips, Natalie. "Literary Neuroscience and the History of Mind: An Interdisciplinary fMRI Study of Attention and Jane Austen." In *The Oxford Handbook of Cognitive Literary Studies,* edited by Lisa Zunshine. New York: Oxford University Press, 2015.

Picard, Rosalind W. *Affective Computing.* Cambridge: MIT Press, 1997.

Pinchbeck, Daniel. *Breaking Open the Head: A Psychedelic Journey into the Heart of Contemporary Shamanism.* New York: Broadway, 2003.

Pisters, Patricia. *The Neuro-Image: A Deleuzian Film-Philosophy of Digital Screen Culture.* Stanford: Stanford University Press, 2012.

Pitts-Taylor, Victoria. *The Brain's Body: Neuroscience and Corporeal Politics.* Durham: Duke University Press, 2016.

——. "I Feel Your Pain: Embodied Knowledges and Situated Neurons." *Hypatia* 28, no. 4 (2013): 852–69.

——. "Social Brains, Embodiment, and Neuro-Interactionism." *The Routledge Handbook of Body Studies,* edited by Bryan S. Turner. New York: Routledge, 2012.

Powers, Richard. *The Echo Maker* (2006). New York: Picador, 2007.

——. *Galatea 2.2: A Novel* (1995). New York: Picador, 2004.

Prinz, Jesse L. *Beyond Human Nature: How Culture and Experience Shape the Human Mind.* 1st ed. New York: W. W. Norton, 2014.

——. *The Conscious Brain: How Attention Engenders Experience.* 1st ed. New York: Oxford University Press, 2012.

Ramachandran, V. S. *A Brief Tour of Human Consciousness: From Impostor Poodles to Purple Numbers.* New York: Plume, 2005.

——. *The Tell-Tale Brain: A Neuroscientist's Quest for What Makes Us Human.* New York: W. W. Norton, 2011.

Ramachandran, V. S., Sandra Blakeslee. *Phantoms in the Brain: Probing the Mysteries of the Human Mind.* New York: William Morrow Paperbacks, 1999.

Rapp, Rayna. "A Child Surrounds This Brain: The Future of Neurological Difference According to Scientists, Parents and Diagnosed Young Adults." In *Sociological Reflections on the Neurosciences,* vol. 13, 3–26. Bingley, UK: Emerald Group, 2011.

Ray, Sarah Jaquette. "Normalcy, Knowledge, and Nature in Mark Haddon's *The Curious Incident of the Dog in the Night-Time.*" *Disability Studies Quarterly* 33, no. 3 (May 23, 2013). http://dsq-sds.org/article/view/3233/3263.

Requarth, Tim. "Bringing a Virtual Brain to Life." *New York Times,* March 18, 2013. http://www.nytimes.com/2013/03/19/science/bringing-a-virtual-brain-to-life.html.

Richardson, Alan. *British Romanticism and the Science of the Mind.* Cambridge: Cambridge University Press, 2005.

——. "Once upon a Mind: Literary and Narrative Studies in the Age of Cognitive Science." *MFS Modern Fiction Studies* 61, no. 2 (2015): 359–69.

Rickards, H., N. Hartley, and M. M. Robertson. "Seignot's Paper on the Treatment of Tourette's Syndrome with Haloperidol. Classic Text No. 31." *History of Psychiatry* 8, no. 31, pt. 3 (September 1997): 433–36.

Ricoeur, Paul. *Freud and Philosophy: An Essay on Interpretation.* New Haven: Yale University Press, 1970.

Robison, John Elder. *Be Different: My Adventures with Asperger's and My Advice for Fellow Aspergerians, Misfits, Families, and Teachers.* New York: Broadway, 2011.

——. "I Resign My Roles at Autism Speaks." *Look Me in the Eye,* November 13, 2013. http://jerobison.blogspot.com/2013/11/i-resign-my-roles-at-autism-speaks.html.

——. *Look Me in the Eye: My Life with Asperger's.* New York: Three Rivers, 2007.

——. *Raising Cubby: A Father and Son's Adventures with Asperger's, Trains, Tractors, and High Explosives.* New York: Broadway, 2013.

——. *Switched On: A Memoir of Brain Change and Emotional Awakening.* 1st ed. New York: Spiegel and Grau, 2016.

Rose, Nikolas, and Joelle M. Abi-Rached. *Neuro: The New Brain Sciences and the Management of the Mind.* Princeton: Princeton University Press, 2013.

Roth, Marco. "The Rise of the Neuronovel." *n+1.* August 3, 2009. https://nplusonemag.com/issue-8/essays/the-rise-of-the-neuronovel/.

Roy, Deboleena. "Asking Different Questions: Feminist Practices for the Natural Sciences." *Hypatia* 23, no. 4 (2008): 134–57.

Ruddick, Lisa. "When Nothing Is Cool." In *The Future of Scholarly Writing* (71–85), edited by Angelika Bammer and Ruth-Ellen Boetcher Joeres. New York: Palgrave Macmillan, 2015.

Ryskamp, Dani Alexis, ed. *NeuroQueer.* http://neuroqueer.blogspot.com/.

Sacks, Oliver. "The Abyss." *New Yorker,* September 24, 2007. http://www.newyorker.com/magazine/2007/09/24/the-abyss.

——. *An Anthropologist on Mars: Seven Paradoxical Tales* (1995). New York: Vintage, 1996.

——. *Awakenings.* London: Duckworth, 1973.

——. *The Man Who Mistook His Wife for a Hat: And Other Clinical Tales.* New York: Simon and Schuster, 1985.

——. *On the Move: A Life.* New York: Knopf, 2015.

Satel, Sally, and Scott O. Lilienfeld. *Brainwashed: The Seductive Appeal of Mindless Neuroscience.* New York: Basic, 2013.

Savarese, Ralph James. *Reasonable People: A Memoir of Autism and Adoption.* New York: Other, 2007.

Savarese, Ralph James, and Lisa Zunshine. "The Critic as Neurocosmopolite; Or, What Cognitive Approaches to Literature Can Learn from Disability Studies: Lisa Zunshine in Conversation with Ralph James Savarese." *Narrative* 22, no. 1 (2014): 17–44.

Scarry, Elaine. *Dreaming by the Book.* Princeton: Princeton University Press, 2001.

Schaber, Amethyst. "Ask an Autistic," YouTube channel. https://www.youtube.com/user/neurowonderful.

——. *neurowonderful.* http://neurowonderful.tumblr.com/.

Schacter, Daniel L. *Searching for Memory: The Brain, the Mind, and the Past.* Rev. ed. New York: Basic, 1997.

Schleifer, Ronald. "The Poetics of Tourette's Syndrome: Language, Neurobiology, and Poetry." In *Literature, Speech Disorders, and Disability: Talking Normal,* edited by Christopher Eagle, 137–61. New York: Routledge, 2013.

Schofield, William. "A Journey to Shock and Enlighten." *The Guardian,* January 29, 2004. http://www.theguardian.com/books/2004/jan/29/whitbreadbookawards2003 .costabookaward.

Searle, John R. *The Mystery of Consciousness.* New York: New York Review Books, 1997.

Sedgwick, Eve. *Touching Feeling: Affect, Pedagogy, Performativity.* Durham: Duke University Press, 2002.

Sellers, Heather. *Don't Look Like Anyone I Know: A True Story of Family, Face-Blindness, and Forgiveness.* New York: Riverhead, 2010.

Semino, Elena. "Pragmatic Failure, Mind Style and Characterisation in Fiction about Autism." *Language and Literature* 23, no. 2 (2014): 141–58.

Seung, Sebastian. *Connectome: How the Brain's Wiring Makes Us Who We Are.* Boston: Houghton Mifflin Harcourt Trade, 2012.

Shakespeare, Tom. "Review of *An Anthropologist on Mars,* by Oliver Sacks." *Disability and Society* 11, no. 1 (March 1996): 137–39.

Shinn, Austin. *A Flickering Life: A Memoir of Autism.* Amazon Digital Services, 2016.

Shore, Stephen M. *Beyond the Wall: Personal Experiences with Autism and Asperger's Syndrome.* 2nd ed. Shawnee Mission, KS: Autism Asperger Publishing, 2003.

Shulman, Alix Kates. *To Love What Is: A Marriage Transformed.* New York: Farrar, Straus and Giroux, 2009.

Shuttleworth, Sally. "Psychological Definition and Social Power: Phrenology in the Novels of Charlotte Brontë." In *Nature Transfigured: Science and Literature, 1700–1900,* edited by John Christie and Sally Shuttleworth. Manchester: Manchester University Press, 1989.

Siebers, Tobin Anthony. *Disability Aesthetics.* Ann Arbor: University of Michigan Press, 2010.

Silberman, Steve. *NeuroTribes: The Legacy of Autism and the Future of Neurodiversity.* New York: Avery, 2015.

Slater, Lauren. *Lying: A Metaphorical Memoir.* New York: Penguin, 2001.

——. *Prozac Diary.* New York: Penguin, 1999.

Smith, Sidonie, and Julia Watson. *Reading Autobiography: A Guide for Interpreting Life Narratives.* 2nd ed. Minneapolis: University of Minnesota Press, 2010.

Snow, C. P. *The Two Cultures and the Scientific Revolution.* London: Cambridge University Press, 1959.

Solms, Mark, and James Rose. *The Feeling Brain: Selected Papers on Neuropsychoanalysis.* London: Karnac, 2015.

Solms, Mark, and Oliver Turnbull. *The Brain and the Inner World: An Introduction to the Neuroscience of Subjective Experience.* New York: Other, 2003.

Spolsky, Ellen. *Gaps in Nature: Literary Interpretation and the Modular Mind.* Albany: State University of New York Press, 1993.

Starr, G. Gabrielle. *Feeling Beauty: The Neuroscience of Aesthetic Experience.* Cambridge: MIT Press, 2013.

Stiles, Anne. "Christian Science versus the Rest Cure in Frances Hodgson Burnett's *The Secret Garden.*" *MFS Modern Fiction Studies* 61, no. 2 (2015): 295–319.

——. *Popular Fiction and Brain Science in the Late Nineteenth Century.* New York: Cambridge University Press, 2014.

Straley, Jessica. "Wilkie Collins's Experiment in Heart and Science." *Nineteenth-Century Literature* 65, no. 3 (December 2010): 348–73.

Straus, Joseph N. "Autism as Culture." In *The Disability Studies Reader,* edited by Lennard J. Davis. 4th ed., 460–84. New York: Routledge, 2013.

Swaab, Dick. *We Are Our Brains: A Neurobiography of the Brain, from the Womb to Alzheimer's* (published in Dutch, 2010). 1st U.S. ed. New York: Spiegel and Grau, 2014.

Szalavitz, Maia. "The Boy Whose Brain Could Unlock Autism: Autism Changed Henry Markram's Family. Now His Intense World Theory Could Transform Our Understanding of the Condition." *Medium,* December 11, 2013. https://medium.com/matter/the-boy -whose-brain-could-unlock-autism-70c3d64ff221#.5q0cryyoi.

Tammet, Daniel. *Born on a Blue Day: Inside the Extraordinary Mind of an Autistic Savant.* New York: Free Press, 2007.

Taylor, Jill Bolte. *My Stroke of Insight: A Brain Scientist's Personal Journey.* New York: Plume, 2009.

——. "My Stroke of Insight." Filmed February 2008. TED Videos, posted December 2011.

Theil, Stefan. "Why the Human Brain Project Went Wrong—and How to Fix It." *Scientific American,* March 27, 2016. http://www.scientificamerican.com/article/why-the-human -brain-project-went-wrong-and-how-to-fix-it/.

Thernstrom, Melanie. *The Pain Chronicles: Cures, Myths, Mysteries, Prayers, Diaries, Brain Scans, Healing, and the Science of Suffering.* New York: Farrar, Straus and Giroux, 2010.

Toga, Arthur W., Paul M. Thompson, Susumu Mori, Katrin Amunts, and Karl Zilles. "Towards Multimodal Atlases of the Human Brain." *Nature Reviews Neuroscience* 7, no. 12 (December 2006): 952–66.

Tougaw, Jason. *Strange Cases: The Medical Case History and the British Novel.* New York: Routledge, 2006.

——. "Touching Brains." *MFS Modern Fiction Studies* 61, no. 2 (2015): 335–58.

Turner, Mark. *The Literary Mind: The Origins of Thought and Language.* Rev. ed. New York: Oxford University Press, 1996.

——. *Reading Minds: The Study of English in the Age of Cognitive Science.* Princeton: Princeton University Press, 1993.

Vermeule, Blakey. *Why Do We Care about Literary Characters?* Baltimore: Johns Hopkins University Press, 2009.

Versaci, Rocco. *This Book Contains Graphic Language: Comics as Literature.* New York: Bloomsbury Academic, 2007.

Vidal, Fernando. "Brainhood, Anthropological Figure of Modernity." *History of the Human Sciences* 22, no. 1 (February 1, 2009): 5–36.

Vonnegut, Mark. *Just Like Someone Without Mental Illness Only More So: A Memoir.* New York: Delacorte, 2010.

Walker, Nick. *Neurocosmopolitanism: Nick Walker's Notes on Neurodiversity, Autism, and Cognitive Liberty.* http://neurocosmopolitanism.com/.

———. "Neurodiversity: Some Basic Terms and Definitions." *Neurocosmopolitanism,* September 27, 2014. http://neurocosmopolitanism.com/neurodiversity-some-basic-terms-definitions/.

———. "Neuroqueer: An Introduction, by Nick Walker." *NeuroQueer,* May 4, 2015. http://neuroqueer.blogspot.com/2015/05/neuroqueer-introduction-by-nick-walker.html.

———. "Neuro-what?" *Neurocosmopolitanism,* July 26, 2013. http://neurocosmopolitanism.com/neuro-what/.

Waugh, Patricia. "Memory and Voices: Challenging Psychiatric Diagnosis through the Novel." In *Memory in the Twenty-First Century: New Critical Perspectives from the Arts, Humanities, and Sciences,* 316–24. London: Palgrave Macmillan, 2016.

Williams, Donna. *Nobody Nowhere: The Remarkable Autobiography of an Autistic Girl.* New York: Doubleday, 1992.

———. *Somebody Somewhere: Breaking Free from the World of Autism.* New York: Three Rivers, 1994.

Williams, Raymond. *The Long Revolution* (1961). Rev. ed. Harmondsworth, UK: Penguin, 1965.

Wood, James. *How Fiction Works.* New York: Picador, 2009.

Wooden, Shannon R. "Narrative Medicine in the Literature Classroom: Ethical Pedagogy and Mark Haddon's *The Curious Incident of the Dog in the Night-Time,*" *Literature and Medicine* 29, no. 2 (2011): 274–96.

Wray, John. *Lowboy: A Novel.* New York: Picador, 2010.

Wurtzel, Elizabeth. *More, Now, Again: A Memoir of Addiction.* New York: Scribner, 2002.

Yates, Frances A. *The Art of Memory.* Chicago: University of Chicago Press, 1966.

Young, Kay. *Imagining Minds: The Neuro-Aesthetics of Austen, Eliot, and Hardy.* Columbus: Ohio State University Press, 2010.

Zunshine, Lisa. *Introduction to Cognitive Cultural Studies.* Baltimore: Johns Hopkins University Press, 2010.

———, ed. *The Oxford Handbook of Cognitive Literary Studies.* 1st ed. New York: Oxford University Press, 2015.

———. *Why We Read Fiction: Theory of Mind and the Novel.* Columbus: Ohio State University Press, 2006.

INDEX

Sherrington, Charles, in *Neurocomic,*
186
Shinn, Austin, *A Flickering Life: A Memoir
of Autism,* 100
Shore, Stephen, *Beyond the Wall: Personal
Experiences with Autism and Asperger's
Syndrome,* 128
Shulman, Alix Kates, 74, 89–92; and
memory, 78, 84–86; *To Love What Is,* 6,
77–78
Silberman, Steve, 127; *NeuroTribes: The
Legacy of Autism and the Future of
Neurodiversity,* 66, 99
Simmel, Marianne, "An Experimental
Study of Apparent Behavior" (with Fritz
Heider), 22
Singer, Tania, 32
Smith, Sidonie, *Reading Autobiography*
(with Watson, Julia), 76
Snow, C. P., "The Two Cultures," 25–26,
28, 39
Solms, Mark, 18; *The Brain and the Inner
World: An Introduction to the
Neuroscience of Subjective Experience*
(with Turnbull, Oliver), 9
Spolsky, Ellen, 28–30; *Gaps in Nature:
Literary Interpretation and the Modular
Mind,* 29
Starr, Gabrielle, *Feeling Beauty: The
Neuroscience of Aesthetic Experience,*
33, 62, 177–78
Straus, Joseph, "Autism as Culture," 118
Suarez, Daniel, 200
Swaab, Dick, 3; *We Are Our Brains: A
Neurobiography of the Brain, from the
Womb to Alzheimer's,* 11–12
synesthesia, 101–102

Taylor, Jill Bolte, 74, 89–92; *My Stroke of
Insight,* 6, 63, 77–78, 86–87
theory of mind, 31, 102. *See also* autism:
and mindblindness
Tourette Association of America, 70
Tourette's syndrome, 42–44, 46, 137,
141–44, 146–47; as "moral disease,"

43, 137; treatment with haloperidol,
43. *See also* Lethem, Jonathan
Tourette Syndrome Association (TSA),
43
transcraniel magnetic stimulation (TMS),
112–15; experience of, 115–16. *See also*
Robison, John Elder
transorbital lobotomy, 74, 77
Tuke, William, 180. *See also* moral
treatment; Tourette's syndrome
Turnbull, Oliver, *The Brain and the
Inner World: An Introduction to the
Neuroscience of Subjective Experience*
(with Mark Solms), 9
Turner, Mark, 28–30; *The Literary Mind,*
29; *More than Cool Reason: A Field
Guide to Poetic Metaphor* (with Lakoff,
George), 29; *Reading Minds: The Study
of English in the Age of Cognitive
Science,* 29

Umiltà, Carlo, *Neuromania: On the
Limits of Brain Science* (with Legrenzi,
Paolo), 27
Umwelt, and narratology, 146, 153
U.S. National Council on Disability, 72
universalism, 29
unreliable narration, 135–37, 139–40

Vermeule, Blakey, 28; "Can 'Neuro Lit
Crit' Save the Humanities?" (*New York
Times* article), 26; *Why Do We Care
about Literary Characters?* 31–32,
123
Versaci, Rocco, 191
Vessel, Ed, 33
Vidal, Fernando, 27, 55, 63, 110; "Brains
in Literature / Literature in the Brain"
(with Ortega, Francisco), 35

Walker, Nick, *Neurocosmopolitanism*
(blog), 67, 72; and the neurodiversity
paradigm, 67
Watson, Julia, *Reading Autobiography*
(with Smith, Sidonie), 76